Francis
of Assisi

The Wandering Years

Francis
of Assisi

— ✿ —

The Wandering Years

Anthony Mockler

PHAIDON
Oxford

Phaidon Press Limited, Littlegate House, St Ebbe's Street, Oxford
Published in the United States of America by E. P. Dutton & Co., Inc.

First published 1976
© 1976 by Phaidon Press Limited

ISBN 0 7148 1715 5
Library of Congress Catalog Card Number: 76-15923

Printed and bound in Great Britain by The Pitman Press, Bath

Contents

This book is dedicated to the memory of Frances, who was inevitably much in my thoughts while I was writing it; but it is also dedicated, and with more feeling, to Clare.

Preface

'When you read a work of history,' a well known modern scholar has said, 'always listen out for the buzzing. If you can detect none, either you are tone deaf or your historian is a dull dog.' History, he added a little later, means interpretation and indeed he even went on to suggest – he was lecturing at Cambridge, and so could be sure of a sympathetic reception for the provocative paradox – calling history 'a hard core of interpretation surrounded by a pulp of disputable facts.'

In a sense the life of Francis of Assisi is nothing but a mass of pulp of disputable facts; and very bitterly and learnedly have they been disputed. Yet in another sense the disputes touch mainly on points of detail and there is no argument about what occurred in his life; that is to say, it is generally agreed that there are now no new facts to be discovered, no earth-shaking revelations to come. 'The papers' are there; and it is, if not impossible, at least highly unlikely that new documents of first-class importance will come to light. This being so, it might be thought that there is no place for a new biography since there can be nothing new for the biographer to say. That is not so; that is to forget the 'hard core of interpretation'. To quote Professor Carr's words again (and I can quote them not because I attended his Trevelyan lectures in 1961 but because they have been reprinted by Penguin in a short book entitled *What is History?*), facts are not laid out 'like fish on the fishmonger's slab. They are like fish swimming about in a vast and inaccessible ocean; and what the historian catches will depend partly on chance but mainly on what part of the ocean he chooses to fish in and what tackle he chooses to use.'

When I was initially asked to write a book about St. Francis I was distinctly wary. There were three reasons for this. The first was a kind of antipathy to the very name of Assisi. I had learnt Italian many years before at Perugia, and anyone who stays long enough in that entrancing city is affected by the prejudices of its citizens – first and foremost among which is a freely expressed contempt for the hereditary enemy across the valley, the city of Assisi. This may seem rather a frivolous reason, at least to those who have not lived in the small cities of Italy. The second will be more easily appreciated: as a Catholic writing for a mainly non-Catholic body of readers, I was not at all sure that I would be able to find the right approach. This was never intended to be a devotional biography or in any sense a propaganda exercise; the risk lay rather in going too far in the opposite direction and yielding to the temptation to discover feet of clay where there were none, precisely in order to prove total impartiality. Furthermore, within the context of English Catholicism – which has its own particular quirks – I was uneasily aware that it was no advantage, for the purposes of this book, to have been educated by the Benedictines. It would be unfair to say that we were brought up to view St. Francis as a rather lower-level saint, for indeed I cannot recall any mention ever having been made of him at all. But we did end our formative years with the very distinct feeling that monks and the monastic orders were the serious branch of the Church Militant, and that friars of all sorts were rather a poor and later imitation, suitable perhaps for the sentimentalists and the female element in the Church, but to be taken with a pinch of salt outside the sphere of illustrated devotional manuals and their addicts.

Nevertheless to recognize these prejudices was halfway to overcoming them. The third reason that gave me pause concerned, not pitfalls which could perhaps be avoided, but professional training which would need to be adapted. Briefly, I had always written military history: was this not a disqualification for writing religious history?

The answer, obviously, is that I decided in the end that it was not. Indeed the more I studied Francis' life and Francis' world the more I became convinced that it was a positive blessing only superficially in disguise. Had I been asked to write a biography of Ignatius of Loyola, a professional soldier by training and by temperament, this would have been fairly obvious. But Francis – the peaceful, gentle, animal-loving saint of Assisi – what possible help could an interest and training in military history be in interpreting his life?

It will be for the reader, the critics and other historians to judge. But I would, now that this biography has been completed, go almost as far as to say that religious history and military history are two categories that overlap rather than lie far apart; and that in particular the study of any saint in the Middle Ages can only benefit from being undertaken by those whose speciality is not religious history, indeed by those whose buzzing is distinctly unholy. For, to go back to Professor Carr's metaphor and Professor Carr's point, the study of St. Francis has attracted very many learned scholars – but most of them have fished in the same part of the ocean. They have used as tackle mainly the contemporary documents relating directly to Francis and the Friars Minor; and that part of the ocean is very nearly fished out. So if the present biography has any new value, it lies in this – that it has attempted to cast its net rather wider, though no doubt less profoundly, and to study the effect not of Francis on his environment, but of his environment, in the widest sense, including both contemporary history and contemporary literature, on Francis' life. And this has led me to believe that the culminating event in his life was the event that his biographers of the Middle Ages dismiss very briefly and even his modern biographers treat as a mere *incident de parcours* – namely his going on crusade.

This belief explains both the format and the title of the present biography; and I hope that it will justify them. There are bound to be readers who will be disappointed at not finding a more substantial account of the last years of Francis' life and who will feel therefore that what purports to be a biography is not properly balanced. I would plead that these years, the passive years, the years of suffering, have already been treated in innumerable excellent lives of the saint, and that occasionally formal balance should be sacrificed if a different tilt, and therefore a new perspective, is to be obtained. I plead guilty therefore to a deliberate choice, a sin of commission – but not to culpable negligence, to a sin of omission. Let me add merely that there is a slightly misleading nuance in the phrase that has been chosen as subtitle – 'The Wandering Years'. This seems to imply purposeless movement, and that would be incorrect. Francis was a wanderer, yes; but the whole purport of this book is to show that he wandered with a purpose, and that – literally, or metaphorically – he wandered under the embroidered sign of the Cross.

I could not have written this book without the kindness, the hospitality and the assistance of many Franciscan friars and nuns, in Italy, in France and in England. They will not all agree with my conclusions; they may even be a little hurt at certain opinions expressed; but I hope that they will accept my heartfelt gratitude. In particular my thanks are due to everyone at the Franciscan Study Centre at Canterbury where St. Francis' gaiety of spirit and open-hearted friendliness so well lives on.

Donna Anna Fortini of Assisi was particularly helpful; Mrs Howard typed the manuscript with enormous precision and speed. Hope Leresche, my agent, was, as always, both long-suffering and stimulating. As for my editors, they were particularly encouraging and unprecedently speedy – John Calmann, Jean-Claude Peissel and Mark Ritchie. To all of them go my thanks. And in a very special way to Gwenda Marsh without whose constant and cheerful companionship and encouragement this book would never have been completed.

Canterbury
April 1976

Legends,
✤ Lives and Literature ✤

1: Legends, Lives and Literature

'Paris, Paris'

St. Bonaventure never lost his head. It was lost for him at the French Revolution – which, however, it approached with the distinct advantage, unlike the
heads of many other saintly persons, of being already detached from its body.[1]
This was typical of the man; other saints have preserved various bits and pieces,
ranging from sliver of finger to heart. But in death as in life, St. Bonaventure
– unlike his saintly predecessor, the subject of this biography – concentrated on
keeping intact one organ, one organ only, and that detached from all others,
the organ that, encompassing his brain, symbolized his intellect.

The General Chapter of 1260 of the Friars Minor, popularly known as the
Franciscans, opened on 23 May in Narbonne. 'Likewise we order,' the Chapter
decreed – and 'we' were the representatives of by this time over 17,000 friars –
'that a good "Legend of St. Francis" be written based on all those in existence.'
St. Bonaventure complied; for the next General Chapter, held three years later
at Pisa, he produced twenty-four manuscripts (one for each of the Provinces
into which the Order was then divided), copied out in Paris, of his own work,
which came to be known as the *Legenda Major*. (A *Legend* had, at least in theory,
nothing legendary about it. It meant simply a history or, as in this case, a
biography written in Latin prose and designed to be read aloud – particularly
in the choir or in the refectory.)

'I know,' St. Bonaventure, eighth Minister-General of the Order and (though
he knew it not) second saint to hold that position, wrote in the preface to his
Legenda, 'that I am unworthy and incapable of writing the life of a man so
deserving of our imitation and all our veneration, and I would never have
attempted it, were it not for the eager desire of the friars and the unanimous
request of the General Chapter.' Such a modest disclaimer, coming from an
ordinary friar, might be convincing; penned by the Minister-General, it rings
very false. The decision to write was deliberate and his own. St. Bonaventure
went on to explain his literary methods, style and aims: 'I wanted to be perfectly sure of the truth about his life and have a clear grasp of it before setting
it down to posterity, and so I went to his birthplace and visited the country
where he lived and died. There I was able to speak with some of his close
friends who were still alive and to interview them carefully, especially those
who had first-hand experience of his holiness and had tried to imitate it themselves. The honesty of these witnesses and the obvious fact that they are telling
the truth means that we can trust their testimony implicitly. In recording
what God in his goodness accomplished by means of his servant, I decided

deliberately to avoid using a literary style. A straightforward account will do the reader more good than an attempt at any elaborate literary style. The story does not always follow chronological order.'

This sounds fine and reasonable. It is not; it is – with the exception of the last sentence – a farrago of misleading half-truths. The manuscript consists of 150-odd pages, divided into two parts: part one, fifteen chapters on St. Francis' life; part two, ten chapters on the miracles which took place after St. Francis' death. (And either then, or shortly afterwards, Bonaventure also produced the *Legenda Minor* – a sort of devotional resumé of his major work, thirty-five pages divided into seven chapters, of no interest to the historian.) The Chapter General at Pisa approved, to the surprise of no-one, the Minister-General's text.

The statutory three years passed and the next Chapter General of the Order was held in Paris, Bonaventure's home ground. 'Paris, Paris,' Fra Giles, Francis' tried companion, used to say, 'thou hast ruined Assisi.' Bonaventure, like Francis, came from Umbria – he was born at Bagnoregio, near Orvieto, probably in 1217, the year when the Friars Minor really started to spread their wings and flutter out from Italy across the Alps and across the seas – but he had spent over twenty years of his life in Paris, a third as an ordinary student at the Faculty of Arts till he entered the Faculty of Theology and at the same time the Order, studying under the Englishman Alexander of Hales to whose post he eventually succeeded – after passing through the stages of *Baccalarius Biblicus*, then *Baccalarius Sententarius*, then *Baccalarius Formatus*, after the requisite doses ˙ of *Disputationes* and *Praedictiones*, after the honours of the *Inceptio* and the *Licentia* – as *Magister Regens in actu Facultatis Theologiae Minorum*, or one of the eight Regent Masters in Theology. 'Paris, Paris!' indeed; it was a far cry from the unlettered simplicity of Assisi.

The General Chapter of 1266 at Paris, the first to be held in the city that was now in both a very symbolical and a very real sense the centre of the Order, the city of books that had replaced Assisi, the city of prayers, was Bonaventure's triumph. All the old companions of Francis, including the crusty Fra Giles, all except his secretary Fra Leo and Clare's cousin Fra Rufino, were dead; and learning had triumphed over simplicity. The Narbonne Constitutions – 250 new regulations devised by Bonaventure – were in force and proving a success. With the year 1260 far behind the Joachimite controversies which had ruined Giovanni of Parma, St. Bonaventure's predecessor, were losing their sting.[2] The Order appeared united and peaceful, for the first time for forty-five years. And St. Bonaventure determined to continue to impose his policy, apparently so successful, of enforced and pacifying uniformity in that most dangerous and most tempting of all fields – the literary. Jesus Christ had had the right to four biographers; Francis was to be allowed only one; and that one himself.

The General Chapter passed a decree ordering that all the lives and histories of St. Francis previously written should be destroyed – to be replaced everywhere, not only in the 1,500-odd Friaries and 400 Poor Clare houses but also outside the Order, by the standard biography of the Minister-General, the *Legenda Major*.

This dastardly decree was diligently put into force: older manuscripts by other authors were sought out and presumably burnt; and it is only thanks to luck, the will of God, and the Cistercians that St. Bonaventure's *Legenda* is not the one and only source we have – bar a few contemporary chronicles and documents – for the life and character of Francis and of his first companions. Had this iniquitous scheme succeeded, it is horrible to contemplate the hagiographical portrait that alone would survive. We would know St. Francis only through the eyes of St. Bonaventure; we would see only what St. Bonaventure desired to be seen; we would have a long, long list of miracles accomplished by St. Francis alive and St. Francis dead; we would have an almost equally long list of visions;[3] we would hear a great deal about faith, humility and prayer, fasting, poverty and fervour, all in exhortatory language bordering on the flowery, we would have a few good stories more simply told – and a few extravagant sayings, very few really, that would just leave us with a tantalizing glimpse of a man who was more eccentric and more outrageous and indeed more loony than ever his careful biographer would wish to admit. But what is really intolerable is Bonaventure's implied assertion that after talking to Francis' old friends in Umbria and making every effort to find out the objective facts he is setting them out fully and honestly for posterity. This was just not so. The inner censor was hard at work, a saint was a saint, and must be a model of sanctity, and therefore unlike Fra Leo, Bonaventure felt, for example, no curiosity as to whether Francis was a virgin or not. The question was the sort of question that, in Bonaventure's view, did not arise: and in order that it should not arise all the tales of Francis' dissipated youth must be censored. They were. 'With the help of God's grace,' wrote St. Bonaventure, 'even when he was with his gay companions . . . he never followed the lure of his passions.' This was typical. The plaster-cast saint was born.

About 400 copies, dating from the thirteenth and the fourteenth century, of the *Legenda Major* survive. There had been two preceding official lives, both written by the same friar, Thomas of Celano. They were both almost obliterated by the Paris decree; of the *Second Life*, only two complete copies have survived – the Assisi MS and the Marseilles MS; of the *First Life*, earlier, shorter and more accurate, only one copy survived in Franciscan hands; but fortunately the

Cistercians kept eight (and the Benedictines three) – an interesting sign of the rather paradoxical admiration the monastic orders felt for the friars, their supplanters.

Are these *Lives* more valuable than the *Legenda Major*? There is a short and simple answer: yes.

Thomas was only four or five years younger than Francis, he came from Celano in the Abruzzi, about eighty miles away from Assisi, joined the order in its early years and was one of the Friars Minor sent to Germany later on, with Fra Caesar of Speyer. He was probably in Germany when on Saturday 3 October 1226 Francis died.[4]

Cardinal Ugolino, the Cardinal Protector of the Friars Minor, was elected Pope Gregory IX on 19 March 1227, and next year came to Assisi where amidst great celebrations he canonized Francis, on 26 July 1228. It seems that Thomas of Celano was present at the ceremony, and either then or shortly before he was commissioned by the Pope to write the *First Life*, which was presented to Gregory IX very soon afterwards, on 25 February 1229, and approved.

The *First Life* is divided into 151 sections, on average rather less than a page long, and is certainly the first[5] and in many ways the best account that we have of Francis' life; for it was written by a friar who knew him personally, who knew his friends and best companions well, at a time when memories were fresh and plentiful and above all at a time when a writer could not risk distorting facts, faced as he was bound to be with a highly critical audience who themselves knew what had and what had not happened.

Thomas, unlike St. Bonaventure, described Francis' life in chronological order; he split the *First Life* into three 'books'; the first, eighty-seven sections long, described his active life; the second, thirty sections long, concentrated on the last two years of his life, namely on the period running from the stigmata to his death; the third, and least interesting, took in his canonization and the miracles following his death. The first two 'books' are therefore a most important source for anyone concerned with St. Francis' life; miracles and visions abound but do not dominate; and though one can only echo Thomas when he writes in his *Prologue*: 'I wish however that I might truly deserve to be a disciple of him who always avoided enigmatic ways of saying things and who knew nothing of the ornaments of language,' in fact his prose, though studied and at times edifying, only rarely gushes.

Four or five years later Julian of Speyer wrote a short life based entirely on Thomas of Celano's *First Life*; and Bartholomew of Trent, a Dominican, one even shorter. A more quizzical biographer, inspired by the same source, is Henri d'Avranches. In the *Bibliotheca Comunale* at Assisi there is a fine bunch of medieval manuscripts, carefully bound together – MSS 338 – that used to be held at the *Sacro Convento*. There, copied out in different hands at different times during the thirteenth century, are various Franciscan writings – the *Offices*, the *Hours*, the two *Rules*, the *Testament* and many others. But the pride of place – for it is more beautifully illustrated and more decoratively coloured even than the *Canticle of the Sun*[6] – is held by a long poem entitled the *Legenda Versificata*. filling folios 54–71 inclusive.

'*Gesta sacri cantabo ducis*' ('I will sing of the deeds of the sacred leader') it begins, and it continues for over 2,500 Latin hexameters. Anyone handling this MS can hardly doubt that this was the most popular and best loved version of Francis' '*gesta*', the life the friars preferred to hear. It, too, like Thomas' *First Life*, is dedicated to Gregory IX. Whether it was commissioned by him is another matter. It seems that Henri d'Avranches, a secular cleric born in Germany of a Norman father about 1190, was a genuine and successful '*gyrovagus*', a wandering scholar and poet. He wrote poems for great men wherever there was a great man to write a poem for; for Otto IV, the Emperor, in Germany; for Frederick II, Hohenstaufen, in Sicily; for St.Louis of France; and at the end of his life for Henry III of England, at whose court he was '*versificator*'. He was at the papal Curia from 1232 to 1234, and again from 1238 to 1239, when he probably wrote the *Legenda Versificata*. It has been suggested therefore that he studied the written evidence leading to St. Francis' canonization, the *Acts* as they were called, which have now been lost – and that his *Legenda* is therefore full of nuggets of new information. Alas, this seems to be untrue. What Arnaldo Fortini, mayor and then *Podestà* of Assisi, author of the monumental four-volume *Nova Vita di San Francesco*, took as interesting new sidelights have turned out to be mainly borrowed half-lines from Ovid and others. Indeed Henri would hardly have had time to do much original research: he is known to have written at least 162 'epic' poems, and there were those of his contemporaries[7] who thought him a wandering nincompoop, 'telling mad, strange tales.' But these were remarks typical of goliards, jealous of the success of a court poet, probably themselves starving, irreverent, biting and bitter. Henri d'Avranches may not have added much to the story of Francis of Assisi; but he followed pretty accurately Thomas of Celano in his *First Life*.

1229 then – one official biography, the first, written by an ordinary friar shortly after Francis' death. 1263 – another official biography, written by the Minister-General when personal memories of Francis had faded. Between these two biographies there was a gap, therefore, of thirty-four years; and this is the period of the so-called 'Franciscan Question', over which innumerable scholars have sharpened their learned fangs: who wrote what, where, when, why, how and for whom?

The starting point at least is simple; at least the question 'for whom' can be answered. After St. Francis' death there was a period of conflict in the rapidly expanding Order that centred around two points: first of all, should the Order be dominated by priests or by non-priests? Secondly, should the intentions of the founder be respected or adapted? The first conflict was dominated by the personality of Fra Elias, Francis' companion and like Francis not an ordained priest. It ended, in 1239, in his defeat and deposition, and the triumph of the clergy; Haymo of Faversham, basically a Dominican in style, neither simple nor forgiving, was elected Minister-General. He died, however, in 1244, to be succeeded by Crescentius of Iesi, stern but ineffective,[8] under whose rule the second conflict was also apparently settled by Innocent IV's Bull 'Ordinem vestrum' which consigned Francis' *Testament*, his last wishes, to oblivion. It seemed therefore – false claim as it turned out to be – that controversy was stilled; and so, without fear of creating factions, Crescentius 'directed that all the friars make known to him in writing all that they might know with certitude concerning the life and miracles of St. Francis.' Obviously the general feeling in the Order was that Thomas of Celano's *Life* omitted too much; and that, before they died, all the friars who had been Francis' companions should set down their reminiscences for posterity.

How many documents came in? It is impossible to say: but probably the most important roll or sheaf was that which came accompanied by a letter from the hermitage at Greccio outside Rieti. The letter read as follows:

'To the Reverend Father in Christ, Fra Crescentius, by the grace of God Minister-General. To him Fra Leo, Fra Rufino and Fra Angelo, unworthy companions of our blessed father Francis, offer their dutiful and devout reverence in our Lord.'

Of all Francis' companions Fra Leo was likely to be both the most literate and have the most information. Fra Leo – 'Little Sheep,' as Francis used affectionately to call him – had been his companion and secretary in his last days and in particular had been his sole body-companion on Monte La Verna when the saint received the stigmata. Fra Rufino was a first cousin of St. Clare, a member therefore of one of the noble families of Assisi and a witness to Francis' early life. Fra Angelo had been one of the first twelve companions, a knight of Francis' Round Table, as he loved to describe it, before the Order as such properly existed; he too was probably of noble birth and therefore more likely to be literate, or at least capable of expressing himself, than the totally uneducated who appear to have formed the mass of the early companions. They must have been the three informants on whom the Minister-General relied most.

'The command of the last General Chapter,' the letter proper began, 'is also that of Your Reverence and it orders all the friars to communicate to Your

Paternity any signs and wonders of our blessed father Francis which they either know personally or can truthfully vouch for. Therefore it has seemed to us who, though unworthy, conversed at length with him, that we ought truthfully to recount to Your Paternity some of the many facts of which we were eye-witnesses or heard from holy friars, especially from Fra Filippo, Visitor of the Poor Clares, Fra Illuminato of Rieti, Fra Masseo of Marignano, and Fra Giovanni who was the companion of Fra Giles and heard many of these facts either from Fra Giles himself or from Fra Bernard of holy memory, the first companion of blessed Francis.'

Here the roll-call was almost complete. Fra Bernard of Quintavalle, the first companion, the man without whom the Order could hardly have existed, had recently died; Fra Giles, the third companion, was still alive – but a grumpy if beloved recluse, living at Perugia, certainly not one to write down his memoirs. Fra Illuminato had been with Francis to the Saracens and Fra Masseo was often his travelling companion inside Italy. The three therefore seem to have spoken for all – except for the eccentric Fra Juniper – though, strangely, they do not claim to speak of what they had heard from three other dead but famous friars, Silvester, Leonardo and Pacificus. Probably, though, Bernard of Quintavalle was, among the dead, by far the most important name to bring up.

'We do not intend merely to report on miracles, which are not the cause of sanctity although they prove it; we wish to relate some notable facts of his holy life to the praise and glory of the most high God. . . . We shall not recount these things in the form of a *Legend*, since other *Legends* have been written of his life and of the miracles which God has deigned to work through him. Using our own judgement we wish rather to gather the most beautiful of the many flowers blooming in a pleasant field: we do not propose to follow an historical sequence and are studiously omitting those things which have already been told in the aforesaid *Legends* with words as accurate as they are polished.'

In other words this was intended to be totally new material, not arranged in a chronological order with a beginning and an end as was the rule for *Legends* and biographies, but rather on the basis of a '*florilegium*', a flower garden, the other medieval form of prose description.

'If you consider it advisable,' the letter ended, 'the few things we shall here tell might be inserted in other *Legends*, and we are convinced that had venerable men who wrote these *Legends* been acquainted with the things we recount they would on no account have omitted them; rather they would have embellished them with their own eloquent words and thus have transmitted them to posterity. . .

Written at Greccio on the 11th day of August 1246.'

This promises the sort of raw material on which scholars love to pounce:

unadorned, unordered, unembellished and unknown. It took, however, a local expert, an Arnaldo Fortini, to point out that the letter was written on the feast day of San Rufino, first bishop and patron saint of Assisi,[9] a point which, had there been any doubt about the letter's authenticity (it is a touch over-elegant in style), might have greatly helped in proving it genuine.

In any case the rolls, the *rotuli*, that accompanied this letter were sent in to Assisi, and after a failed attempt to make something out of them himself[10] the Minister-General, Crescentius, handed them over to Francis' first biographer, Thomas of Celano.

Thomas at once set out to write a new biography, not so much to replace as to supplement his original work. His *Second Life* was almost exactly half as long again as his *First Life*; it consisted of 224 sections divided into two 'books'; the first 'book' was very short, composed of twenty-five sections adding details and incidents to his original account of Francis' early life and conversion; the second 'book' more or less abandoned the chronological method and was divided into chapters with different headings under which were grouped stories and sayings that were linked by the title – for instance, 'Of St. Francis' Compassion for the Poor' or 'Against Familiarity with Women.'

In the *Second Life*, Fra Elias, prominent in the *First Life* as Francis' right-hand man, is nowhere mentioned by name. Does this mean, as some critics have asserted, that the *Second Life* is not to be trusted, that Thomas has deliberately avoided all painful subjects, and twenty years older and wiser, set out to write a more cautious work? This does not seem to be so. Elias was a very special case; not only had he been deposed as Minister-General after making himself generally loathed throughout the Order but he had gone over to the Emperor Frederick II, and both he and his master were excommunicate. Indeed the Emperor had been solemnly deposed by the Pope at the Council of Lyons (July 1246) and all his vassals released from their oaths of loyalty to him. These were high politics, and it was wise for reasons of personal safety, both spiritual and corporal, to avoid the very mention of the name of Elias. But in other ways[11] Thomas was more outspoken than he had been in his *First Life*, eager to explain and illustrate Francis' intentions and not avoiding the three great questions: the meaning of Absolute Poverty, the relations between the friars and the clergy, the interpretation of the *Rule* and the *Testament*.

The next Minister-General, Giovanni of Parma, invited Thomas to round off the *Second Life* by writing what Fra Salimbene later described as 'a very beautiful book about the miracles' of St. Francis. His *Treatise on Miracles* was probably written between 1250 and 1253; it was very long – 198 sections, many of which repeated stories already related in the *First Life* and *Second Life* and is of no more interest than most collections of miracle stories.

This was not the end of Thomas' work. He also wrote a shortened *Legend of St. Francis for Use in the Choir*, a *Legend of St. Clare* (probably in 1255–6; she died in 1253) and probably, though rather astonishingly, the tremendous *Dies Irae*. But the extraordinary thing is this: with the *First Life*, the *Second Life* and the *Treatise on Miracles* to hand, it becomes immediately apparent that the *Legenda Major* (and *Legenda Minor*) are fit merely for the wastepaper basket.[12] In other words, despite all his protestations of first-hand interviewing, visiting the site, careful sifting of facts, etc., what St. Bonaventure did was simply sit down and embellish Thomas' work – and then, three years later, order that Thomas' work should be destroyed.

So much then, for the 'official' biographies of St. Francis.[13]

The Mystery of the Book Cupboard

The traveller from Rome heading up the Spoleto valley past Foligno will see on his right halfway up the hillside a beautiful, thin, straggling medieval town; that is Spello. A little further on lies a large, dark, wooded, slightly sinister, humped mountain – Monte Subasio. The mountain ends in a range of hills; and on these hills, rather further away, is another beautiful, thin, straggling medieval town, walled, gated and turreted. This is Assisi. At the far end of the line of buildings, like a castled king at the end of a row of chessmen, stands a most impressive church, stern and high against the skyline. This is the Basilica of Saint Francis, the church that Fra Elias built with quite extraordinary speed, on the model of the crusaders' fortress-churches he had known in Outremer, to house the body of St. Francis. The body of the saint lies in the Lower Basilica; most of the great frescoes of Giotto decorate the Upper Basilica. Attached to the Church proper is the *Sacro Convento*, the residential headquarters of the Franciscan Order. From the first the *Sacro Convento* had a library; and inside the library there was, as the writings of Fra Ubertino da Casale prove, an *armadium* or book-cupboard. What was inside the book-cupboard?

Actually this is a rhetorical question. We know what was inside the book-cupboard because Fra Ubertino tells us: the rolls or *rotuli* of Fra Leo. Which rolls? They must have been, most scholars agree, the rolls that were sent in with the letter of 11 August 1246 and contained the reminiscences of Fra Leo, Fra Rufino and Fra Angelo. In other words these rolls had survived (after all, they were only unadorned raw material) the years of the Bonaventure book-burnings, for they were seen sometime after the year 1305[14] by Fra Ubertino; and that greatly to his surprise. For he, too, had considered them lost.

'Listen, reader,' wrote Fra Ubertino, 'and store this in the depths of your heart. What follows comes from the holy Fra Conrad (of Offida) and he heard it from the mouth of the holy Fra Leo in person, for he was present and wrote the *Rule*. This story is said to be contained in some *rotuli* written in his own hand which he entrusted to the Convent of Santa Chiara (in Assisi) to be preserved as a memorial for posterity. *He wrote many stories in them, such as he had heard from the holy father's mouth or seen him do*; in them are contained accounts of the saint's wonderful works; also prophecies of the *Rule*'s future corruption, and of its restoration; about the mighty events surrounding the institution and renewal of the *Rule* by God; of St. Francis' intention on the observance of the *Rule*, according to the intention he said he had received from Christ. *These stories were purposely omitted by Fra Bonaventure*, who did not wish to write them for all to see in his *Legend*, especially because some of them openly showed how they were departing from the *Rule* at that time, and he did not wish to disgrace the brothers prematurely before those outside the Order. Manifestly it would have been far better to include them, since such a fearful falling-off would perhaps not have happened, and the one which follows was especially ignored from that time. *With great sorrow I heard that those* rotuli *had been scattered [distracti]* and possibly lost – especially some of them.'

One must be logical about this. The rolls had clearly existed in 1246, when they had been sent to the Minister-General. Thomas of Celano had used them for his *Second Life*; and then? . . . Then nothing is known or heard of them for almost sixty years; but though the names of Fra Angelo and Fra Rufino have disappeared (for obviously Fra Leo, the scribe, was the one who wrote out the stories which all three contributed) the 'many stories' to which Ubertino refers *must*, by all the rules of commonsense, refer to the same collection. Just as it is highly unlikely that Thomas of Celano destroyed them – why should he have done? – so it is more than probable that Bonaventure, as Ubertino implies, cast an eye through them between 1260 and 1264 when he was visiting Assisi and included them, by implication, in his book-burning order of 1266. But by 1266 Bonaventure was far away in Paris, and the discreet Superior of the Convent of St. Clare could quite easily have moved them down the road to the rather safer refuge of the book-cupboard in the library of the *Sacro Convento*, where five years later, probably writing in August 1311, Fra Ubertino found them himself.

'Of all the things which in this reply I say Francis intended,' – he was writing at this time about the saint's desire for small churches rather than grandiose basilicas – 'many are evident enough in the *Rule*, the *Testament* and the *Life*; but all without exception are revealed by his own words which were written down with pious care (*solempniter*) by the holy man Leo, his companion – both on the saint's command and out of his own devotion – in the book which is preserved in the friars' book-cupboard in Assisi and in his *rotuli*, which I have by me, written in the handwriting of Fra Leo, in which the intention of St. Francis as to the poverty of the Rule is perfectly declared, against all abuses and transgressions, which these folk strive to defend . . .'[15]

How many learned scholars would have loved to burrow into that book-cupboard. But, alas, rolls and book-cupboard alike disappeared – though not before the *rotuli*, in part or in whole, accurately or inaccurately, by themselves or with other documents, had been transcribed. In one form or another the writings of Fra Leo, Fra Rufino and Fra Angelo, the most simple and therefore most accurate source of the history of Francis of Assisi, exist. The whole question – what is known as 'the Franciscan Question' – is: in what form? Blood has not yet been spilt in the efforts to resolve this question, but ink and passion have not been spared. I do not intend to go deeply into it here, but merely to give a glimpse of its intricacy and, hopefully, a taste of its fascination.

After centuries of devout hagiography, usually by Irish or Italian friars, the study of St. Francis attracted at long last an outsider – a characteristically lucid Frenchman.

Paul Sabatier was born in 1858, the son of a Provençal mother and of the Protestant pastor of the small village of St. Michel de Chabrillonaux in the Cevennes. The village was split into two hostile communities, Protestants and Catholics. In 1880 Sabatier went to Paris to study at the Protestant Faculty of Theology and attend the lectures of the notorious Ernest Renan, whose *Vie de Jésus*, in which the second person of the Trinity was described as merely 'an incomparable man', had created an unimaginable furore two decades earlier.

'Towards the end of 1884,' Paul Sabatier wrote later[16] 'Renan, after his lecture, talking to some of his students said: "When I began to work I dreamt of devoting my life to the study of three periods. Blessed be the illusions of youth! Three periods! The origins of Christianity in connection with the history of Israel, the French Revolution, and the marvellous renewal of religion realized by St. Francis of Assisi. You, M. Leblond, must write the religious history of the Revolution, and you" (he said, putting his hand on Sabatier's shoulder), "you will be the historian of the Seraphic Father." '

M. Leblond, ungratefully, disappointed Renan and his own comrades by dying. Sabatier, stimulated by an essay of the *maître* published in *Nouvelles Etudes d' Histoire Religieuse*,[17] four years later set to work to write a totally new, lucid and exact Life of St. Francis. It came out in 1893 and had immediately an immense success; Renan, by a displeasing irony, had died in 1892 and so did not see even the first of the forty-seven editions of his pupil's masterpiece, the most deservedly popular biography of a medieval saint ever to be published in Europe.

Sabatier's book was as controversial as it was brilliantly written; and since its publication interest in Franciscan studies has continually increased, perhaps reaching its climax between the wars. Sabatier was only thirty-seven when his masterpiece came out; he had still thirty-three years to live and he devoted many of them to studying the sources of St. Francis' life – for he had based his biography on the *First Life* and the *Second Life* of Thomas of Celano, the *Legenda Major* of Bonaventure – and a simpler, shorter document which had survived in later compilations attached to the famous letter of the three brethren and was therefore known as the *Legenda Trium Sociorum*, the *Legend of the Three Companions*. In 1900, Père Van Ortroy in a learned article[18] demolished the *Legenda Trium Sociorum* as 'une pièce apocryphe, un habile pastiche', a bad parody of the 'official' biographies. Sabatier countered the following year with a defence published in *Revue Historique No. 75* entitled 'De l'Authenticité de la Legende de Saint François dite "des trois compagnons"' – and the Franciscan Question was born.

There followed a regular flurry of ransacking of medieval archives: the first new manuscript to be triumphantly produced was by Sabatier himself – a text entitled the *Speculum Perfectionis*, the *Mirror of Perfection*, and dated MCCXXVII – 1227, a year after St. Francis' death. This then, proclaimed Sabatier, was Fra Leo's original work; and he edited it in 1898 as such. Unfortunately other manuscripts, discovered in other libraries, were dated MCCCXVII – 1317. Complications arose, controversy raged, and confusion momentarily increased when Père Ferdinand Delorme produced in 1922 a further manuscript – MS 1046 of the *Bibliotheca Augusta Comunale* of Perugia – known as the *Legenda Antiqua*, which claimed to be stories of the Saint written by eye-witnesses and companions.[19] Let us say nothing of the additional head-scratching occasioned by the discovery of the Lemmens or San Isidoro MS, the Little Bodleian MS, and the so-called *Lives and Sayings of Fra Giles*. But there is one other manuscript that cannot be ignored, the *Anonymous of Perugia*, written by another apparent eye-witness,[20] and describing vividly and simply the first days of the Order.

How are these four manuscripts related? Which is based on which? Which is copied *from* Thomas of Celano and which is copied *by* Thomas of Celano? Which, above all, most closely represents the *rotuli* of Fra Leo? Which ought to be used by the would-be biographers of St. Francis? These are questions to which it is impossible to give a simple answer; and almost impossible to give any definite answer at all. Perhaps the 'Question' will one day answer itself – perhaps the *rotuli*, complete, unmistakable, in Fra Leo's own handwriting will still, like Bonaventure's head, turn up. Till then, it is largely a matter, as Sabatier recognized, of intuition aided by textual criticism.

Of the four texts I personally prefer the short *Anonymous of Perugia*; its 'feel' is right and, provisionally, I would accept the theory that it was probably written between 1260 and 1270 by Fra Giovanni, Fra Giles' friend and confessor. The *Speculum Perfectionis* is now generally agreed to be a later compilation that adds little or nothing to the other three texts, a polemic. The *Legenda Antiqua* is over twice as long as the *Anonymous of Perugia*, 115 sections as opposed to forty-eight. It is, in the words of Père Théophile Desbonnets,[21] 'with all its faults and deficiencies one of the most authentic eye-witness accounts and the most vivid we have of St. Francis.' Following him, following almost all authorities, I accept at least sections 42–115 as being copied directly from Fra Leo's *rotuli*. As for the *Legend of the Three Companions*, the truth about its origin and composition now matter much less than was the case before the discovery of the *Legenda Antiqua*; almost all the stories and incidents contained in it can be found either in that work or in the *Anonymous of Perugia*, except for the early life of St. Francis, for which it is indispensable.

To sum up: the reader, expert or layman, has a right to know his author's sources.[22] This having been said, I will avoid what seems to me the rather finickety habit of giving precise references for every incident and every saying; for this is a history, not a thesis for a doctorate – though nowadays, for better or for worse, every 'serious' study has to be adorned with the fig-leaves of scholarship, and pages nude of footnotes are frowned upon by the neo-Victorians of academia.[23]

Little Flowers and Larger Chronicles

No sooner was St. Bonaventure safely dead and disposed of, and his long, long rule over, than – as always happens after a period of dictatorship, literary or otherwise – curiosity came to life again. The Chapter General of 1276 called for new material about Francis and his life; and at least one young friar, Fra Ugolino Boniscambi, set to work in the hills and hermitages of Le Marche, the area around Ancona, to write down the stories and memories of old friars. It was rather late in the day, of course; Francis had been dead for fifty years and even the longest-living of his companions, Fra Leo and Fra Rufino, were buried too.

Fortunately old Fra Giacomo of Massa had known them both, and Fra Juniper and St. Clare too; and from others of the second generation of Friars Minor, or from their younger friends, Fra Ugolino collected tales and stories. He did not write them down, or at least not put them together, for another fifty years or so, waiting till he was, in his turn, a dangerously old man; but then he collected all the stories of his friends in Le Marche, about each other and about the first days, and wrote the *Actus Beati Francisci et Sociorum Ejus*, a long, long collection of colourful legends divided into seventy-five chapters. Another fifty years passed; and another brother, who never revealed his name, took fifty-three of these chapters and translated them into Italian to produce the first book written in any language but Latin about St. Francis – the first and still the best loved, the *Fioretti* or *Little Flowers*, a title that was very fashionable at the time.

How true are the stories told in the *Little Flowers*? No-one has answered that question better than Paul Sabatier. 'Here,' he wrote, 'are words that were never uttered, acts that never took place, but the soul and the heart of the early Franciscans were surely what they are depicted here.'

In a sense the *Little Flowers* are – again to borrow Sabatier's phrase – a higher truth. It is one of the more melancholy servitudes of present-day historians to feel irretrievably bound to the searching-out of the lower truths. To turn a cold eye on the tale of 'How St. Francis tamed the very fierce wolf of Gubbio' seems preposterously pedantic: yet, though it need not be insisted upon, it must be done. It is all part of the much more difficult question of how to treat the miraculous element in St. Francis' life. As G. K. Chesterton said, if you deny the miracles *en masse*, you might as well deny that St. Francis ever existed; but, as he also said, there are many of them that are obvious fairy stories; and it is these that dot the pages of the *Little Flowers*.

In 1262 Fra Giordano of Giano dictated his *Chronicle* at Halberstadt, fifty pages or so of autobiography and memories, half about the life and organization of the Province of Germany, half his own personal experiences as a young friar who had known Francis. It is strange that tradition should use the same word *Chronicle* for this old friar's short reminiscences and for the immense work of Fra Salimbene of Parma, written about twenty-five years later (for the benefit of his niece Agnes who, at the age of fifteen, had joined the Poor Clares) – an account of his life and times which is now recognized as one of the greatest sources of information for the student of thirteenth-century Europe. Halfway between the two, in length and in interest, lies the *Chronicle* of Thomas of Eccleston, an account of the coming of the Friars Minor to England in 1224 and their establishment first at Canterbury, then at London and Oxford.

Even if none of the works mentioned before had survived, it would still be possible to write a short history of Francis of Assisi, and the founding of his Order on the basis of these three chronicles alone – though a very different, and perhaps a truer, perspective would emerge, with Francis himself, the founder, becoming a figure of minor rather than of legendary importance.

Later friars made immense compilations, piling together vast collections of material with little artistry or respect for truth and much repetition.[24] Further-more, in almost all the contemporary thirteenth-century chronicles and his-tories there is some reference, long or short, accurate or inaccurate, to St. Francis and the Friars Minor; and, of course, many more in papal Bulls and Letters, in the Registers of Cardinal Ugolino, etc.

Nor have I mentioned all the contemporary sources: the *De Laudibus* of Bernard of Besse, St. Bonaventure's secretary, and the allegorical *Sacrum Commercium Beati Francisci cum Domina Paupertate*; the writings of the 'Spirituals', in particular the *Chronicle of the Seven Tribulations* of Angelo Clareno (not strictly contemporary); or the *Liber Exemplorum* of Fra Nicola of Assisi. As the reader will appreciate, it is possible to get very bogged down.

Sabatier et al.

A final word about modern biographies;[25] they can be divided rather cavalierly into two main categories, the documented and the undocumented; and, rather puritanically, these two categories can be labelled the serious and the non-serious.

Of the undocumented biographies there must be scores; G. K. Chesterton's, no doubt the shortest and the most brilliant, was first published in 1924, with a revised edition in 1957.

There are four serious modern biographies. First came Sabatier's, in 1894. The next was that of a Danish poet, Johannes Jorgensen, an exalted and at the same time scholarly work first published in 1907. This was almost as popular as Sabatier's biography and was translated into many languages; the poet died aged ninety, in 1956, a converted Catholic after a long spiritual (and physical) odyssey in which his life was dominated by St. Francis and Umbria. Personally I find his style and approach gratingly romantico-Nordic; the street known as Via Santa Maria delle Rose in Assisi has been officially renamed Via Johannes Jorgensen and leads up to Villa Fortini; this is just the sort of change one fears he might have approved of.

In 1912 Father Cuthbert, a Capuchin friar, published his biography. Born of a German father and an English mother he became a professed Franciscan at the age of fifteen, in 1881. His *Life* has been praised (by Dr. Little) for its 'complete honesty, charming simplicity, accurate learning' but damned (by Little and others) for not being a work of art. This seems most unfair; is the aim of a biography accuracy and honesty – or art?

Father Cuthbert was transferred from Oxford to Assisi at the age of sixty-one; he died at Assisi in 1939 and is buried there on the hillside.

The last and latest of the 'serious' biographies is that written by the Abbé

Omer Englebert, which was first published in Paris in 1947. The Abbé made great use of the new material available, in particular of the *Legenda Antiqua*. His second and revised edition (1959 Albin Michel), was translated and published in Chicago in 1965 for the Franciscan Herald Press, together with a most useful bibliography of sources.

All these four biographies are of much the same length, about 400 pages long; all four have been translated into different languages, and printed in revised editions. All four are worth reading – but to my mind Sabatier's is still, by far, the best.

NOTES

1 The facts are these: St. Bonaventure, eighth Minister-General of the Friars Minor, died on 15 July 1274 at the Council of Lyons – poisoned, if we are to believe (and why not?) his secretary Peregrinus of Bologna. He was buried with some haste that same evening in the Franciscan church at Lyons.

  A hundred and sixty years later his remains were transferred to the new Eglise Saint François; it was then that his head was found to be perfectly preserved.

  In 1562 his shrine was plundered by the Huguenots who burnt the urn containing his body in the public square. But still his head survived – saved by the Guardian at the risk of his own – only to disappear two centuries later at the time of the Revolution.

  Since then, all efforts to trace it have been in vain. No doubt it is still lurking in some remote corner of Europe, waiting to be brought to light again, like some missing medieval manuscript in dim archives. If found, it apparently can be recognized by the lifelike redness of the tongue.

2 For the Joachimite controversies see the next chapter and also chapter seven and (especially) its notes. By many scholars Abbot Joachim of Calabria is considered to be the most important of Francis' predecessors. His theories certainly influenced many of the early Franciscans – and in particular his forecast of a New Age due to begin in the year 1260. Indeed controversy, particularly at the University of Paris, became so sharp that the seventh Minister-General of the Order, Giovanni di Parma, a lover of poverty cast in St. Francis' mould, but a Joachimite, was summoned to Rome to answer before an extraordinary Chapter General in the presence of the Lord Pope. There he resigned, nominating as his successor Bonaventure – a boon which that saint repaid shortly afterwards by the fraternal gesture of hailing the deposed Minister-General up for trial at Castello della Pieve and sentencing him to life imprisonment. (See, especially, the *Seven Tribulations* of Fra Angelo Clareno.)

3 In the first four chapters alone of the *Legenda Major* there are accounts of no less than fifteen visions, including dreams, apparitions, visions in prayer, and visions accompanied by miraculous phenomena such as fiery chariots – mainly undergone by Francis but not sparing his companions nor indeed the Pope.

4 One of the very few dates of which we can be absolutely certain in Francis' biography. And even with this there is a typical medieval confusion, worth mentioning if only to show how

difficult it is to be accurate about days, months and years in medieval times. Francis died after dusk but before midnight. Therefore according to the style of Assisi – and of many other cities – he died on Sunday, 4 May; for a day ended and a new day began at sundown.

The dates of very nearly every important event in his life have been the subject of immensely entangled and highly learned disputations – usually more over the year than the month. Into these, in this book, I will not try to enter but will normally plump for the date at the moment most widely accepted.

It is even unsure whether Francis was born in 1181 or 1182. And in any case the question of Francis' date of birth pales into insignificance besides that of the *year* of birth of his great patron, Cardinal Ugolino, later Gregory IX – who was born either in 1170 or in 1140; and so was either of a totally different generation than St. Francis or roughly his contemporary. At any rate we know that Francis was either forty-four or forty-five when he died.

5 Except of course for Francis' own writings. But these are few – various *Letters*, various *Admonitions*, various *Laudes* or Praises, plus the two *Rules* and the *Testament*. They are vital as a source for Francis' thought but of very little direct use for his biography in the strict sense.

6 Francis' famous poem, composed shortly before his death (see page 250).

7 For example, Michael of Cologne who, in the fashionable and lilting rhyming verse of medieval Latin, wrote scornfully of him and his heavy old-fashioned hexameters:
'*Immo per terras vagus erras, si quod oberras*
Narrans res miras, deliras; nec tibi liras
Eligis, immo liras res diras, dignus et iras . . .'

8 'The choice was not inspired.' Brooke, R., *Early Franciscan Government* (Cambridge, 1959), understating.

9 There is a tendency, particularly among French and Anglo-Saxon experts to adopt rather a condescending tone towards Fortini, and certainly his prose is of that exuberant proto-fascist style that wearies and repels. Yet the basis on which he set to work was surely right. It was this: Francis was a man of Assisi; therefore let us rummage around through all the communal archives and local documents of the time; for the more we know about Assisi, where he lived and died, the more we know about Francis. The result was the sort of minor but important detail, like the feast day of San Rufino, that confirms or contradicts the genuineness of many a story.

10 '*Opusculum quoddam in modum dialogi fecit*' Bernard of Besse wrote of Crescentius. cf. Moorman, *Sources for the life of St. Francis* (Manchester, 1940), p. 110, footnote 1.

11 As Moorman points out. *Op. cit.*

12 One page in ten should be saved from the rubbish-dump. Moorman is a little more generous. 'About eighty-five per cent of Bonaventure's *Legend* is taken directly, and often verbally, from Celano,' he writes [*op. cit.* pp. 142, 143] 'and supplies us with practically no new information.' He goes on to analyse the remaining fifteen per cent; and boils it down to seven additions to incidents in Francis' life; plus a number of new miracle stories. He notes that Bonaventure apparently interviewed neither Fra Giles nor Fra Leo, undoubtedly the two best witnesses still living; but that he certainly did interview Fra Illuminato, who went with Francis into the Sultan's camp – in my view the *only* interesting and accurate episode that the whole of the work of St. Bonaventure adds to earlier and better accounts.

13 To help the reader and the student, here is a chronological table:

1226, 3 October. Death of Francis at Assisi.

1227, 19 March. Cardinal Ugolino, Cardinal-Protector of the Friars Minor, elected Pope as Gregory IX.

1227, Pentecost Chapter General. Fra Giovanni Parenti, Minister-Provincial of Spain, elected second Minister-General of the Order.

1228, 26 July. Francis canonized by Gregory IX at Assisi. At or about this time Thomas of Celano commissioned to write his *Life*.

1229, 25 February. *First Life* of Thomas of Celano approved by Pope.

1232, Pentecost Chapter General. Fra Elias of Cortona elected third Minister-General of the Order.

1239. Fra Elias deposed. Fra Albert of Pisa elected fourth Minister-General of the Order.

1240, 23 January. Death of Fra Albert of Pisa.

1240, November. Fra Haymo of Faversham elected fifth Minister-General of the Order.

1244, early. Death of Fra Haymo of Faversham.

1244, Pentecost Chapter General. Fra Crescentius of Iesi elected sixth Minister-General of the Order. Request for memoirs of Francis' life and miracles.

1245, July. First Council of Lyons. Emperor Frederick II, already twice excommunicated, deposed by Pope Innocent IV.

1246, 11 August. Fra Leo, Fra Rufino and Fra Angelo send in their memoirs.

1247, 13 July. Fra Crescentius of Iesi deposed by Pope for 'insufficiencies'.

1247, Chapter General at Lyons. Fra Giovanni of Parma elected seventh Minister-General of the Order.

1247, July. *Second Life* of Thomas of Celano finished.

1250–3. *Treatise on Miracles* of Thomas of Celano finished.

1253–5. Great scandals at Paris over the Joachimite controversy.

1257, 2 February. Giovanni of Parma 'resigns'.

1257, Chapter General at Rome. Bonaventure nominated by him his successor as eighth Minister-General of the Order.

1260, Pentecost Chapter General at Narbonne. A new 'Legend of St. Francis' asked for.

1263, Pentecost Chapter General at Pisa. *Legenda Major* of St. Bonaventure presented and approved.

1263, *Legenda Minor* of St. Bonaventure composed.

1266, Pentecost Chapter General at Paris. Decree that all previous biographies of St. Francis should be destroyed, wherever possible.

1274, 15 July. Death of St. Bonaventure (poisoned?) at the Second Council of Lyons.

14 In which he wrote his *Arbor Vitae Crucifixae*.

15 Both extracts quoted in Brooke, R., *Scripta Leonis, Rufini et Angeli* (Oxford, 1970), pp. 54 and 55. My italics. She makes light of the slightly worrying distinction between the book and the rolls, and emphasizes Ubertino's unusual accuracy in citing his sources.

16 In *Etudes Inédites sur Saint François d'Assisi* (Paris, 1932). For a sympathetic essay on Sabatier, see Dr. A. G. Little's lecture to the British Society for Franciscan Studies (now defunct) printed in his *Franciscan Papers, Lists, and Documents* (Manchester University Press, 1943).

17 In which Renan described St. Francis in a phrase that, at first sight banal, seems on reflection sadly most true: '*On peut dire que depuis Jésus François d'Assisi a été le seul parfait chrétien.*'

18 In *Analecta Bollandiana*, 19, pp. 119–97.

19 Section 79: *Nos qui fuimus cum Beato Francisco . . . et nos (tot) oculis nostris vidimus.*

20 As claimed in the prologue: '*Ego qui actus eorum vidi, verba audivi, quorum etiam discipulus fui.*' The full title of this manuscript is: *De Inceptione vel Fundamento Ordinis et Actibus Illorum Fratrum Minorum Qui Fuerunt Primi in Religione et socii Beati Francisci.* A critical edition of the text, with a massive introduction, the main thesis of which I accept, is published in *Miscellanea Francescana*, Vol. 72, Fasc. i–iv, 1972, by Fra Lorenzo di Fonzo.

21 In his introduction to the translation contained in the invaluable *Omnibus* collection of sources for the life of St. Francis published by the Franciscan Herald Press in Chicago, 1972. It is from the *Omnibus* that all the translations of the works mentioned will be taken, bar the extracts from the *Little Flowers* which are taken from the Everyman Edition and bar the *Anonymous of Perugia*, which for some extraordinary reason is not included in the *Omnibus* and which therefore I have translated, where necessary, myself.

22 In this book, or at least in those parts of it which treat directly of St. Francis and his companions, the *Legenda Antiqua* and the *Anonymous of Perugia* and the *First Life* are the basic sources, then, on which I have worked, plus the *Three Companions* for Francis' early life, supplemented by the *Second Life* of Thomas of Celano, with certain very minor additions from the *Legenda Major* and the *Speculum Perfectionis*.

23 The temptation to follow a Berserker like Chesterton and charge on boldly, as he did in his famous and brilliant biography, all footnotes discarded as a coward's shield, with more concern for impetus and empathy than for dates and facts, was almost overwhelming. All the same the critics of his *St. Francis* have a point; it is infuriating to find in it those casual references to 'some Pope or other' or to the *Canticle of the Sun* being composed as the saint 'wandered through the fields'. One does think, meanly, that he should have done a little more work on his subject. On the other hand if he had spent more time on Francis, he would have had less time to spend on Father Brown, and his myriad other books, and that would have been a tragedy. 'Franciscanisants' may frown; but the subject of their scholarship would surely agree.

24 Here, however, is a list, more or less complete, of these compilations, some of which are confusingly entitled *Chronicles*.
   (i) *Speculum Vitae Beati Francisci et Sociorum Ejus* (Anonymous) *c.* 1300–50.
   From this compilation Sabatier extracted, by deduction, the text of the *Speculum Perfectionis* – which he later discovered as a separate manuscript; a most brilliant feat of scholarship.
   (ii) *The Chronicle of the Twenty-four Generals* by Arnaud de Sarrant, *c.* 1350.
   Buried in this text are the *Life of Fra Juniper* (which I use) and the *Longer Life of Fra Giles*. (I rely on the *Shorter Life*, since discovered in manuscript form and attributed by Brooke and other scholars most definitely to Fra Leo. She publishes it after the *Legenda Antiqua* in her O.U.P. edition of the *Scripta Leonis, Rufini et Angeli*.)
   (iii) *Liber de Conformitate Vitae Beati Francisci ad Vitam Domini Nostri Jesu Christi* by Bartholomew of Pisa, *c.* 1385.
   Still more monumental. Much used by Sabatier.
   (iv) *La Franceschina* by Giacomo Oddi of Perugia, *c.* 1450.

Hagiography – the lives of twelve Franciscans. The only one of these texts written in vernacular Italian.

(v) *Chronica* by Nicholas of Glassberger, *c.* 1508.

A continuation of the *Chronicle* of Fra Salimbene. Much used by Father Cuthbert.

(vi) *Fasciculi Chronicarum* by Mariano of Florence, *c.* 1510.

(vii) *Cronaca* by Mark of Lisbon, *c.* 1500?

Written in Portuguese and Castilian.

(viii) *Annales Minorum* by Luke Wadding.

This row of seven great volumes, first published in 1625, was the history of the Order from its beginnings up to the year 1540 compiled by an Irish friar on the basis of almost all his predecessors' work: it was therefore the climax, the *ne plus ultra*, of the compilations.

25 Fortini's *Nova Vita* (first published 1926, revised edition 1959) is, despite the title, more a documented study of Assisi than a documented biography of St. Francis; hence it is not included in this admittedly arbitrary list.

In the field of studies as opposed to biographies British academics such as Rosalind Brooke, Dr. John Moorman, and Dr. A. G. Little, seem to excel; and particularly as regards Fra Elias I have tended to follow Miss Brooke.

Of present-day Franciscan writers Father Kajetan Esser appears to be both the most erudite and the most readable. Unfortunately – and it is a source of frustration – his books and articles have not generally as yet been translated from German into other languages.

Pietro Bernadone –
🌿 An Unorthodox Character 🌿

2: Pietro Bernadone – An Unorthodox Character

The Counts of Champagne

The great medieval trade fairs were held in the county of Champagne. There were six fairs, each lasting six weeks, none overlapping. The *Foire de Janvier* was held at Lagny, the *Foire de Carême* began on the Tuesday before mid-Lent at Bar-sur-Aube; they were followed by two fairs at Provins and two at the chief city and residence of the count, Troyes: the *Foire de Mai* at Provins, the *Foire Chaude de la Saint Jean* at Troyes, the *Foire de Saint-Ayoul* at Provins and the *Foire de Saint-Rémy*, the last of the year, at Troyes.

Merchants from all over Europe came to these fairs; there were dealings in spices, jewels, slaves, carpets, furs, peppers and a thousand and one other goods; but above all there were dealings in cloth and clothes. Raw wool from England, shipped to Bruges, was dyed and woven in Ghent and Ypres to be sold at the great trade fairs to merchants and dealers from Germany, Sweden, Norway, Denmark, England, Portugal, Castile, Catalonia, and all the other states of Europe – even, occasionally, to Saracens. But the mass of the buyers came from Italy: from the sea-cities of Genoa, Venice and Pisa, from the great inland centres of Milan, Florence and Siena, and from smaller towns and cities too.

The fairs were highly organized; the Consuls of the Cities welcomed the Captains of the Caravans; the Count's Sergeants kept order. And the Clerks of the Fairs set up clearing houses to change the different coins that were just coming into use all over Europe: Saracen besants, Luccan pounds, Venetian and Papal ducats. A sophisticated banking and credit system grew up; contracts between merchants of all sorts and bills of exchange were marked to be settled 'at the next fair of Troyes'. As the wealth brought by trade poured in, the court of Champagne, enriched and liberal, became the centre of almost a new civilization, knightly but not militaristic, poetic but not degenerate.

Thibaud the Great had reunited the county of Champagne. His eldest daughter Adèle married the King of France; his eldest son Henry the Open-Hearted married Marie, a daughter of the same king by his first wife, Eleanor of Aquitaine. His third son Thibaud, Seneschal of France, married Marie's sister, Alix. The rulers of Champagne were, if not kings themselves, very much more than mere counts; their knights were the proudest and probably the richest in Europe; and when Thibaud the Great died the courts of Marie of Champagne at Troyes and of her mother Eleanor of Aquitaine at Poitiers became the most famous and renowned in Europe.

Eleanor's grandfather, Guillaume IX of Aquitaine, had been the first of the troubadours; the first to sing of the Dame whose secrets must be kept: '*Par elle seule je serai sauvé*' – not the sort of sentiment that the Church could approve of – and of Love and its rules:

'*D'amor je sais qu'il donne aisement grande joie*
A celui qui observe ses lois.'

These laws, *Mesure, Service, Prouesse, Longue Attente* and (insistently) *Chastité* led to *Joie*, the sign of *Vrai Amor*.

These were the sort of notions that fashioned the courts of Champagne; and were not only discussed but debated. For Marie of Champagne, herself a poet, held at Troyes her famous Courts of Love where the rules of this new form of chivalry that honoured the Lady, and the techniques of the *gai savoir*, were debated. There marriage was condemned and *cortezia* praised, the Anglo-Norman *trouvères*, equivalent of the Provençal troubadours, sang their songs in the *langue d'oil*; and Chrétien de Troyes wrote the first of his famous romances, *Erec et Enide*, in which for the first time the stark stories of the Arthurian cycle were embroidered with enchanted castles, knights errant, tournaments, favours, demoniac opponents, and heroic combats. Of all the crimes against the Lady, copulation was the chief; that was why, according to the *leyes d'amor*, Tristan and Isolde were doomed and Lancelot, the *Chevalier de la Charette*, was not worthy to achieve the Graal. For the Lady must be adored and served and desired, but the desire, however sensual in tone, must never be satisfied by the senses.

In 1181 Henry the Open-Hearted died, leaving Marie his widow as Regent of Champagne till the boy-count Henry II should come of age. At about this time a merchant of Assisi, Pietro Bernardone, was at one of the great fairs of Champagne. He had left his wife Pica pregnant behind him; when he arrived back in Assisi with his bales of cloth and merchandise, he found that she had given birth to a son.[1] Much to his annoyance, she had baptized him Giovanni. The merchant, a strong-willed man, immediately changed his son's name to Francesco, the Frenchman – Francis.

If this was a mere whim, it was an extraordinarily drastic way in which to display it; more of the gesture one would expect from a poet or a sentimentalist, which Pietro Bernardone certainly was not, than from a hard-headed business-man which is what he appears to have been. If it was not a mere whim, it was a deliberate and calculated and rather provocative move: for it can be imagined that the changing of the baptismal name of the son of one of the leading merchants of the community must have created a considerable stir in a small town like Assisi. At the very least it indicates that Pietro Bernardone was a great enthusiast for French ideas and that he wanted to flaunt this enthusiasm openly.

There can be no doubt that it was he who later on brought up his son to speak French and to sing French songs, a notable habit that is often referred to as if it were extremely unusual.

There is a considerable mystery about the father of St. Francis. He is cast by all the saint's biographers, without exception, as the villain of the piece, both harsh and avaricious – and yet, on any normal view of human relations it was the father who behaved well and even over-indulgently, spoiling his son, putting up with his extravagances, fitting him out as a knight with all the expense that that involved – until he was provoked almost beyond endurance; and it was the son Francis who, as the next chapter will show, behaved badly and indeed in an abominably insulting way. 'Honour thy Father and thy Mother,' says the Bible, which both Francis and his friars were so fond of quoting. Yet no-one seems even to have reproached Francis for committing what was presumably a mortal sin in failing to honour his father; and even the Bishop of Assisi, a very worldly man and none too generous himself, supported the son against the father. Why? It is more usual, to say the least, for the established authorities to support men of substance of their own generation against extravagant, insolent and rebellious young men than vice-versa. And why, furthermore, was Pietro Bernardone so ill-thought of in Assisi that, in the documents of the Commune, drawn up at that period, his other son Angelo was always referred to as 'the son of the Lady Pica' and never, though it would have been normal, as 'the son of Pietro'?

What, in any case, was Pietro Bernardone's background? There is a late document that implies that he came from Lucca and a still later one that attempts to find a noble origin for his wife Pica. These can both be discounted. There is a possibility that Pica was a nickname, that in fact she was a Picard from northern France (her grandson, one of Angelo's two boys, was also called Piccardo); but this is mere guesswork. What is certain is that, in the communal documents, she is always referred to as *domina*, but her husband is never given the honorary title of *dominus* despite his status as a leading merchant of Assisi and as a considerable landowner of various orchards and farms, both in the plain below Assisi and on the slopes of Monte Subasio. For some reason he seems to have been extremely unpopular with the powers-that-were and to have been relegated almost to the status of a non-person by Francis' biographers. He was, at the same time, clearly a great admirer of French ideas. Can this have been the cause of his unpopularity? I think it can and it must have been. It is important to know because clearly Pietro Bernardone was a very strong character and his ideas, as in the case of all fathers with strong characters in close-knit families, directly formed his son's ideas – either in the sense that Francis accepted his father's views or in the opposite but equally important sense that he reacted against them. It will become clear that Francis was, even as a grown man, terri-fied of his father; and it took him twenty-five years of his life before he formally broke loose. That is a long and most important period in the life of a man who only lived to the age of forty-four or forty-five. And it is worth while to dig hard and wide and deep in the attempt to get to the roots of their relationship.

The Wool Trade

No striking tales have come down to us of Francis' childhood. His formal education was minimal. He learnt 'Grammar' from the canons at the parish church of San Giorgio – reading and writing, at neither of which does he appear ever to have been very skilled, and the elements of Latin. At the age of fourteen, that is to say in 1195 or 1196, he started helping in his father's business, both buying and selling.

The family house of the Bernardones was probably just off the main square in Assisi, where the *mercatus* or market was held. It was normal for the *fondaco* of a merchant, the shop itself, to occupy the front part of the ground floor of the house where he and his family lived; the merchandise was displayed both inside the building and outside, in stalls on the street. At this stage in Italian history the merchant class, the bourgeoisie, was becoming increasingly power-ful, and within the Commune was on almost equal legal footing with the nobility. The nobles were gradually being forced by the economic and social changes of the period to abandon their isolated castles and fortresses in the out-lying countryside and to come and live inside the walls of the cities and towns of Italy, submitting much against their will to the power – and the rules and regulations – of the urban *Comune*, the Commune. This was a gradual and bitter process; while it was occurring and indeed long after it occurred the nobles retained their pride of blood and their social prestige, even if they lost a considerable part of their actual power. They remained the knightly class, the *militares*; but the guilds of the merchants, the *mercatores*, were becoming the dominant and directing body; of these merchants the élite were the merchants who dealt in cloth and clothes.

It is not easy nowadays to grasp the idea of the extraordinary importance of the wool trade and its offshoots in the Middle Ages. It gave employment to incomparably more people than any other single industry. The mere process of turning wool into cloth, as Iris Origo explains in that fascinating book *The Merchant of Prato*, required six months: 'The wool was beaten, picked, greased, washed, combed, carded, placed on the distaff, and spun (in this case by ninety-six different peasant women on their farms), then it was measured off the warp and woven, then curled, shorn (while still damp), stretched out to dry, teasled and shorn again, handed over to the dyers (in this case to be dyed blue), napped and shorn again, and at last pressed and folded – each of these processes requiring a set of specialized workers.'

The merchants, even of the smaller cities like Assisi in Umbria and Prato in Tuscany, grew prosperous; Pietro Bernardone may have been nothing like, as affluent as the merchant of Prato, Francesco di Mario Datini, whose trade extended all over the Mediterranean, but he was certainly very far from being a mere shopkeeper. He, like Datini, had travelled abroad; and probably he was of much the same stamp as Datini, a self-made merchant, energetic, obstinate, querulous, self-willed and egoistic, ambitious, ostentatious, disdainful towards the minor nobles of his own town but immensely conscious of his own lack of breeding, dazzled therefore by the great nobility, impatient with opposition in his own family, unhappily married, dissatisfied and – here the parallel with the present-day self-made businessman ends – in a sense genuinely religious.

'On the first page of Datini's great ledgers stood the words "In the name of God and of profit," and these were the only goods to which these merchants aspired, profit in this world or in the next, as if the whole of life were one vast accounting house – and at its end, the final Day of Accounting.'[2] For all that Datini may not have had the slightest inkling of the true meaning of religion, he was, as the Marchesa Origo has portrayed him, an assiduous sermon-goer, a great alms-giver, a reader among whose few books was, interestingly enough, the *Fioretti di San Francesco*, and the sort of man who in his late middle-age was ready to go on a barefoot penitential pilgrimage.

Datini's papers – not only his account books but also his letters to his wife – have survived, but none of Pietro Bernardone's. Yet in a sense this hardly matters; for the portrait of Datini is the portrait of a whole class; to know the merchant of Prato is to know all the rich merchants of the *Arti della Lana*, the wool guilds, in the Italian cities of the Middle Ages. We know something of Bernardone's character, everything of Datini's, and again and again the parallel rings true. They were both men cast in the same mould. Yet there were two hundred years between them: in those two hundred years life, in its essentials, had changed very little for the merchant classes. But in one essential it had changed enormously, and that was in their attitude to the Catholic Church. By Datini's time the wool merchants had become ultra-respectable supporters of the established ecclesiastical authorities. In Bernardone's day it was very different.

The Heresy of the Cathars

God cannot have created the world. The world is evil and God is the supreme Good. That which is the supreme Good cannot have created evil. Therefore, in the universe, there are and always have been two opposing principles, one of Light which man calls God, and one of Darkness which man calls the Devil. The God of Light has created the soul of man, and heaven for the soul to live in; the Demiurge of Darkness has imprisoned man's soul in its earthly flesh and surroundings. Redemption is the process by which the element of Light is freed from the element of Darkness.

That, very briefly and superficially, is the basis of the Dualist heresy – which rather than a Christian heresy might be called a non-Christian religion. It provides a satisfactory answer to the 'problem of evil' which Christian apologists have always found so difficult to explain or explain away. For if God is all-powerful, there is no reason why he should ever have allowed evil to exist; but if there were two forces in the universe, almost equally balanced, then God is not all-powerful and it is logical that evil should both exist and persist.

Dualism, erected into a system by Mani of Ctesiphon in the third century A.D., flourished briefly and was then suppressed – in so far as any powerfully attractive idea can be suppressed. The title of Manicheans may have become a mere historical memory, but Dualist sects flourished in the Eastern Empire. From the Paulicians of the Upper Euphrates sprang the Bogomils of Bulgaria; persecuted in their own land, the Bogomils moved west towards the Adriatic, settling finally in Bosnia and Croatia. And about the year 1000 the Dualist religion, under a score of different forms and names, began spreading through the West. As early as 1022 ten canons of Orleans were condemned, and apparently burnt, as Manicheans. In 1030 there were reports of an organized Dualist sect in Italy, at the castle of Monforte by Alba. The policy of severity was abandoned; a hundred years later western Christendom was awash with different movements of reform; the Church has rarely been so powerless to impose its ideas or so uncertain as to what those ideas were or ought to be. For a brief period, however, it seemed as if a new orthodoxy might be imposed by a group of ascetic young nobles in Burgundy who had set out to reform the monasteries: the white monks of Cîteaux, vowed to poverty, simplicity and hermit-like solitude, set out to counter the scandalously lax and rich and powerful black monks of Cluny. But by the time their violent and impetuous champion, Bernard of Clairvaux, had died, in 1153, their very success had inevitably tangled them up with politics and possessions: 300 great Cistercian monasteries, centrally controlled and highly organized, inspiring in their turn the great Military Orders of the Templars in Outremer and of Calatrava in Spain, were unlikely to be hot-beds of evangelical poverty, nor their abbots devotees of solitude. Indeed in Calabria Abbot Joachim of Corazzo, whose tastes ran towards that solitude that had always been a tradition of southern Italy, which had been settled (monastically speaking) by the hermit-monks of St. Basil from Eastern Christendom, abandoned his abbey to live as a wandering hermit in the vast wooded mountains of La Sila, and ignored his condemnation by the Cistercian Order, solemnly reunited in Chapter General, as a 'fugitive monk'.

Meanwhile, often confounded with reforming movements more lowly-based than that of the nobles of Burgundy, with the Petrobrusians of northern France or the Henricians of Tours, the Dualist religion spread. Bernard of Clairvaux found them entrenched at Albi in the county of Toulouse and called them the Albigensians; in northern France they were known as the Bougres;[3] at Milan they were confused with the reforming Patarines, who, a century earlier, had been enlisted by Pope Gregory VII in his campaign to impose celibacy on the clergy; in other parts of Italy they were known (there were slight differences of doctrine between the three) as Albanesi, Concorrezzesi and Bagnolesi. But gradually one name and title came to embrace all the rest – Cathars, from the Greek $\kappa\alpha\theta\alpha\rho oi$ meaning 'the pure'.

In the early 1100s there seem to have been Cathar communities scattered all over western Christendom; particularly in the towns, particularly where the newly powerful trading classes were conscious of their growing strength and of their lack of any status in the feudal system. Yet it would be wrong to see it as merely a class movement: it was all a great deal too complicated, in structure and influence, to be explained away by simplistic identifications. Just as the feudal ideal attracted the bourgeois who, by the mischance of birth, were in fact prevented from ever taking an active part in chivalry, so the Cathar notions and practice, though middle-class and urban in origin, attracted certain of the nobility. 'The agents through whom the nobles were converted,' Steven Runciman has written, 'seem to have been heretic cloth merchants and doctors of medicine. The cloth merchant, particularly the travelling draper with goods from the East, was always welcome in noble houses ... his business connections kept him in close touch with Lombardy and with Constantinople.' The itinerant cloth merchant, in Runciman's view, would pass the new religion onto the resident cloth merchant who in turn would pass it onto the weaver, who in turn would pass it onto the noble lady for whom dresses were made: hence the preponderant influence of women among the Cathars. Hence, too, yet another name by which they were known – 'textores.'[4]

In theory the Cathars disapproved of marriage, considering it to be merely licensed fornication. This belief was logical, if self-destructive; for marriage led to procreation, and by procreation souls were imprisoned in flesh. Their ideal was perfect chastity. And to those who had had the misfortune to be born, death was a joyous release that might even, in certain circumstances, be hastened by the ritual of the *endura*, a self-imposed fasting designed to lead to death.

Within the Cathar church there were two classes. The mass of adherents were simple Believers (*Credentes*), mere acolytes (as it were) of the second class, the Perfect. The *Perfecti* were initiated by the *consolamentum*, a Latin ritual based on the ceremonies of the early Christians that combined elements of most of the Church's sacraments, and ended with a ceremonial kiss of peace and ritual prostration that was strangely similar in detail to the ritual of *'domnei'* as laid down by the Courts of Love, in which the perfect knight swore vassalage to his Lady. At about the time when Francis of Assisi began helping in his father's business, the Lady Esclarmonde of Foix, sister of Count Raymond-Roger of Foix, took the *consolamentum* at a ceremony attended by all the nobility of Languedoc; the ceremony involved renouncing Rome and the priesthood; it was therefore an open defiance of the Church. By this time, however, the extent of Cathar influence had shrunk; it had disappeared from northern France and was concentrated south of the Loire, in Toulouse, and in Italy north of Rome, around Milan – in both regions very strongly affecting (though never accepted by) all the population and all classes and coinciding, at its focal points, with a new if confused spirit of nationalism and desire for political independence. From these focal points it radiated more weakly: from Toulouse eastwards into Provençe; and from Milan southwards into Umbria. The southernmost Cathar 'church' was that of the valley of Spoleto.

It is not my intention to build up a laborious thesis – one, furthermore, which could never totally be proved or totally disproved. But it is now widely accepted that the *troubadors* of France south of the Loire and the *trouvères* of northern France, when they sang of the Lady to whom they had taken their vows and to whom they owed perfect chastity, the Lady to whom so often death alone could unite them, were singing not of women of flesh and blood but of a symbolic Lady, as much a symbol as that Lady Poverty to whom Francis of Assisi was in his turn to take his vows. In their case the Lady stood for what its adepts called *L'Eglise d'Amour*, the religion of perfect love. They were not gospel-spreaders of the Cathar beliefs, but their lyrics were inspired by the hushed and rather mysterious ideals of the Cathars.[5]

What is undeniable in Languedoc in or about the year 1200 is more tenuous in northern France two or three decades earlier. It may or may not be true that Chrétien de Troyes' romances were a secret, symbolic chronicle representing the history of the persecuted Church of the Cathars; what cannot be denied, however, is that there were curious ideas on marriage and chastity rampant at the court of Marie de Champagne; that within the territories of Champagne were the greatest toings and froings of wool merchants in Europe; that the traders in wool were known as the propagandists of Cathar beliefs; that Pietro

Bernardone was a wool merchant and a declared admirer of France; and that the Cathar church had in his time spread down into the valley of Spoleto, in which Assisi stands.

I am not suggesting that Pietro Bernardone was a Perfect. I am suggesting that he was either a Believer or an open sympathizer with Catharist teachings; that he belonged to a minority but to a powerful minority in Assisi, and that for this reason when the majority, the traditional believers in the traditional Church, established their position of dominance he became, despite his riches and influence, a highly unpopular man.

He was not perhaps a very intelligent or discriminating man; he probably did not distinguish too clearly between the aristocratic traditions and feudal panache that had dazzled him at the courts of Champagne and the strictly Catharist beliefs and practices. What I am suggesting is that he was a forceful personality who tried to impose all that he had learnt or heard in France upon his son Francis; and that Francis, all his life, was to be influenced by this informal education he had received from his father – enjoying parts of it, detesting other parts, but always strongly reacting. As for his mother, *domina* Pica, all the evidence seems to show that she was a traditional Italian *mamma*, of the weak not the strong variety, doting on her *figliolo*, afraid of her husband's temper and shocked by his views, conventionally accepting the Church and its teachings. One need hardly delve into psychology to conclude that Francis both hated his father and longed for his approval; and that this relationship is the key to at any rate the first half of his life.

Outremer ~

Imagine Francis as a little boy of five or six just beginning to ask intelligent questions and take an interest in the world. Suddenly and unexpectedly news came that shuddered all Christendom. There had been a great battle in Palestine; the knights of Outremer, with the Grand Masters of the Military Orders, had been defeated by the Saracens at the Horns of Hattin, and Jerusalem had fallen.

This was the one great event, totally overshadowing all others, that took place in Francis' childhood; it was to affect, directly or indirectly, his life and the lives of most of his contemporaries.

It is hard to give an idea of the alarm that the news of the loss of Jerusalem caused. It seemed almost like a betrayal by God himself. When the news reached Rome, the shock killed the Pope, Urban III. For almost a hundred years the Holy City had been safe in Christian hands: it had fallen to the first crusaders to the cry of *'Deus le vult'* – *'God wills it'*. But did God no longer will it? In the five Latin states of Outremer almost all was lost. In the kingdom of Jerusalem, the greatest of the states, only Tyre held out, thanks to Conrad of Montferrat. The queen, sister and successor of Baldwin the Leper, took refuge in Cyprus with her husband Guy of Lusignan. Christendom rallied. The new Pope sent out a circular letter calling for a new crusade, proclaiming a fast on every Friday for the next five years, with abstinence on Wednesdays and Saturdays. In January 1190, at Gisors, Richard the Lion Heart, King of England, and Philippe Auguste, King of France, swore a pact and took the Cross. It was decided that the French crusaders should wear red and the English white crosses. Following them, Frederick I, Barbarossa, the Emperor, took the Cross. That meant excitement even at remote Assisi; for Assisi, like all the towns and cities of Umbria and Tuscany, was ruled, indirectly and fairly benevolently, by the Emperor, who ten years earlier had installed one of his Swabian south Germans, Conrad of Lutzen, as Duke of Spoleto and Count of Assisi.

Barbarossa was the most legendary figure in Europe, and for over thirty years had been the most powerful. Dominating the Popes of his day, he had reunited under his rule all the territories of the Empire. The Lombards alone had baffled him; forced to concede virtual independence to Milan and the other communes of the Lombard League, he had built up his power in central Italy. Despite certain atrocities perpetuated by his raw German knights in the Lombard wars, he himself, tall, blond and magnificent, was considered a model of knightly virtue. But he was a German; the Third Crusade, like its two predecessors, was first and foremost a crusade of the French or at least of the French-speaking nobility.

Richard the Lion Heart himself was more of a Frenchman than an Englishman. The ruling house of the Kingdom of Jerusalem was also descended from the Counts of Anjou. And William the Good of Sicily, whose fleet saved Tyre and Tripoli, was himself a Hauteville of Norman descent. Although Philippe Auguste, the King of France, was a lukewarm crusader, the same was not true of his cousin Henry II of Champagne. Even before their young lord had taken the Cross, knights from Champagne were helping Guy of Lusignan and his fleet to besiege the Sultan at Acre. On 4 October 1189 Count Erard of Brienne, whose château dominated a hill near Troyes, led his men right to the Sultan's own tent, before he was killed; his eldest son Walter buried his body there. Meanwhile Richard the Lion Heart wintered in Sicily, holding Messina against the successor of William the Good, the misshapen bastard Tancred of Lecce, intriguing for the rights of his sister Joan, William's widow, and summoning the saintly Abbot Joachim over the Straits from Calabria to see him.[6]

In the summer of 1190 Henry of Champagne reached Acre before the kings, and as the greatest nobleman there took command of the siege. The disastrous news of the death of Barbarossa, drowned at the crossing of a river in Asia

Minor, was balanced by the arrival of Richard the Lion Heart, Philippe Auguste, and Duke Leopold of Austria. In July 1191 Acre fell to the crusaders; two months later, at the great battle of Arsuf, Richard the Lion Heart and Henry of Champagne scattered the Saracen armies and avenged the Horns of Hattin. The queen was restored if not to Jerusalem at least to her realm; Conrad of Montferrat was chosen by the barons of Outremer to marry her; shortly after the wedding he was murdered by the Assassins. Although only twenty-one, the young queen was soon twice married; by popular consent and with Richard the Lion Heart's approval, Henry of Champagne was chosen as her second husband. A truce for five years was made with the Saracens; Saladin guaranteed that Christian pilgrims would be permitted once again to visit Jerusalem; and on 9 October 1192 Richard the Lion Heart left the Holy Land only to be arrested in Vienna, contrary to all the rules and privileges that protected returning crusaders, by Duke Leopold of Austria on the trumped-up charge of having instigated the murder of Conrad of Montferrat. So ended, but even so, unsordidly, with the tale of a minstrel's song and the freeing of the hero, the legendary Third Crusade. We must imagine the little boy at Assisi, who perhaps even before the crusade had begun had been taught a few lines of the *Chanson de Roland* and learnt of the wickedness of the Saracen and the heroism of the paladins, hearing as he grew up all the stories of the adventures of kings and crusaders, of the death of the Emperor whose subject he was and, no doubt, tale after tale from his father of the Court of Champagne and of the young Count Henry whom Pietro Bernardone could well have known by sight, who had conquered the Saracens and married the Queen of Jerusalem.

Henry of Champagne, like his vassal Count Erard of Brienne, never saw Troyes again. On a late summer evening in 1197 he was standing by an open window in his palace in Acre; his dwarf Scarlet slipped, clutched onto him, and they both together fell backwards through the window to their deaths.

At Troyes he was succeeded by his younger brother, the twenty-year-old son of Marie, Thibaud of Champagne, married to Blanche of Navarre, herself daughter of a great warrior against the Saracens of Spain, Sancho VI. It is easy to imagine how all this knightly heroism and tales of crusaders, battles and kingdoms to be gained and won, had revived the traditional feudal spirit and put women and their courts of love and their new religious beliefs and practices in the background. In November 1199, Count Thibaud held a joust at the Chateau of Ecri on the Aisne; there the talk of the knights turned to a new crusade. They called in a wandering preacher, Fulk of Neuilly, parish priest of a little village near Lagny, and a famous man in Champagne. So inspiring was his preaching that a messenger went to the Pope: and so the Fourth Crusade, with the Pope Innocent III's warm approval and blessings, was born.

Once again – even more so than the time before – it was the knights of Champagne who inspired and led it. Count Thibaud and Bishop Garnier of Troyes took the Cross; and with them all the nobility of Champagne, Walter of Brienne, Geoffrey of Joinville, Robert his brother, Walter of Vignory, Walter of Montbeliard, Eustace of Conflans, Guy of Plessis, Henry of Arzillières, Oger of Saint Cheron and, as the chronicles put it, 'many other right worthy men whom this book does not here mention by name.' On Ash Wednesday, Count Baldwin IX of Flanders, married to Thibaud's sister Marie, took the Cross, too, and Count Louis of Blois and many other young and boyish nobles; but they all agreed on two things: first that Count Thibaud should be their leader and secondly, remembering the advice of Richard the Lion Heart as he sailed away from Acre, that Egypt, the real source of Saracen power, should be their objective. Early in 1201 Count Thibaud sent Geoffrey de Villehardouin, Marshal of Champagne,[7] to Venice to negotiate with the Doge for ships; by April a treaty had been drawn up – Venice was to have a fleet ready to sail by June the following year. Thereafter nothing seemed to go right with this noble and knightly enterprise: first news reached Geoffrey that his master Count Thibaud was sick and despaired of, then on the way back to Troyes at one of the Alpine passes he crossed Walter of Brienne with a score of the best knights of Champagne off to conquer the lands of his wife in southern Italy. They said they would come to Venice the next year, but they did not; and when, in November 1202, the fleet carrying the crusaders finally sailed from Venice under the leadership of a veteran crusader and patron of the troubadours, Boniface of Montferrat, there was a disastrous episode at Zara across the Adriatic, and almost half the host decided to leave and join Walter of Brienne in Apulia – for he, too, was fighting for the Cross – and it took all of Geoffrey's begging and persuasion to induce them to go on.

What was this distraction? What were Walter of Brienne and his followers from northern France doing in the heel of Italy – and what relevance could this possibly have had to the boy in Assisi? These are questions that will be answered in the fourth chapter of this book. For, chronologically speaking, the tale has jumped rather too far ahead; by the time the knights of Champagne were in Apulia, the boy in Assisi had become a grown man – he would have known of the great doings of the outside world but he had taken no part in such deeds. On the other hand his life in Assisi, though for years placid, had not been entirely uneventful. On the contrary he, too, had had his adventures within the little world of the Spoleto duchy – both his triumphs and his disasters.

NOTES

1 There is no proof that Pietro Bernardone was in Champagne when his son was born. We are simply told that he 'had gone to France on business.' But the presumption is very strong. There were other trade fairs, particularly in Provence; Provence, however, at this time was imperial, not French territory.

As for the date of Francis' birth, my inclination is to place it in early 1182 when his father would have been at the Lagny fair. For if anyone was by natural bent an Aquarius, it was Francis.

There are various legends about his birth – mysterious visitors arriving to prophesy, the simultaneous birth in Assisi of an Antichrist, etc. – which are probably accretions. The stable which is shown in Assisi as his birthplace is unconvincing.

2 Origo, I., *The Merchant of Prato* (Jonathan Cape, 1957; Peregrine Books, 1963).

3 A corrupt French version of 'Bogomil.' It became pejorative: in the derived Anglo-Saxon six-letter word 'bugger'.

4 Runciman, S., *The Mediaeval Manichee* (Cambridge University Press, 1955). A slim volume – unlike his massive *History of the Crusades* on which I have also relied – which concentrates on the Bogomils of Bulgaria.

A vast literature has, in recent years, grown up around the Cathars. Sabatier (in a footnote to page 41 of the English edition) wrote as follows: 'I would say that between the inspiration of Francis and the Catharist doctrines there is an irreconcilable opposition; but it would not be difficult to find acts and words of his which recall the contempt for matter of the Cathars: for example, his way of treating his body, some of his counsels to his friars: *Unusquisque habet in potestate sua inimicum suum, videlicet corpus, per quod peccat.* (Assisi MSS 338, folio 20b 2, *De Conformitate*, 138b 2) *Cum majorem inimicum corpore non habeam.* (2, Celano 3, 63.) These are momentary but inevitable obscurations, moments of forgetfulness, of discouragement, when a man is not himself, and repeats mechanically what is said about him.' That is Sabatier's interpretation. It only needs a slight shift of perspective to see that Francis was not repeating what was said about him at the time but the doctrines, possibly even the phrases, which had been instilled in him as a child and which as an adult he had rejected. In Runciman's view (page 129): 'By the middle of the fourteenth century it was all over. The only trace of Cathar doctrine was now to be found in certain of St. Francis' own teachings. Consciously or unconsciously, he had absorbed something of their ideas of the evil of matter and of the identity of the human with the animal soul.'

Both of these great men, however, agree on the essential: that St. Francis was influenced by the Cathars. My own view, which I will attempt to substantiate in the course of this book, is that he was never interested in or influenced by their weird cosmogony, their complex theology or even their esoteric ceremonies. What did affect him was the way of life they practised, and their attitudes towards their fellow men.

5 Those who know Denis de Rougemont's masterpiece, *L'Amour et L'Occident* (1939 Editions Plon. Revised edition 1956), will be aware of how much this chapter owes to him. Briefly, the thesis on which he founded his ideas was this: it is unthinkable that two movements should co-exist at the same period in the same centres without affecting each other. Therefore, despite superficial contradictions, the lyric poetry of the troubadours and the religious ideals of the Cathars, both of which flourished in southern France, and particularly in Toulouse, in the twelfth century must necessarily be linked.

This study of St. Francis is based on very much the same idea, more loosely and more widely applied: namely that Assisi did not exist in a vacuum.

6 It is difficult to disentangle truth from legend in the story of St. Francis of Assisi; but it is almost impossible in the case of the Abbot Joachim. Strangely enough, English chroniclers alone give what appears to be an objective glimpse. A fellow Cistercian abbot, Ralph of Coggeshall, visited Italy in 1195 and was curious enough to seek an interview with the 'renegade'. Joachim looked about sixty; and, reports Ralph, he and the new Order he had founded at San Giovanni in Fiore were much supported by the Emperor Henry VI, Barbarossa's son and successor, and his wife Constance. Religion and politics were totally intertwined in the Middle Ages.

Earlier it is Benedict of Peterborough (II, pp. 151–5, in the first redaction of Roger Hoveden's *Chronicles*) who reports the meeting of Christmas 1189 between Richard the Lion Heart and the wandering abbot. Joachim prophesied that the king would be victorious in Palestine and Saladin slain – which was diplomatic. He also explained the seven Heads of the Dragon in the Apocalypse; they represented Herod, Nero, Constantius, Mohammed, Melsemuth (Abdul Muneim of Almohar), Saladin – and Antichrist, who had been born fifteen years earlier in Rome and would become Pope. But the chronicle may, deliberately or not, have got this a little wrong: Joachim, as his writings show, was a master of that turgid medieval style in which it is impossible to be sure if a phrase is meant literally or symbolically.

At this stage the reader may be wondering what is the importance of the Abbot Joachim. It is twofold: first of all, he was in Sabatier's view not merely the precursor of Francis of Assisi but 'his true spiritual father.' Secondly, thanks to Joachimite prophecies and theories of history, according to which the Third Age was due to begin in the year 1260, St. Francis very nearly became, after his death, that which he had never desired to be in his life. As Chesterton puts it, 'St. Francis was so great and original a man that he had something in him of what makes the founder of a religion. Many of his followers were more or less ready, in their hearts, to treat him as the founder of a religion. They were willing to let the Franciscan spirit escape from Christendom as the Christian spirit had escaped from Israel. . . . That was the point the Pope had to settle: whether Christendom should absorb Francis or Francis Christendom.'

7 Geoffrey de Villehardouin's *Chronicle* describes the Fourth Crusade; and the part that he, as Marshal of Champagne, played in it.

There Was a
❦ Young Man of Assisi ❦

3: There Was a Young Man of Assisi

Francis' boyhood and early youth had been, like his childhood, peaceful and undisturbed. Years before he was born the Emperor had descended with his Germans on Umbria; the infamous warrior-archbishop, Christian of Mainz, had razed Terni and sacked Narni. Assisi, wisely, had submitted; and for twenty years Duke Conrad ruled, from Spoleto, a duchy that like all central Italy under German domination was fairly contented and increasingly prosperous. Inside Assisi, dominated by the duke's fortress, the Rocca, the merchants increased their wealth; the bishop, from his palace in the lower part of the town, squabbled with the canons of the cathedral of San Rufino, in the upper part, over revenues and rights. Outside Assisi the local nobles, mainly of German descent, lived with their gangs of retainers in their isolated little castles and towers and squeezed the merchants with the toll-fees they demanded for passing through their territory. High up on Monte Subasio the great Abbey of St. Benedict looked out over the valley of Spoleto, through which the Tiber wound; on the other side of the rich and fertile plain stood the free imperial city of Perugia.

Probably Francis did not go with his father on Pietro Bernardone's long journeys. He had finished his schooling at the age of fourteen; and for two uneventful years he helped in the *fondaco* on the market square. It must have been a dull life for a romantic boy dreaming of crusades and knight-errantry and the service of fair ladies. It must have been a dullish life, come to that, for all the citizens of Assisi; twenty years without freedom, without change.

In 1198 all that came to an end, and Assisi lived through a tumultuous twelve years. The age-old pattern of events obtained. Sudden freedom, joyfully celebrated, gave place to a class struggle and civil strife; civil strife led to civil war, the calling-in of outsiders and war in earnest. Whether on a small or a large scale, this process is always immensely stimulating to those caught up in it. Their initial exhilaration may disappear, and disillusion set in. Life becomes distinctly unsettling. But young men bored with trade need to be unsettled, they desire to be unsettled; they are all the better for being unsettled. After all, had Francis not been unsettled, he would not have become a saint.

The Emperor Henry VI

Medieval political history resembles nothing so much as a perpetual series of games of chess between two antagonists, one named the Pope, the other the Emperor. There would be long intervals between the games when both players would remember that they were old friends; such intervals seemed merely to whet their appetites for the next bout. Games tended to end in stalemate. The chequer-board was the whole of western Christendom, which both players claimed the right to dominate. But the most dramatic contests usually took place in the Pope's section of the board, Italy, rather than in Germany, the Emperor's. The contest was complicated by the lack of any consistent agreement as to the rules: it was, however, agreed that although their pawns and pieces might fall, the two players themselves enjoyed a certain physical immunity.

In 1190 the Emperor Frederick I, Barbarossa, died on the Third Crusade; he had been a grandmaster of the game. Six years before he died he had made a brilliant move, he had married his son and heir Henry to the heiress of the Kingdom of Sicily, Constance.

'Sicily' gives a very bad idea of what shall henceforward be called, simply, the Kingdom. The territories that comprised the Kingdom included the whole southern half of the Italian peninsula – the duchies of Apulia (the heel) and Calabria (the toe), so long held by the Byzantines, the Lombard principalities of Salerno and Capua to the north, the three sea-republics of Naples, Gaeta and Amalfi – and the island of Sicily itself, reconquered from the Saracens, with its great and splendid capital, after Baghdad and Cordoba the most renowned and wealthy city in Islam, Palermo. With all those lands the Popes of the day had enfeoffed the Hauteville brothers, the adventurers from Normandy who had organized the reconquest. Thereafter Roger II the Great had developed at Palermo one of the richest and strangest Christian states in Europe, patronizing Arab geographers, keeping a harem, dominating the Mediterranean with his Saracen fleet commanded by an officer with a Saracen title – the Grand Admiral.

On the eve of the Third Crusade, with the unexpected death of her young nephew, Constance, daughter of Roger the Great, had become heiress to all the lands of the Kingdom. And Constance was married to Henry of Hohenstaufen, who next year on the death of his father Barbarossa was duly elected Emperor. What the Popes had long feared seemed inevitable: they would be at the mercy of an all-powerful ruler dominating both northern and southern Italy.

The Norman barons of the Kingdom had no more desire than the Pope to be dominated by the Hohenstaufen and his Germans. Henry VI was an exceptionally able and energetic man; yet despite his abilities the Norman barons managed to keep him in check for a time. They chose one of their own number, Tancred of Lecce, a bastard grandson of Roger the Great, as king. The Pope of the day, the aged Celestine, blessed their choice; and the Normans with his help held out against the Emperor's first two expeditions.

1194 was the year of great changes. First, the Empress Constance, eight years

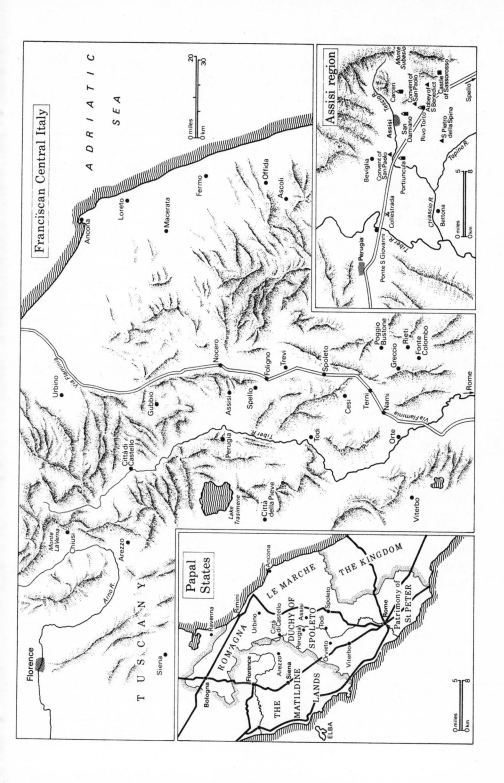

Franciscan Central Italy

A D R I A T I C

S E A

Assisi region

Monte
Subasio

Carceri

Convent of
San Paolo

Assisi

San
Damiano

Abbey of
Rivo Torto   S.Benedict   Castle
of Sassorosso

S.Pietro
della Spina

Spello

Topino R.

Beviglia

Convent of
San Paolo

Portiuncula

Collestrada

Chiascio R.

Bettona

Perugia

Ponte S.Giovanni

Tiber R.

Ferro

Loreto

Ancona

Macerata

Offida

Ascoli

Via Flaminia

Urbino

Gubbio

Città di
Castello

Nocero

Foligno

Trevi

Spoleto

Poggio
Bustone

Greccio

Rieti

Fonte
Colombo

Assisi

Spello

Perugia

Cesi

Terni

Narni

Rome

Tiber R.

Todi

Orte

Lake
Trasimene

Città
della Pieve

Viterbo

Via Flaminia

Monte
La Verna

Chiusi

Arezzo

Arno R.

T U S C A N Y

Siena

Florence

Papal
States

Ravenna

Rimini

Ancona

R O M A G N A

LE MARCHE

THE KINGDOM

Bologna

Urbino

Città
di Castello

DUCHY OF

Florence

Arezzo

Perugia

Assisi

SPOLETO

Spoleto

Rome

Patrimony of
ST PETER

Siena

Todi

Orvieto

Viterbo

THE

MATILDINE

LANDS

ELBA

married and forty years old, gave birth to a son. To allay all suspicion she had her bed brought out into the public square of the town of Iesi in Le Marche and there, attended by two skilful Arab doctors, gave birth. The infant heir to both the Kingdom and the Empire was baptized Frederick Roger in memory of his two renowned grandfathers. Constance left him with her great friend the wife of Conrad of Lutzen, and he spent the first two years of his babyhood in Umbria, not far from Assisi. Francis was nearing the end of his schooling at the time; and it is an unusual schoolboy who does not follow the doings of Emperors, heiresses and kings with passionate interest, particularly when the drama is being played out almost on his doorstep.

In February Tancred of Lecce died. He left a boy son, who was chosen as king, a widow, Sibylla of Acerra, and three daughters of legendary beauty. The Emperor Henry VI descended a third time upon Sicily; and this time by force of arms and fair words at long last seized his wife's inheritance. He was crowned in the cathedral at Palermo on Christmas Day. Despite his promises he took a most bloody vengeance on the Normans. Tancred of Lecce's body was dug up and desecrated; his Admiral, Marguritone, blinded and disembowelled; his supporters crowned with crowns of revolving nails. The last of the Hautevilles, the boy king William, disappeared; his mother and his three sisters were deported to a prison deep in the Emperor's German realms. The tale of the three princesses was told all over Europe; pity and chivalry stirred.

Despite bloody revolts, bloodily suppressed, the Emperor consolidated his grip over all Italy north and south of Rome: he appointed his brother Philip of Swabia ruler of the Matildine lands in Tuscany, Markwald of Anweiler ruler of the Duchy of Ravenna and Le Marche of Ancona on the Adriatic, confirmed Conrad of Lutzen in Umbria, and spread his German nobles throughout the Kingdom. He brought the baby Frederick Roger to Palermo and there had him crowned king. There were talk and dreams of a universal empire and preparations for a new crusade. Then, on 20 September 1197, of a chill in Messina, Henry VI died. His heir and successor, the future Emperor Frederick II, was a baby aged three, half a Hohenstaufen, half a Hauteville.[1]

After the death by illness or old age of a tyrant or dictator there is always a lull while the subject people hesitate and look around and wonder whether they really can be free. The weakness of the whole medieval and feudal system, as will have become apparent from these few preceding pages, was that a man had to be succeeded by another man if the hereditary system was to work smoothly. Women or children alone could not hold turbulent states like the Kingdom or Outremer together. The inhabitants of Palermo had seen it on the death of Tancred of Lecce, they were to see it again on the death of Henry VI. The

Hohenstaufen possessions were to dissolve, at least temporarily, into their component parts.

Freedom for Assisi

In the first week of 1198, while all were hesitating, Pope Celestine died. The Cardinals elected, on 8 January, the youngest Pope for many years, Lothair of Segni, of noble birth on his father's side, and on his mother's side a member of the great Roman family of the Scotti; thirty-seven years old, Cardinal Deacon, a canon lawyer who had studied both at Paris and Bologna. In February he was ordained priest, consecrated bishop and crowned as Pope Innocent III.[2] In the spring he set out from Rome, after due diplomatic preparation, on what was to be a triumphant progress to reclaim suzerainty of the traditional papal lands from the representatives of the imperial usurpers.

Troubadours from Provence had already been stirring up with their songs a wave of national feeling against the Germans. Pierre Vidal had wandered across from the great Cathar strongholds of Laurac, Gaillac, Saissac and Fanjeaux to the court of Boniface of Montferrat; he was followed by Gaucelme Faidit, Raimbaud of Vauqueyras, Peirul of Auvergne, Bernard of Ventadour and many, many others. It seems that there was a great popular movement against the feudal northerners, both French and German, that embraced Languedoc, Provence and Lombardy; and its heralds were the troubadours. Italians began to sing in Provençal. In 1196 Pietro della Caravana had become famous throughout Milan and the other cities of Lombardy for his songs against the Emperor Henry VI. As far south as the Duchy of Spoleto, high-spirited boys learnt the foreign songs and sang them as a gesture of defiance against the Emperor and the German lords and knights.

The old Duke Conrad met the new Pope in April 1198 at Narni, on the southern edge of his duchy. He made no attempt to retain his position by force; but he offered Innocent III complete submission, fealty, 10,000 pounds of silver plus an annual tribute of another hundred, and two hundred of his soldiers as a papal guard – provided he could retain the duchy. The Pope very nearly agreed; but he was powerless against the wave of anti-foreign feeling that suddenly swept over central Italy. Conrad of Lutzen agreed to go, and agreed too, before he went, to ensure an orderly transfer of power by handing over his three major fortresses, at Cesi, Gualdo and Assisi, to the legates appointed by the Pope.

Rather than hand the castle over to the papal legates, the people of Assisi[3] razed it to the ground. It is easy enough to write that simple phrase: but in practice it must have been a weary, back-breaking task. It is impossible to picture a wild rush of infuriated citizenry from the centre of Assisi to the heights above; it is the sort of hill that would bring a wild rush to a plodding halt within fifty yards. However it was done, done triumphantly; the great castle of the imperialists came toppling down.⁴ Freedom for Assisi! From their little castles dotted around the hills and on Monte Subasio the local nobles watched with queasy feelings the act that symbolized the end of an era. Inside the town walls their tall family houses, grouped around the cathedral of San Rufino, took on the air of forts, dour amidst the general good-humour and exaltation. For it must have been a most exulting time; we can picture Francis, a high-spirited youth and one of the wildest in the town, singing the Provençal songs that he knew better than any of his companions and battering bits off the great, empty castle, happy that at long last something was happening in Assisi. It was certainly the greatest and most exciting event in his life so far.

Then came the visit of the Lord Pope, and for the first time free elections. Innocent progressed triumphantly through all the towns of Umbria – Foligno, Gubbio, Todi, Assisi, Città di Castello – and the towns of Le Marche. By September he was in Perugia, issuing Bulls and Charters, granting more or less complete autonomy to the towns and cities under the protection of the Church provided they acknowledged papal suzerainty and paid their taxes. In their first heady joy the Commune of Assisi went too far, they elected a Rector – a title which implied virtually a claim to total independence. Innocent placed Assisi under an interdict; and the Rector disappeared. By December, they had at least one (probably several) elected consul.⁵

The consuls – it was usual in Umbrian cities for there to be at least four of them – were elected annually as the chief executives of the Commune, and as its judges in penal affairs. It was their task to apply the immensely detailed statutes of the Commune, which regulated, at least in theory, the lives, property rights, trading practices and personal behaviour of all the citizens. Once inside the walls and gates of a Commune the traveller was within their jurisdiction. Within the Communes the most powerful bodies by far were the *Arti* or guilds that united all members of a trade, laid down prices, standards, working-hours, forbade competition, kept out (except at fairs) imports, and generally exercised a tyrannical domination over every detail of the lives of their members; of the guilds the most important by far was the Guild of the Merchants, the *Mercanti* – far more wealthy than the shoemakers, the ironworkers or the butchers, the other leading guilds of Assisi.

As the son of one of the richest families in the Commune, Francis lived the best of lives. He was quick and clever at his trade, and as a result his father seems to have allowed him all the money he needed. He was always roaming the city with young men of his own age, eating and feasting, never wearing anything but the finest clothes, well known as a spend-thrift. 'Almost up to the twenty-fifth year of his age,' wrote Thomas of Celano disapprovingly, 'he squandered and wasted his time miserably. Indeed he outdid all his contemporaries in vanities and he came to be a promoter of evil and was more abundantly zealous for all kinds of foolishness.' But though his parents often took him to task for his extravagance, and were particularly peeved by his habit of leaping up and leaving the family table whenever his friends sent for him, they seem to have been extremely indulgent – and indeed proud of the fact that their son had more money to throw about, and finer clothes to wear, than the young sons of noble families. Besides, he was an extremely pleasant and agreeable young man; always high-spirited and gay, always courteous and spontaneous, generous to the poor and to beggars, altogether one of the most popular young men about Assisi. 'Of St. Francis' Birth, of his Vanity, Eccentricity and Prodigality,' the first chapter of the *Three Companions* is headed, 'and how he came to be Liberal and Charitable to the Poor.'

Of course it is clear that there was in all this a certain element of social climbing. All through his life Francis was ashamed of being merely the son of a merchant; or, if not ashamed, at least highly conscious. And it seems evident, from the rather guarded accounts that we have of his youth, that the young sons of noble families, if they elected Francis King of the Revels and admitted him to the companies of the *Tripudiantes*, did so largely because the king was obliged to pay. As Thomas of Celano says, he was easy and affable, ever making himself foolish because of it. It all sounds extremely conventional: the son of a *nouveau riche* businessman trying to get himself accepted by the aristocracy by throwing his father's money around – and never, never quite succeeding.

In a way it was all very sad – and even sadder for the father than for the son. Pietro Bernardone must have despised the local nobility heartily. On one level they were the enemies of his class, fighting a losing battle to retain their powers and privileges; they represented the past, he and his class stood for progress – and he was well aware that he could have bought most of them up. On another level they were pale little echoes of the real knights and great nobles whom he had seen and admired in Champagne. He must have felt that he knew more about chivalry and the ideals and practice of chivalry than they did. It was intolerable that his son Francis should waste time and money in associating with the sons of such men as these; but it was even more intolerable that, if he did so, he should be forced to play second fiddle to them by a mere accident of blood. I picture Pietro Bernardone as being violently ambitious for his son but totally torn between two conflicting ambitions: on the one hand satisfied with the boy's ability as a merchant and determined to groom him as his own successor, with his own beliefs and ideals – but at other times fascinated by the thought that his son, already more cultivated than the local boors of better blood, might become a great knight and possibly even a prince, and play a part on a wider stage than that of Umbria.

War with Perugia

Whatever the relations between the sons of the merchants and the sons of the nobles, there can have been no love lost between their fathers. It has been calculated that tolls had to be paid sixteen times on merchandise brought into Assisi between the river Po and the borders of the duchy; but what the merchants really resented was the further tolls they had to pay to the nobles of the county of Assisi whose lands they crossed.

It was the same all over Umbria; with the growing prosperity of the towns and cities, in two decades of peaceful trade, the nobles had become mere parasites and were hated and resented as such. As soon as their imperial protectors were swept away, it was inevitable that the town-dwellers, led by the merchant class, should turn on the fierce but basically powerless castellans. As for the castellans, they had seen how the town-dwellers had destroyed the great castle of the duke and they had no illusions about their own powers of resistance; besides, the Commune exercised its own attraction. The nobles of the county had always had their footholds within the walls – just as the Abbot of St. Benedict had his town house on the main square; and as more and more of the little castles were abandoned or destroyed for some alleged breach of the Commune's statutes, more and more of the noble families came into the town to live and often indeed, as individuals, to play their parts in the Commune's public life. But this was a slow and jerky process; and the more powerful nobles, like the lords of Sassorosso, clung bitterly to their rights and privileges.

The castle of Sassorosso stood on the far side of Monte Subasio, beyond the Abbey of St. Benedict, at the very edge of the boundary of the county of Assisi, on what was known as 'the knight's road' that led down to the next town, Spello. Gislerio, son of Alberico, lord of Sassorosso, lived on the tolls he charged all travellers who used the road. Despite the strength of the castle, he realized that he alone with his three sons and their retainers could never hold it against an expedition from the town: he needed a protector. And so, followed by other nobles of the countryside, he turned to Perugia.

Perugia, semi-independent for seventy years, had long been following a policy of expansion. The Consuls of Perugia had dominated their own unruly outlying nobles; but they were perfectly willing to support rebellious nobles who offered them fresh territory and alliances outside their own borders, particularly in the case of Assisi, an hereditary enemy. There was no sense of community among the merchant class in different towns: each was concerned only with the greatest possible expansion of its own guild and its power.

By January 1200 the struggle for power in Assisi and its territory had reached the critical stage of civil war. Part of the lands of the lords of Sassorosso lay within the territory of Perugia; and so, on 17 January, the eldest son of Gislerio swore allegiance to the Consuls of Perugia and applied for citizenship; a week later Fortebraccio, the second son, and his nephew Oddo, sought refuge in Perugia – to which, it seems, the old lord Gislerio had already fled. The communal army of Assisi razed the abandoned tower and castle. Under their city's statutes the Consuls of Perugia were obliged to help new citizens to defend and *recover* their goods. Therefore an ultimatum went out across the valley; the Commune of Assisi was ordered to rebuild Sassorosso and pay compensation to the lords. The ultimatum was scornfully rejected. Like the cities of Lombardy three decades earlier, the towns of Umbria were keen to enjoy the most exhilarating of all collective freedoms, the freedom to make war.

It is no longer the fashion to sneer at the little wars of Italy simply because of their scale. War is as dramatic an experience for those involved whether hundreds or millions are involved in them. Indeed it seems far more natural to fight for a town and people one knows and can touch, see, and comprehend than for abstract concepts like a nation or an empire.

For almost two years the war between Assisi and Perugia was an affair of raids down in the valley, crop-burnings, the destruction of towers and reprisals. By October 1201 Perugia had made a pact with Foligno; and Assisi with Spello and Nocera. Most of the nobles of the county of Assisi had taken refuge in Perugia with their families, including the lords of Coriano, the five sons of Offreduccio – the youngest, Favarone, with his wife Ortolana and their three daughters, Agnes, Beatrice and Clare, Francis' future followers. A few of the nobles of Perugia had joined the forces of Assisi. Gradually, as in all wars that begin slowly, the clamour grew on both sides for a decisive action.

The great battle finally took place in the autumn of 1202. The bells rang, and the army of the Commune of Assisi assembled outside the cathedral and marched out of the town, behind their banners, through the Roman Gate. First came the companies of ordinary foot-soldiers, each from their own quarter of the town: the Company of San Rufino, following the banner of the Palm of the Martyr, the Company of Santa Maria Maggiore, the bishop's Church, behind the banner of the Stars; the Companies of Murorotto Inferiore, of Murorotto Superiore, of Il Colle, Il Prato, Il Borgo, of San Lorenzo, and of L'Abbazia; then the foot-soldiers of the guilds, the Mercanti, the Calzolai, the Macellai, the Gabellieri, then the archers and the cavalry escorting the *Carruccio*, a great wagon drawn by white oxen, with on it an altar, candles lighted and a shining cross at which the priests of Assisi, to the sound of trumpets, celebrated

Mass over whatever saintly relics their town could provide. Over the *Carruccio* flew the red and blue standard, the *Gonfalone* of Assisi.

Like all the richer young men of Assisi and the few young noblemen loyal to the Commune, Francis had been armed and mounted by his father and rode with the cavalry; with their allies from Nocera and Spello the army of Assisi must have been two thousand strong. It was a short march down into the plain, then a long morning's trek of about ten miles to the border between the territories of Assisi and of Perugia. The army of Assisi halted before the Tiber and took up position at a place called Collestrada in and around gentle hills dominated by a small fort and the buildings of a hospital; their commander lined up his crossbowmen by the hospital and placed his cavalry in ambush. In the early afternoon the soldiers of Perugia crossed the shallow river and fell upon the men of Assisi.

No clear description of the battle that followed survives; but it seems to have been a bloody affair, particularly when the Assisi exiles came to grips with their low-born countrymen. Two of the lords of Sassorosso were killed; but by late afternoon the Perugians had won the greatest victory they could remember. According to one account, the banks of the Tescio, a tributary of the Tiber, overflowed with the blood of the killed.[6] The victors pursued the vanquished far and wide over the plain, massacring the foot-soldiers till darkness saved the survivors. But the men on horseback, as was usual in medieval battles, were captured where possible. Among the prisoners who were led back that night by the triumphant Perugians to the dungeons underneath the palace of the *Capitano del Popolo* was Francis of Assisi.

Defeat, Dungeons and Depression

It is infuriating that we know nothing either of the part Francis himself played in the battle and in the long months of skirmishing that preceded it, or of his feelings at the first great catastrophe of his life. He never appears to have talked about the fighting later on; or if he did, his biographers, who skate quickly over the episode, have censored his comments and stories. What in a way is very strange is that he, the gentlest of saints, never expressed a horror of war and bloodshed in his later teachings. He had seen, underneath all the trimmings of banners and trumpeters, violent death; and it does not seem to have horrified him. In fact, distasteful though the idea is, in those eighteen months of fighting, in that great battle, Francis may very well have killed one of his fellow-men.

All we know for sure is that, of all the people in the world, the only ones for whom Francis in later life was to show positive distaste were the Perugians. Admittedly they took a year from his life; and a year is a long time, particularly for a spoilt and whimsical young man. He was not treated badly; the reports stress that he was imprisoned with the nobles, not with the commoners, 'because he was noble in his ways.' His perpetual cheerfulness seems to have got on the nerves of his fellow-prisoners occasionally; on the other hand it was he and only he who took the trouble to look after a fellow-prisoner, surly, depressed and ostracized. In many ways Francis was a most conventional young man – he loved what was colourful and loathed what was depressing; he could not bear, as he himself wrote at the time of his death, even to look at lepers – but he had this breezy and generous good-nature that made him always not only courteous but genuinely kind – as even his companions in the prison were forced to recognize.

Their defeat at Collestrada came as a great shock to the over-confident townsfolk of Assisi. Within a few weeks Nocera had submitted to Perugia, and when Gubbio, further north, dared to challenge the new dominant power of the region, they too despite their famous crossbowmen were bloodily cut to bits. A year later, in November 1203, the Commune of Assisi made a determined effort to put their war effort on a sounder footing. In order to end class warfare within the town and its territory three arbitrators were appointed.[7] They decided that the houses and property of the 'loyal' nobility that had earlier been burnt down or demolished should be restored; but that outlaws and traitors should be utterly banished. This was not, however, as some scholars have mistakenly imagined, a form of truce with Perugia. On the contrary, the Consuls of Perugia immediately reacted by promising the said 'outlaws and traitors' their homes and their revenge.

Yet there seems to have been at least some sort of lull in the fighting; for Francis came home. He had for the first time in his life fallen seriously ill while in prison; and a charitable group in Perugia that looked after invalid prisoners had taken him under their protection. At any rate the Perugian authorities allowed him to be ransomed; cheerfully and willingly Pietro Bernardone paid out a sum of money for his unfortunate son. And Francis came home.

Defeat, imprisonment and illness affected even his sunny temperament. Reaction set in; and a long period of depression followed. Gradually, however, he recovered. He walked about the house with a cane, went out again into the fields and vineyards, and eventually began to lead his old style of life with his old good spirits.

As always after a military defeat and an unsuccessful attempt to re-establish the situation – unsuccessful in the sense that the pact of November 1203 had failed to entice back the exiled nobles, having been immediately countered by the Perugians – the political atmosphere on the side of the defeated became both active and embittered. The war had been provoked by the townspeople, led

by the newly powerful bourgeoisie. After the defeat at Collestrada it is reasonable to suppose that the merchant class split into two separate groups, the
moderates and the extremists. The moderates were for reconciling the exiled
nobles and so depriving the Perugians of their pretext for continuing the war;
the November pact was their work. When it failed, as it very soon became
evident that it had, the extremists demanded that the war should be prosecuted
with greater energy and determination, and, with popular support, they insisted
that the consuls should be replaced by a *Podestà*, one man, a sort of temporary
dictator and commander-in-chief, his power limited only by the statutes and
by the general assembly of the Commune. This was a fairly drastic measure,
probably imposed by an active but temporarily dominant minority. In my view
Pietro Bernardone was at this time one of the leaders of this extremist faction;
for the man who at the beginning of the year 1204 was elected as *Podestà* was a
heretic and a Cathar, Gerardo di Gilberto by name.[8]

It was a little late in the day. After the first flush of freedom and the disappearance of the strictly conventional German feudal lords from central Italy,
the Cathars had made a bid for political power. They had been particularly
active at Orvieto, where a *Podestà* sent out from Rome by Pope Innocent had
even been killed by some of their wilder followers, and at Viterbo, where their
women had infiltrated the bishop's congregation. Even the weapon of the interdict had been used in vain against citizens who no longer believed in the
Catholic sacraments. But at Viterbo there had been a long tradition of heresy
and many visits by famous Cathar preachers; even so the Pope had imposed his
will and his men. And at Orvieto the populace had finished by rioting against
the Cathars. By 1200 the menace of Catharism as a real rival to Catholicism
had almost disappeared from the states that owed direct allegiance to the Pope.

And so Innocent III lost little time in reacting against the presumptuous
minority in Assisi. There was never a Pope as ready as he to use the weapon of
the interdict or the even more powerful weapon of excommunication. Assisi
was placed under an interdict and all its normal life interrupted: no bells rang,
the church doors remained shut, Masses were not said, birth, marriage and
death could only be celebrated, if at all, by the most stark formalities. By the
end of the summer Gerardo di Gilberto had been ousted or resigned; Cardinal
Leo of Santa Croce, sent from Rome, received an oath of fidelity and orthodoxy
from Gerardo's successor and from fifty leading citizens. In effect not only did
this mean the humbling of the extremists – very probably Pietro Bernardone
was among the fifty who were made to swear '*amende honorable*', for merchants
can rarely afford to be martyrs – but it also indicated that the Church was
throwing in her weight behind the Perugians; indeed in August of the following year, 1205, there was a serious attempt by the Perugian *Podestà* to impose a

truce and force Assisi to accept the exiles back on terms favourable to them – after which the war spluttered on inconclusively for another five years.

But all that is to look ahead a little. At the time, in the early months of 1204, as Francis was recovering his health, his father Pietro Bernardone had plunged up to his neck in the political life of the town and for a few brief months was riding high. The gamble ended with sudden political defeat and personal eclipse and humiliation. His hopes for an energetic conduct of the war which, if successful, would have ensured the expansion of his trading activities and offered his son a chance of glory and revenge vanished as swiftly as did his dreams of a new and triumphant religion. That, at least, is a reasonable hypothesis. For it alone explains why (and when) the next episode of Francis' life occurred.

For it was at this point that the son of Pietro Bernardone took it into his head, like so many of the real knightly class, to set out for Apulia, and join Walter of Brienne and the nobles of Champagne. His father, apparently without quibble, probably with great pride, equipped Francis with arms and armour; and Francis, attended by a young boy as a shield-bearer, in the company of a genuine nobleman from Assisi, with whom he had long been discussing this adventure, set off to win fame and fortune and to be knighted by Walter of Brienne.

His equipment was magnificent; and though his fellow-citizen was a nobleman, Francis was by far the more extravagant of the two. When the neighbours commented on this to his mother, she told them that she was sure he would become a great prince. For once Pietro Bernardone and his wife seem to have been united in their thoughts, fierce ambition and wishful dreams for their son. He was just under twenty-five years of age.

NOTES

1 (a) Family Tree of the Hohenstaufens (Holy Roman Emperors, Kings of Germany):

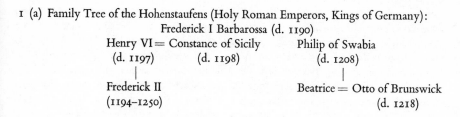

Frederick I Barbarossa (d. 1190)

Henry VI = Constance of Sicily   Philip of Swabia
(d. 1197)   (d. 1198)   (d. 1208)

Frederick II   Beatrice = Otto of Brunswick
(1194–1250)   (d. 1218)

(b) Family Tree of the Hautevilles (Kings of Sicily, Dukes of Apulia and Calabria):
Roger II the Great (d. 1154)

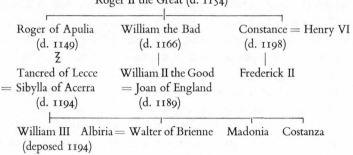

Roger of Apulia	William the Bad	Constance = Henry VI
(d. 1149)	(d. 1166)	(d. 1198)
Tancred of Lecce	William II the Good	Frederick II
= Sibylla of Acerra	= Joan of England	
(d. 1194)	(d. 1189)	

William III   Albiria = Walter of Brienne   Madonia   Costanza
(deposed 1194)

2 The main source for the life of Innocent III are his letters – over 5,000 have been edited – and the chronicle *Gesta Innocentii*.

3 If present-day Assisi has 12,000 inhabitants, it seems reasonable to put its population *c.* 1200 at 8,000. The town was slightly less than two-thirds of the size it is now but was probably more densely inhabited. The cathedral of San Rufino (third and final version) had been begun in 1140; though it was not completed or consecrated till one hundred years later. Of the Abbey of St. Benedict on Monte Subasio only the ruins survive; it was sacked by the towns-folk of Assisi themselves in a later civil war.

4 The castle now dominating Assisi is the papal castle *rebuilt* on the site of the Rocca two centuries later.

5 The archives of the Commune only prove the existence of one consul for the year 1198. But the documents surviving are few; it seems more reasonable to assume that there were several. (As early as 1130 Perugia had two.)

   A judgement recorded for this year begins '*Ego Bonus Baro, Asisinatum Consul.*' Fra Salimbene, talking of Fra Elias (who received him into the Order), writes '*et vocabatur in saeculo Bonusbaro.*' Could these two references be to one and the same person? It is generally agreed that Fra Elias came from a small hamlet outside Assisi, Beviglia. He was certainly an excellent administrator – and a man of violent temper. (The ex-consul Bonusbaro led the army of Assisi at the battle of Collestrada.)

   If indeed he was Assisi's first consul and Francis' commander in battle, that would explain what has so puzzled many people: the extraordinary trust and confidence that Francis placed in this man so unlike himself. But there are difficulties. Fra Elias died in 1253; even if he was very old when he died, this would still make him a very young man to be appointed as Assisi's first consul ever. Furthermore Fra Salimbene (who admittedly was one of his detractors) described him as a schoolmaster and carpet-weaver ('*Suebat cultras et docebat puerolos psalterium legere*') by profession, not a politician, judge, and general. It is impossible to say. I prefer, however, this thesis, supported by Fortini, to Sabatier's suggestion, equally but less convincingly designed to explain Elias' influence, that the old friend who accompanied Francis to the grotto after his return from Apulia was Bombarone da Beviglia, later Fra Elias. As Sabatier himself points out (page 21, footnote) it is very difficult to understand why the *First Life* does not name Elias. On the other hand the same objection does not apply vis-à-vis the battle of Collestrada. Thomas of Celano *does not mention* either the battle or Francis' imprisonment.

6 For the description of the events leading up to the battle of Collestrada I am heavily indebted to Fortini. The precise date of the engagement is uncertain, but the evidence, such as it is, supports the date of November 1202.

An interesting contemporary source, from which the detail of the Tescio overflowing with blood is drawn, is Boniface of Verona's epic Latin poem written to the glorification of Perugia: *L'Eulistea*. He described the killing as '*strages latissima, cedes saevissima*' – which, even allowing for poetic exaggeration, means many dead.

7 The pact of November 1203 was headed: '*Compositio Pacis inter bonos homines et homines populi.*' The wording is of some significance. The attempt to identify Francis' fraternity with the *populo minuto*, the *minores*, as opposed to the *populo grasso*, the *majores*, fails if the terms *minores* and *majores* were not commonly used at the time in Assisi to distinguish the two classes.

8 Sabatier states that the *Podestà*, Gerardo di Gilberto, was a heretic. Fortini queries his evidence and traces Gerardo's background. He was probably not by birth a citizen of Assisi – in 1201 he had been *Podestà* of Spello; and it was normal for *Podestà* to be chosen from 'outsiders' in time of civil strife (though when that convention first became general is none too clear). In any case he had certainly been excommunicated *before* being chosen. The statutes of the Commune (Bk. 1, 2, rubric 21) give the following form of oath to be taken *by the Podestà*: '*Iuro expellare hereticos et sodomitas* [i.e. Waldenses] *et patarenos* [i.e. Cathars] *de civitate et de comitatu Assisii si qui reperirentur.*' This regulation, which clearly cannot be prior to the election of the first *Podestà* (for in that case the oath would logically be imposed on the consuls), could very well have been inserted in the statutes by Cardinal Leo and sworn by Gerardo's successor, Ugolino, Assisi's second *Podestà*. In which case Pietro Bernardone, to avoid expulsion, must have been obliged to swear loyalty to the Church.

For the story of the rise and fall of the Cathars in central Italy as a whole see Canon Giovanni's *Chronicle*, in 'Archivo Storico Italiano', Series III, Vol. XXII, pp. 52–81; and Innocent III's Letters and Bulls, *passim*. Generally any reference to '*haeretici*' meant the Cathars; cf. their condemnation by Alexander III at the Third Lateran Council in 1179, '*quos alii Catharos, alii Patarenos, alii Publicanos, alii aliis nominibus vocant.*'

Daydreams and Voices Off

4: Daydreams and Voices Off

Walter of Brienne: Vox Populi?

Count Walter of Brienne had ridden out from his castle by Troyes into the realm of the Emperor and rescued the three princesses of Sicily and their mother Sibylla, the queen, from four weary years of prison in Alsace. It was a deed of knight-errantry in the old style, worthy of a Lancelot or a St. George; the tale was told all over Europe and great glory was won by the bold and gallant knights of Champagne.[1] Next year their liege lord, Count Thibaud, took the Cross; Count Walter of Brienne was the first of his knights, as has already been recounted, to take the Cross. He made ready to return to the Holy Land, where ten years earlier he had buried his father.

Sibylla, the deposed queen, journeyed to Rome; in the name of her eldest daughter, the princess Albiria, she claimed from the Pope the rightful inheritance of the Kingdom. Innocent temporized; his policy was in a state of total flux, for the Empress Constance had followed her husband Henry VI to the grave and the Pope had accepted the wardship of the orphaned baby in Palermo, Frederick Roger. Sibylla was sent back to France.

She appeared at the court of the King of France, the wary Philippe Auguste, no friend of Pope Innocent. The king summoned his barons and presented them with the landless queen. 'Here is Sibylla,' he proclaimed, 'who asks for our aid and promises to give in marriage her daughter endowed with Sicily and Apulia to whoever sets out to reconquer it. Would that I could go myself!'

The barons of France hung back. Three generations had passed since the seven sons of Tancred de Hauteville had set out from Normandy on a similar venture; times had changed, there were wars to be fought and land to be gained or lost nearer home, against the English; the attractions of a powerless queen and her penniless daughter were few.

But Sibylla was not to go unsuccoured. Walter of Brienne stepped forward. He, their rescuer, would marry the princess and reconquer their lands. Possibly it was love; possibly it was ambition; certainly with the young Count Thibaud ill to the point of death the proposed crusade appeared more nebulous. In the presence of the king, Philippe Auguste, Walter of Brienne married Albiria, princess and, according to some, rightful heiress of Sicily. He then set off in his turn to visit Rome. This was about the time when Perugia was declaring war on Assisi; like Umbria, all Italy was troubled with local wars.

Not all the German lords had retired as gracefully and as peacefully as the aged Duke Conrad. Markwald of Anweiler lorded it in the north, Dipold in the south; in Sicily itself, in the name of the baby heir, there were power struggles.

Walter of Brienne was summoned to appear before a Consistory of Cardinals. The Pope was left in deep perplexity.[2] He could not afford to reject outside aid if Italy were to be rid of the turbulent Germans; in the days of his predecessors the Normans had generally been loyal allies of the Papacy in southern Italy; and the knights of Champagne now had the prestige that the Normans had enjoyed in their great days. On the other hand Innocent was a canon lawyer, and could hardly be expected to support an illegitimate line against the legitimate; he was also ward and guardian of the rights of a defenceless baby.

In the end there was a compromise. The Pope conceded Albiria's rightful claim to the personal lands of her dead father Tancred of Lecce, the county of Lecce and the principality of Taranto, in other words to most of Apulia. But Walter of Brienne was made to swear that he would in no way diminish the rights of the baby Frederick but rather would oppose his enemies. With this the knight of Champagne had, for the moment, to be satisfied.

Walter of Brienne returned to Champagne and raised his bands; with him, on his return to Italy, came his younger brother John of Brienne, and of the famous knights who had taken the Cross, Robert of Joinville, Eustace of Conflans, and Walter of Montbeliard. Jangling down into Italy, they passed Geoffrey, marshal of Champagne, on his way back from Venice. God, what great deeds they did in the Kingdom! Though there were only 200 of them, they routed Dipold the German and 5,000 of his men in the spring at Capua; and then defeated him again at Cannae in the autumn. Walter of Brienne boasted that Germans even when armed would not stand up against unarmed Frenchmen. It was a famous but unfounded boast. Drama followed drama in the south; Markwald of Anweiler sailed down from Ravenna and captured Palermo and the imperial baby. Frantically Innocent urged his knight, Walter of Brienne, to sail out and rescue the young Frederick, writing even to his own relations to borrow money for the expedition. Markwald summoned Duke Conrad back from Swabia; only for first the one, then the other to die. But William of Capparone seized Palermo and proclaimed himself Guardian of the King and Captain-General of Sicily. In the autumn of 1203 Innocent lay very ill at Anagni; rumours of his death spread; all the cities revolted; James the Marshal, the Pope's cousin, and Walter of Brienne proclaimed themselves 'Masters and Justiciars of Apulia and the Terra del Lavoro.' Although the Pope recovered, Dipold the German built up his power again.

Between campaigns, the knights of Champagne led a brilliant courtly life at Lecce. It was as if all that was most chivalrous in France has shifted to the realm of the south.

Francis had recovered his health, his spirits and his ambitions. The catastrophe at Collestrada had not sickened him with war and its glories; on the contrary it seems merely to have resolved him to do better the next time around. Even in prison he had boasted to his companions that one day he would be honoured by the whole world.

By the whole world possibly. But, in the autumn of the year 1204, there was very little chance of Pietro Bernardone's son being honoured in Assisi. In the early months of the year Pietro may have been grooming his son to lead the great counter-attack against Perugia; and we can well imagine Francis proudly accepting that patriotic role, polishing up his arms and armour, keeping his hand in with the correct knightly gestures and preparing for the great day of Assisi's revenge. But then came Cardinal Leo's visit, the deposition of the *Podestà*, the change of regime and policy, and his father's humiliating disgrace. It meant the end of any dreams Francis may have had of being a champion of his city.

Bitterly Pietro Bernardone weighed up his own position and his family's future. He had at least saved his wealth; he might manage to safeguard his future as a merchant, but his own ambitions were over and done with. He belonged to the beaten faction, and that in a small town marked him down. He can have had no illusions as to how his fellow-citizens viewed his outward submission to the Church; he must have been both disgusted with himself and yet, as a realist, totally resigned. All his hopes were now pinned on his son. The boy was probably not cut out to be a trader; fortunately – as it had turned out – he had never shown any real interest in theology or politics, he simply wanted to be a knight and win honours. Very well then; at least the family was rich enough to set him up properly – and seeing that the Church was the master, by all means let him fight for the Church. And so Pietro Bernardone fitted out his son most magnificently with new arms and armour and prepared to send him off to win honour and knighthood in the wars.

It seems to have been Francis' idea originally; or rather the idea of a noble of Assisi, possibly one of his companions in prison. This noble had vowed he would go to Apulia, and there join Walter of Brienne and win wealth and fame. Francis, 'who was flighty and not a little rash,' says Thomas of Celano, arranged to go with him.[3] And there can be no doubt that his father threw himself heart and soul behind Francis' scheme; for everyone remarked how Francis' apparel was far more magnificent and luxurious than that of the noble whom he was accompanying.

Probably they had thought of joining the Fourth Crusade; it would have been the natural aim of two ambitious young men. But, though ambitious, they were distinctly provincial. It is unlikely that Francis had ever been further from Assisi than the neighbouring towns of Umbria; and in any case the Fourth

Crusade had deviated from its original purpose and was regarded with a mixture of horror and admiration by all Christians, from the Pope downwards. For though the crusaders had imposed a Latin Emperor in the East, by the autumn of 1204 full accounts had reached Rome of the horrors they had perpetrated in doing so. In the name of Christ they had sacked the greatest city in the Christian world, Constantinople, massacred thousands of fellow-Christians and looted hundreds of Christian churches. It was not for this that the knights jousting at the castle of Ecri had heard Fulk of Neuilly preach and taken the Cross. In a sense Walter of Brienne and his knights had proved truer to their oaths: for though they, too, were fighting against fellow-Christians, not Saracens, it was at least with the Lord Pope's approval and as his liege-men against excommunicated Germans. And what perhaps weighed most in the minds of Francis and his companion was that Innocent III had authorized the followers of Walter of Brienne to embroider the Cross on their surcoats. Therefore, at least technically, they could boast that they too were going on crusade. And in any case, though Apulia was very far away and a great adventure and quest, they could at least be certain of getting there. Whereas Constantinople! Let us not forget that Umbria is the one region in Italy that is totally landlocked; there is no reason to suppose that Francis, in the twenty-fourth year of his life, had ever seen the fearsome sea.

Before they set out, Francis had a dream. This is the first of many dreams and visions and apparitions and voices; and here readers will forgive me if I pause in the narrative and ask them for a moment to consider the difficulties the historian faces in reporting these dreams.

The first difficulty is to know exactly what was seen. For instance, in the first version of this dream it is reported that Francis saw his own house filled with saddles, shields, lances and all the trappings of war – which, as Thomas of Celano says, caused him to wonder greatly, 'for he was not accustomed to see such things in his home but rather piles of cloth to be sold.' As he wondered, he was 'told' that all these arms would belong to him and his soldiers – which naturally enough he considered to be a very good omen for the expedition to Apulia. But in the *Second Life* Thomas of Celano varies the story. Francis was shown 'a splendid palace' – not his home – 'and a most beautiful bride.' And in the *Three Companions* this is how the story goes:

'While Francis was asleep a man appeared who called him by name and led him into a vast and pleasant palace in which the walls were hung with glittering coats of mail, shining bucklers and all the weapons and armour of warriors. Francis was delighted and reflecting on what could be the meaning of all this he asked for whom the splendid arms and beautiful palace was intended; and he received the answer that they were for him and his knights.'

Now I do not want to labour the contradiction: obviously dreams and visions are confused and Francis might very easily have seen both his own home and a beautiful palace. But the point is this: there is only one person who actually knows what he has seen or heard in a vision or in dreams, and that is the person who has experienced it. There is no-one else who can prove or disprove his account. Therefore if Francis had wanted to invent a dream or vision, he could easily have done so: wealth of detail is no proof.

Not, I think, that such was the case with this particular dream. The pious biographers may have interpreted it as symbolic of the knight of Christ promised the Kingdom of Heaven; but that is their affair. The version given in the *Three Companions* rings true; it was just such a dream as a boyhood soaked in the romances of Chrétien de Troyes would have produced: magical palaces, empty but for magnificent apparel, were commonplace thoroughfares for the knights of the Round Table.

Francis was so full of glee the next morning that people stopped him in surprise in the street. 'I know that I shall become a great prince,' he told them. And as for the beautiful princess, perhaps she too was sighing for her true knight-errant at Lecce. Albiria was married to her rescuer; but as far as we know (and as far, probably, as Francis knew) her two sisters, the princess Madonia and the princess Costanza, were waiting in Apulia to bestow their favours on the knights who should vow them devotion. Dreams and daydreams mingled.

Spoleto: Vox Prudentiae?

What happened next is quite extraordinary. Anyone reading the accounts is forced to conclude that there is much missed out, or some decisive event glossed over. At any rate the story as we have it is this: Francis rode out boldly, with a company that included the nobleman of Assisi; magnificently arrayed and even accompanied by a shield-bearer; not exactly to be described as his squire, for he himself was not yet a knight but certainly the harbinger of squires to come. At Spoleto, however, he fell ill: and while he was half-asleep ('*semi-dormiens*') he heard someone asking him where he was going to. He replied that he was going to Apulia. The following exchange then took place:

Voice: Who would it be better to serve, the servant or the master?
Francis: The master.
Voice: Why then do you seek out the servant rather than the master?
Francis: What do you want me to do, Lord?
Voice: Return to the place of your birth and be ready to do what is told to you.

That, at any rate, is the simple version. And so Francis, unable to get to sleep properly, woke up, got up and hurried back to Assisi very joyfully, expecting God's will to be shown to him and new orders to come through.

This whole story leaves one distinctly uneasy. It is a very different sort of vision from the previous dream, just the type of thing a young man waved off to the wars might have invented as he was jogging back to explain away his unexpected and distinctly bathetic return. Not even the most devout can be convinced by it: for it was no blinding revelation on the road to Damascus, it was not followed by a total and sudden devotion to God; and the expected instructions for future action, the mention of which has all the air of a rather pathetic attempt to appease a distinctly angry and unsympathetic parent, not surprisingly failed to materialize.

No; something certainly happened at Spoleto of which no account has survived. Possibly Francis, who was always rather frail, was simply exhausted even by that brief ride and realized that physically he was not up to being a knight. But, more probably, as Sabatier suggests, the noble whom he was accompanying, outraged by his airs and graces, by his ostentatious equipment and by his boasts of conquering principalities and winning princesses, quite suddenly had had enough; and pointed out, brutally, to Francis a few blunt facts: namely that he was a nobody and as the son of a merchant and a discredited merchant at that had as much chance of being knighted as a Saracen of being saved.[4] Or else Francis' nerve simply failed him. He had never been far away from home and he suddenly realized that he was not an adventurer or a knight-errant but simply a homesick young man missing his mother, ineffective without his pushful father, and indeed a coward.

Most conventional young men – and Francis was an extremely conventional young man – live up to what is expected of them rather than what they expect of themselves. Physical courage was expected of the sons of nobles; it was not expected of the sons of merchants; they were not trained for it. And I for one, from personal experience, understand very well how Francis may have been brave as a lion at the battle of Collestrada, surrounded by friends and companions, almost within sight of his home, only to find a little yoyo of fear jigging up and down inside his stomach as he rode further and further from Assisi, under no compulsion to go further but his own, and closer and closer to a pointless and probably trivial death in a distant land. So, perhaps, he reasoned to himself; and it must have been with an overwhelming feeling of relief that he finally – or suddenly – decided to turn back, though people who do so in such circumstances eventually suffer an extreme jolt to their good opinions of themselves.

That is what appears to have happened to Francis on his return: this extreme jolt sent him veering from feverish activity to extremes of depression. It is a very confused and unhappy picture, that of the next few months of his life; scattered and disordered, as indeed he must have been. On the surface he was still extraordinarily boastful and uncowed; but there seems to have been a note of desperation in his constant claim that he would – still! – become a great prince. His companions elected him King of the Revels and profited, as before, from his generosity, allowing him to pay for the meals they ate and to lead them singing through the streets. But from time to time he would hang back and go into a sort of trance. 'What are you thinking about?' they would shout rather mockingly. 'Why didn't you follow us? Were you thinking of getting married?'

'You are right,' Francis answered, 'I was thinking of wooing the noblest, richest and most beautiful bride ever seen.' At which reply his friends, naturally enough, redoubled their mockery; his later biographers professed to see in it a symbolic declaration of a spiritual vocation. There is no need for us to strain words as they did; for after all Francis could, quite simply, have been in love.

I do not think he was; Francis was one of those out-and-out romantics who could never have been satisfied with anything less than perfection in a woman, and that perfect woman was to be found only in the songs of the troubadours or the pages of the romances, certainly not in flesh and blood at Assisi. But I do think that at this time he was under intense pressure to marry and settle down.

Let us once again consider his father's probable attitude. Pietro Bernardone had spent a great deal of money in setting Francis up for the expedition to Apulia; and the mockery that Francis' hurried and ignominious return gave rise to must have been even more painful for the father than for the son. No doubt he felt inclined to wash his hands of Francis; particularly as his other son Angelo[5] was by now installed in the family trade, for which he showed all the aptitude that would make him Pietro's eventual successor. The problem of the unsatisfactory son remained: he seemed to show no taste for trade and no appetite for a higher calling. We can imagine Francis' mother Pica pleading first with her scornful husband, pointing out that the boy was nearly twenty-five, that with a good, steady wife he would soon settle down and find his niche in the life of Assisi – and then pleading with her edgy son, pointing out the virtues of this or that merchant's daughter, begging him to forget all his dreams of chivalry and princesses, only to come up against the uneasy obstinacy of the romantic who will not give up his ideal. We can imagine the father contemptuously agreeing to support his son for a little longer, taking him back as a sort of parasite partner in the family business and tossing him the odd purse of gold for his extravagances. And we can imagine Francis hating all this, half-convinced that he should do as his mother wished, yet unable to resign himself to a mediocre marriage and an even more mediocre future.

Above all, we can imagine the tension in the relations between father and son. They had to live under the same roof but there was no sympathy between them. Francis reacted against all that his father stood for; he had always been too generous to be a really successful merchant but now, more ostentatiously than ever, he gave money away to beggars and food, too, from the family table when his father was away on journeys. Even more calculated to infuriate Pietro was a sudden and rather suspect interest in the Catholic religion. Francis bought vases and other ornaments for the churches of Assisi, went on a pilgrimage to the tombs of the apostles in Rome, and – what must have been the most cruel blow of all – took to asking advice from the new Bishop of Assisi, Guido, rather than from his own father. These would have been three calculated insults to a Cathar; for the Cathars rejected churches (and *a fortiori* their ornaments), relics and pilgrimages, and above all the clergy as extraneous to true religion.[6] Francis could hardly have said more clearly to his father: 'I reject everything you tried to teach me. I reject your heretical ideas and theories, I accept the established order and the Church. And if there is anyone I will treat as my father, it is not you but the bishop.' And there could be no pretence either that the bishop was a particularly saintly man. On the contrary Guido was much of a muchness, as far as character and temperament went, with Pietro Bernardone: authoritarian, worldly, ambitious, avaricious, quarrelsome. If Francis chose him as a father-substitute, it was not for his personal qualities but for his position.[7]

There are two curious episodes that occurred about this time that do not quite fit into the picture of tension and disappointment. Both can be interpreted as signs of future holiness in Francis, the conclusion of the biographers. Both can also be interpreted as symptoms of near-lunacy: the conclusion of Francis' contemporaries.

First, Francis overcame his conventional disgust for lepers; though the memory of this disgust haunted him all his life. And leprosy is a disgusting disease. Its warning symptoms are the appearance of reddish or brownish blotches with a white body. These appear and disappear, to be replaced by smaller tumours of a yellowish substance that quickly turns darker, rising usually at the articulations of the toes or fingers. The disease, in its severest form, then spreads rapidly, affecting both the skin and the nerves. Ulcerations appear first on the little finger, then on all the joints of hands and feet, leading eventually to the dropping-off of fingers and toes. Nodules the size of walnuts affect the face, thickening the nose and lips, chin, cheeks and ears. Motor paralysis sets in. The muscles of the face are contracted and distorted by atrophy; ectropion of the lower lids prevents the leper from shutting his eyes. Death after eight years is the ordinary conclusion of every case; in the final stages of the disease the leper suffers from unquenchable thirst and complete inability to move; the skin shrinks; hair, teeth and nails fall off. But, worst of all, the mind is unaffected; with complete helplessness the leper watches the slow and unrelenting process of his own physical decomposition.

Nowhere were the Middle Ages more admirable than in their treatment of these poor creatures. Thousands of *leprosaria*, leper hostels, were scattered all over Europe in which the leper communities led a secluded and religious life tended by clergy and particularly by members of the Order of St. Lazarus who lived with them as brothers and sisters. Then as now it was known that leprosy was an infectious disease; but then as now the means of infection and transmission were not fully understood; what experience had and has proved, however, is that most people have a natural immunity. Yet, with the risk of infection and of certain death following, the lepers had to live an isolated life. They were forbidden to frequent public buildings, talk with children, marry non-lepers, wash in still water. They were obliged to wear gloves and sound a bell when they walked outside the *leprosarium*. In all cases they gave off a peculiarly offensive smell, like that of a male goat.

One day, riding near Assisi, Francis met a leper. Making a great effort, he conquered his aversion, dismounted, gave the leper a coin and kissed his hand – receiving in exchange the kiss of peace. Previously, his horror of lepers had been so great that he could not even bear to look at them; and if by chance he passed near a *leprosarium*, he would turn his face away and hold his nose.

Having taken this possibly suicidal risk, Francis plunged ahead. Some days later he took a large sum of money down to the *leprosarium*[8] and, gathering all the lepers together, gave it away, kissing each leper's hands. To a certain extent he was clearly proving his own courage to himself, and indeed to others, showing that whatever had happened on the road to Apulia, he was not afraid of risking death. But it must have been an enormous relief when the tell-tale blotches of red and brown did not appear. It was the first totally unconventional, as opposed to merely extravagant, act of his life – and the first that put him on a level no longer with knights or merchants but with the religious. And, whatever his original motives may have been, it was as such that he saw it even on his deathbed.

'This is how God inspired me, Brother Francis, to embark upon a life of penance.' These are the opening words of the *Testament* that he dictated as he lay dying. 'When I was in sin, the sight of lepers nauseated me beyond measure, but then God himself led me into their company and I had pity on them. When I had once become acquainted with them, what had previously nauseated me became a source of spiritual and physical consolation for me. After that I did not wait long before leaving the world.'

The second episode appears to have occurred after the gesture of defiance with the lepers. It is distinctly more mysterious.

Francis was becoming more and more detached from his companions of the Revels; and he took to leaving Assisi and seeking out remote and solitary spots. There was one companion of his own age, however, whom he would take with him, and the two of them together would frequently discuss a great treasure that Francis claimed to know of. Then they would go hunting through caves up in the mountains – or rather Francis would go into the caves, and his friend would be left at the entrance as a look-out. And then when Francis came down to the town again, his old companions would quizz him about 'the secret'; and Francis with, as a chronicler says, 'his habitual caution' would only let out occasional hints of his secret, and would declare that he no longer wished to go to Apulia but would do great things in his own land. Was he thinking of marrying, they asked again? And again he replied, though in slightly different words and a more confident tone: 'I shall bring home a bride, more beautiful, richer and nobler than any you have ever seen.'

All this seems on one level incredibly childish; on another level of course the pious biographers took it as highly significant and added details about long prayers and groanings in the cave, mental anguish, and the Lord revealing the future. In my view Francis was once again living in his fantasy world of chivalry: he would not conquer his princess by knightly prowess in Apulia. He would not have to, for he would discover a great treasure which would bring her from Apulia to him. I believe that in his disordered mind were floating visions of the Graal, that perhaps by risking death from the lepers rather than from warfare in Apulia he was trying to persuade himself that he, Francis, if not a Lancelot, could be a Galahad; and that during this period he really did persuade himself that he could still be a great prince and win a beautiful and noble bride. How? By discovering the greatest and most secret of treasures, the Graal, in the caves of the mountain.[9] He was certainly living in an atmosphere of magic and witchcraft; all the accounts tell of a humpbacked and deformed old woman in Assisi and how Francis was terrified that her lump would be cast on him. Perhaps disordered is too meek a term for his state of mind at the time; diseased might be a truer description. Though in that sense half the young men of the medieval world were probably diseased; for castles, princesses, knights, witchcraft, quests and treasures were real enough – and dwarfs, giants, dangers, enchantments, the stuff of the romances, lay only just over the borders of the real; and might very easily be true.

At any rate this period passed. Reality hit back at Francis, as reality was all his life to hit back at him and bring his fantasies toppling to the ground. No treasure was found, no bride was won. The excursions up to the mountain caves stopped. But Francis, too, as he was to do all his life, hit back at reality. He had an eminently practical and rather convincing vision.

San Damiano: Vox Dei?

This is how the *Three Companions* tells the story:

'A few days after this, while he was walking near the Church of San Damiano, an inner voice bade him go in and pray. He obeyed, and kneeling before an image of the crucified Saviour, he began to pray most devoutly. A tender, compassionate voice then spoke to him: "Francis, do you not see that my house is falling into ruin? Go, and repair it for me." Trembling and amazed Francis replied: "Gladly I will do so, O Lord." He had understood that the Lord was speaking of that very church which on account of its age was indeed falling into ruin.

. . . On leaving the church he found the priest who had charge of it sitting outside, and taking a handful of money from his purse he said, "I beg you, Father, to buy oil and keep the lamp before this image of Christ constantly alight. When this is spent I will give you as much as you need." '10

At long last Francis had something active, tangible and comparatively easy to do. And, to continue the story in Chesterton's inimitable words, 'Francis sprang up and went. To go and do something was one of the driving demands of his nature; probably he had gone and done it before he had at all thoroughly thought out what he had done. In any case what he had done was something very decisive and immediately very disastrous for his singular social career. In the coarse conventional language of the uncomprehending world he stole. From his own enthusiastic point of view he extended to his venerable father Pietro Bernardone the exquisite excitement and inestimable privilege of assisting, more or less unconsciously, in the rebuilding of the church of San Damiano.'

He went to the *fondaco*, loaded his horse with cloth of different colours, rode off to Foligno, sold not only the merchandise but also the horse, returned to San Damiano, kissed the poor priest's hand and offered him the money.11 The priest, who knew all about Francis and his way of life, not unnaturally imagined him to be joking and refused the money; and despite Francis' insistence he went on refusing it for fear of Francis' relatives.

All family quarrels seem to come to a head in quarrels over money. The obvious thing for Francis to have done would have been to have given up his plan, or at least postpone it, and take the money back to his father. But he did not do so; he obstinately placed the money in a small cupboard inside the church and begged the priest, if he would not accept the money, at least to accept him, Francis. as a benefactor and guest. Probably the priest did so merely in order that he should not be landed with the responsibility for the money; as long as the young man was there, it was the young man's responsibility. It was not an enviable position for the wretched cleric.

And of course he was quite right. Pietro Bernardone missed his son, went round asking for news and very soon – San Damiano is only about twenty minutes walk from the centre of Assisi – found out exactly what had happened and where Francis was. His reaction was so disproportionately violent that it can only be explained by the last-straw theory. Instead of walking down to San Damiano himself, he called together a posse of his friends and neighbours and they all set off down the hillside below the walls presumably to chase the young thief from his lair. Francis' courage evaporated, as it always seems to have done when he was faced with his father, and he hid in a secret cave or pit which, according to two baffling accounts, he had already prepared as a refuge for just such an emergency.[12] And in this cave or pit he hid for no less than a month, hardly daring to leave it even 'to provide for his human needs', as Thomas of Celano puts it, and having meals brought to him secretly by the only person in his father's household who knew where he was.

There must be something very wrong with a man of about twenty-five who spends four weeks hiding in a hole rather than face an angry father. It sounds more like a boy of ten running away from home than a would-be knight or potential great prince. But there was always something in Francis' relationship with his father, even in the final famous scene, that in the expressive Italian phrase left him '*rimbambito*' – re-babyfied. And when he finally plucked up the courage to come out and face the world again, he was certainly treated as an infant, which, one cannot help feeling, is no more than he deserved, even if it was no less than he feared.

After a month of pit-life the usually elegant Francis made a distinctly bedraggled entrance into Assisi. He seems to have decided, foolishly, instead of sneaking in by night or sending an apologetic message to his father, to put a brave face on it. This was a mistake. As soon as his friends and relatives saw him, the cry went up '*Al pazzo! Al pazzo!*'; jeers and taunts were followed by the usual treatment reserved for madmen, stones and mud-slinging. The tumult brought Pietro Bernardone out of his house, and when he heard that the 'poor madman' being pilloried in the streets was his son, Francis, he appears to have gone half-mad himself with anger and humiliation. In the words of the *Three Companions*: 'Throwing moderation and discretion to the winds, he sprang on his son like a wolf on a lamb; and, his face furious, his eyes glaring, he seized him with many blows and dragged him home. Francis was then shut up in a dark cellar, and for many days his father used threats and blows to bend his son's will . . .'

The scandal in a small town like Assisi was of course enormous, and must have given the enemies of Pietro Bernardone great pleasure. From any normal point of view Francis' behaviour was both inexplicable and perverse. Instead of showing the slightest gratitude to his parents for a cosseted upbringing in which his whims had only to be expressed to be satisfied, he had despised his father's profession, had come back all the same to live unabashedly off his family, repaid Pietro Bernardone for his tolerance by stealing and selling his goods, refused to hand back his father's money even when the person for whose benefit he had allegedly taken it had refused to accept it, created an open scandal, disappeared for a month without apparently the least consideration for his very worried mother – and finally after all his boasting of princesses and treasures had come back yet again looking dirtier and more ragged than any tramp, without a word of regret or apology, expecting, to judge from his brazen air, the fatted calf to be slaughtered once more.

By the statutes of the Commune Pietro Bernardone was perfectly entitled to keep his son fettered, and he did so.[13] The battle of wills between masterful father and defiant young man continued inside the family house, out of the public gaze. Quite clearly it was less about the money than about Francis' future and the family fortune. Pietro Bernardone was determined that his son should not become a restorer of half-ruined churches, Francis was just as determined to prove at last he had found the right and noble way to dispense money. Neither would give way. Statutes or no statutes, it must have made for a somewhat strained family life. Eventually Pietro Bernardone had to leave for one of his trading journeys; inevitably Pica could not bear to see her son fettered in the cellars. She tried to persuade her son to obey his father, but when she found him totally obdurate, 'moved by motherly compassion and loosening the chains, she let him go free.' It was perhaps the first time that she had ever dared to defy her husband. When Pietro returned and found that Francis was not only free but had immediately gone back and installed himself openly at San Damiano, he 'added sin to sin by abusing his wife.' Poor Pica! Her gesture – the only decisive gesture of her life that we know of – did little good. With his usual determination Pietro Bernardone soon abandoned abuse for action; there was, possibly, one more painful shouting match down at San Damiano's (for once Francis stood his ground) and then the father decided that not only would he wash his hands of his ungrateful son but that he would have him driven from the territory of the Commune. This time the rupture was final and formal. Pietro Bernardone went to the *Palazzo Comunale* and denounced his son under the statutes. The penalty for filial disobedience and misuse of paternal goods was banishment from the town and the district. The legal procedure, once under way, followed its course. With grim satisfaction Pietro Bernardone must have watched the judge's messenger, Rainuccio di Palmerio, set out to San

Damiano to call out in front of the accused's dwelling place the summons to appear before the communal court of Judge Egidio. His satisfaction soon changed to stupefaction. The summons had been called and a writ served. But Francis had refused service. 'Your letter does not concern me,' he had told Rainuccio, 'already by the grace of God I have been freed of the power of the consuls, having become the servant of the Most High.'

This was an astute move. For the first (and last) time in his life Francis turned the complexities of canon and civil law to his own advantage. Shorn of its verbiage, his statement simply amounted to this: that, having attached himself to the church and priest of San Damiano, he was *ratione materiae et loci* under the bishop's jurisdiction. On pain of excommunication no civil authority could cite a cleric or 'a person staying on the lands of the bishopric,' to appear before the secular courts 'without the consent of the bishop.' The bishop did not give his consent. There was no legal loophole. The civil authorities of Assisi could proceed no further.[14]

The Bishop's Judgement

It is always humiliating for a father to be outwitted by a son, particularly when the father is an experienced man of the world and the son is a timid and dreamy wastrel. Francis must have been feeling impishly satisfied; even his choice of words was designed to irritate his father. 'Servant of the Most High' indeed, when the whelp was just a runaway from his own kennel! And was it 'by the grace of God' that the rascal had stolen the money and was now crowing over its rightful owner, his own father? Blinded by rage Pietro Bernardone blundered wildly ahead. He cited Francis before the ecclesiastical court. This time Francis accepted the summons, again with a grandiloquence obviously designed to irritate: 'I will willingly appear before the Lord Bishop who is the father and lord of souls.'

It was probably on or about St. Agatha's day, 5 February 1207 (we know that the snows were heavy that year), that the bishop held his court. Mitre in hand, wearing a blue mantle, he sat in state on a throne on the steps of his church, Santa Maria Maggiore. The trumpets sounded, the audience began. The people of Assisi crowded into the square in front of the bishop's palace to hear Pietro Bernardone denounce his own son. Turning to Francis, Bishop Guido gave his judgement: 'Your father is highly incensed and greatly scandalized by your conduct,' he said. 'If therefore you wish to serve God, you must first of all return him his money, which indeed may have been dishonestly acquired. God would not wish you to use it for restoring the church through sin on the part of your father, whose anger will abate when he gets the money back. Trust in the Lord, my son, and act manfully, fearing nothing, for he will help and provide you with all that is necessary for repairing the church.' Just, but safe and platitudinous words.

Then came the famous gesture. Heaven knows whether Francis had been preparing for it or whether he acted in a sudden wild fit of temper. He accepted the bishop's judgement and, having announced his intention, went into the hall of the bishop's palace. There was a hush and a craning of necks. What was the madman going to do now? Even Pietro Bernardone must have felt a momentary qualms.

Francis reappeared stark naked. He dumped his fine clothes down and placed the money on top of them.[15] And then, fully exposed in every sense, he turned to the bishop, to his father, and to the crowd. 'Listen all of you,' he said, 'and mark my words. Hitherto I have called Pietro Bernardone my father, but because I am resolved to serve God I return to him the money on account of which he was so perturbed and also the clothes I wore which are his; and from now on I will say "Our Father who art in heaven" and not my father Pietro Bernardone.'

The crowd had certainly had their entertainment; very rarely can a father have been repudiated by a son in so exhibitionistic, scandalous and sneering a manner. Pietro Bernardone, the account tells us, 'rose up burning with grief and anger and gathered up the garments and money and carried them home.' Perhaps, even at this last minute, he could by a generous gesture have won his son back again. He could have gone forward warmly, embraced him, publicly forgiven him, wrapped him again in his clothes and given him the money. Certainly public opinion seems to have expected some gesture of magnanimity. 'Those present at this scene took the side of Francis because Pietro had left him without any clothing, and moved with pity they started to weep over him.' I do not think he deserved their tears. After all, it was not Pietro Bernardone who had ripped the clothes off his back but Francis who had, of his own free will, made an absolutely needless gesture designed to embarrass and scandalize.[16] Bishop Guido put an end to the public spectacle by covering Francis with his own mantle – a gesture for which he was much praised by local commentators. Yet this did not signify, as they suggest, that he approved of Francis' behaviour. It was a mere expedient of the moment; the bishop reclaimed his cloak and Francis was sent out to face the world in a tunic belonging to one of the bishop's farmhands. It was cold, and he was now, very definitely, alone.

NOTES

1 Walter of Brienne's rescue of Sibylla and the three princesses may, alas, be somewhat legendary. It is possible on the Emperor Henry VI's death that they simply walked out of the convent where they were confined; and Walter himself may have been, earlier, negotiating with the Emperor for lands in Apulia. The versions are confused. However the important thing is that the legend of a latter-day St. George was widely believed all over Europe. I believe that Francis never lost his interest in the family of Brienne; and that for him Walter and his brother John stood out as an example of knightly perfection, linked to the service of the Church.

2 In the phrase of the chronicle, '*coepit multipliciter indubitare*'.

3 The whole chronology of this part of Francis' life is based on the one date of which we are absolutely certain: the death of Walter of Brienne, surprised and killed by his old enemy Dipold the German outside the castle of Sarno in June 1205. Therefore Francis must have set out for Apulia to join him *before* this date. The rest is, as always with Francis' life, a matter of jigsaw-timing.

4 We do not know the name of the noble of Assisi who first had the idea of setting out for Apulia. It is probably incorrect technically to say that Francis could not have been knighted because of his non-noble birth (certainly in Languedoc sons of merchants were often knighted); but he could never have become a great knight, still less a great prince.

5 Francis had at least one brother, Angelo by name, '*frater eius carnalis*' (*First Life*). The *Three Companions* says that his mother loved Francis more than her other sons: '*ipsum prae ceteisr filiis diligebat*'. However, as the communal archives give only Angelo's name, I wonder whether '*filiis*' may not refer to Angelo and a daughter – though there is no record of Francis having had a sister; nor does he ever refer to her. But then Francis' whole attitude towards women was very strained. Although his mother did so much for him, he never seems to have expressed the slightest gratitude to her or even to have gone to see her after he had broken with his father. She was dropped flat. As for other women, despite the wild reputation of his youth he was, as Fra Leo who had been unjustly suspicious, eventually discovered, a virgin. Probably, like many romantics, he had a natural distaste for the physical side of love; which would in his case have been reinforced by the literary ideals of '*cortezia*' of the later troubadours and the spirit of the romances of Champagne. As for marriage, any Cathar influence would have made him view it with distaste.

6 At the risk of over-emphasizing this Cathar influence, let me restate my thesis:
    (i) Pietro Bernardone, like many in the cloth trade, was a sympathizer and possibly a Believer. As such, he would naturally have attempted to instil Cathar ideas and practices in his family. Yet, being neither an intellectual nor an idealist, he probably stressed the more negative side of Catharism – i.e. their condemnation of the practices and hierarchy of the Catholic Church. Church buildings were unnecessary, the clergy corrupt and parasitical, the eucharist a fabrication, pilgrimages and relics were superstitions, the sacraments outmoded.
    (ii) Pica, Francis' mother, was on the other hand a conventional and devout Catholic both in belief and practice.
    (iii) Francis reacted violently against his father and his father's ideas. In later life, over and over again, he would proclaim his own orthodoxy, his submission to the clergy and his devotion to the eucharist. Yet Cathar practices were so familiar to him that he never freed himself from their influence.

(iv) Pietro Bernardone's ideas were themselves confused. Despite his professional and therefore almost automatic acceptance of the 'new religion', he was himself attracted and impressed by high feudalism as he had seen it in Champagne. This was the part of Francis' education that the boy loved; the stories he heard influenced him as an ideal all his life.

(v) After the '*compositio pacis*' of 1203, Pietro Bernardone, disillusioned with the actual practical benefits of Catharism, made '*amende honorable*' and at least overtly accepted the official religion. Like many uneasy converts and collaborators, he even at moments pushed his son towards the Church – though at other times inner revulsion held him back. His own position in Assisi was therefore insecure; and he transferred his own ambitions for career and power to his son.

7 The Bishop of Assisi owned a whole quarter of the town; his palace and church now stand exactly where they did in Bishop Guido's day. The communal archives give full proof of Guido's quarrelsome and materialistic character; he was always in dispute with the Canons of San Rufino or the Abbey of St. Benedict or the communal authorities over questions of money and authority. This Guido, second of the name, remained Bishop of Assisi from 1204 till his death on 30 July 1228 – thus outliving Francis.

8 The *leprosarium* of Assisi, known as *De Arce*, appears to have been on the plain below the town, near a piece of land owned by Pietro Bernardone. It is perhaps the same as the '*leprosarium et ecclesia Sancti Leonardi de strata francesca*' which, notes the papal Bull of 26 May 1198, is under the authority of the Bishop of Assisi.

9 My explanation of the 'treasure' is of course pure speculation. But certainly it fits. Here, too, there may have been some nebulous Cathar influence – the mysterious 'sacred treasure' of Montségur saved by the Cathars in 1224 and the Provençal legend of the *Grazal*.

10 In the church of San Giorgio (which is now enclosed by the vast Basilica of Santa Chiara) can be seen the painted crucifix that spoke to Francis in San Damiano. Somehow, after seeing the crucifix, one can believe more easily that it spoke.

According to *Anonymous of Perugia* the name of the poor priest of San Damiano was *Petrus*. The church was one of those that belonged directly to the bishop. It is nowadays perhaps the most beautiful and authentic of all the churches of Assisi. It lies outside the walls, in the open country, down the hill. There seem to have been an extraordinarily large number of ruined churches and chapels around Assisi at this time. Can this too have been due to the spread of Cathar influence? Cf. the letter written by Count Raymond V of Toulouse in 1177 to Rome:

'*L'hérésie a pénetré partout . . . Elle a jété la discorde dans toutes les familles, divisant le mari et la femme, le fils et le père, la bru et la belle-mère. Les prêtres eux-mêmes cèdent à la tentation. Les églises sont desertes et tombent en ruines . . . Les personnages les plus importants de ma terre se sont laissés corrompre. La foule a suivi leur exemple et abandonné la foi, ce qui fait que je n'ose ni ne puis rien entreprendre.*' [Modernized French text.]

11 Briefly in this chapter I have followed the account of Francis' youth given in the *Legend of the Three Companions*. It does not always coincide with other sources. For instance, the *Anonymous of Perugia* gives a much simpler version of the San Damiano episode: it was at Foligno on his way back from Spoleto that Francis sold his horse and the court garments he had been taking to Apulia. It was then, passing by ruined San Damiano, that the impulse to restore the church suddenly came upon him. This is both logically and geographically more attractive; but it does run everything rather too closely together to cover the months that passed between the return from Spoleto and the bishop's judgement (see page 82).

12 If Francis had *already* specially prepared his cave or pit as an emergency hiding-place (as both Thomas of Celano and the *Three Companions* recount), this is baffling indeed. It implies that he had plotted the whole episode; and this in its turn means that he invented the words spoken by the crucifix, deliberately provoked his father, and had planned a mysterious disappearance which would leave his family and indeed all Assisi baffled and uneasy. Did he in some way hope to spring a sudden miraculous 'return' on the whole town, perhaps coming down from the mountain with treasure and bride? It is not impossible in view of his state of mind at the time and his desire to make a striking public gesture.

13 For the concept of '*patria potestas*' in Assisi, at this time, see Book II, Rubric 5 of the statutes of the Commune headed '*De Dissipatoribus et male utentibus suis substantiis.*' Those guilty of wasting the family substance – exactly what Francis had done – could be incarcerated and fettered. Furthermore 'the son who does not give obedience to his father and his mother, should, on their demand, be banished from the city and the district and no-one can give them food or drink or help them in any way whatsoever.'

14 The conflict between civil and canon law in Francis' case has been carefully and thoroughly analyzed by Fortini. The legal procedure was as follows: the judge's *nunzio* would have called out, outside San Damiano: '*Francesco di Pietro Bernardone. Sia noto a ognuno essere tu per ordine dei consoli accusato e inquisito.*' The accused had three days in which to present himself for trial; if within three days he had not come forward, there was a further period of grace of eight days during which the accusation was publicly proclaimed. At the end of this period, if he still did not appear, he was automatically found guilty.

   Pope Innocent's Bull of 26 May 1198, which confirmed the Bishop of Assisi in his posses-sions and privileges, over-rode in any conflict of law the communal statutes. The relevant section reads: '*Hoc enim omnino sub pena anatematis interdicimus . . . insuper quod nulli potestati vel potestatis ministro facultas sit, a quibuslibet ecclesiarum vestrarum clericis aut hominibus omnibus in dicta ipsius episcopii . . . exactiones in debitas extorquere vel eos ad placitum, praeter voluntatem epis-copi, temere coercere.*' ('From this we totally forbid on pain of anathema . . . that any authority or the representative of any authority should, in the case of clerics of your churches or of laymen under the protection of the bishopric, be entitled to seize property to settle debts or should dare to hail them before courts, except with the agreement of the bishop.') This exactly covered Francis' case. The Bull was sealed by Innocent himself and thirteen cardinals. There is a long and learned controversy over whether Francis had technically become a *conversus*, a sort of lay serf voluntarily attached to the service of a particular church. This seems fairly improbable – and fairly irrelevant. What is difficult to believe is that Francis himself (who, had he shown the slightest taste or inclination for the law, could immediately have had another and most suitable career open – that of student at Paris or Bologna) had hit upon these tactics. It was not his style at all. He must have been advised. Perhaps the old priest at San Damiano, despite his poverty and his fear of Francis' relatives, knew the law: he had certainly known enough of it to avoid compromising himself by accepting the money.

15 As regards the money, there are again different and contradictory accounts. I have followed the *Legend of the Three Companions*. But, according to Thomas of Celano's first version, Francis threw the money back in his father's face at a stormy interview *before* the bishop's trial. 'Therefore when the money was restored . . . the fury of his raging father was extin-guished a little and the thirst of his avarice was somewhat allayed by the warmth of dis-covery.' Nevertheless Pietro Bernardone still cited his son before the bishop's court 'so that,

renouncing all his possessions into his hands, he might give up everything he had.' This version of course puts Francis' father in an even worse light. Thomas of Celano does not stick to it in his *Second Life*, which agrees with the *Three Companions*. The *Legenda Major* follows the earlier version.

16 Chesterton, whose insight into Francis' character was so great, interprets the bishop's judgement and Francis' behaviour in a very different way. Here is how he describes the scene:
'The bishop addressed some remarks to him (Francis), full of that excellent commonsense which the Catholic Church keeps permanently as the background for all the fiery attitudes of her saints. He told Francis that he must unquestionably restore the money to his father; that no blessing could follow a good work done by unjust methods; and in short (to put it crudely) if the young fanatic would give the money back to the old fool, the incident would then terminate. There was a new air about Francis. He was no longer crushed, still less crawling, so far as his father was concerned; yet his words do not, I think, indicate either just indignation or wanton insult or anything in the nature of a mere continuation of the quarrel. They are rather remotely akin to the mysterious utterances of his great model "What have I to do with thee?" or even the terrible "Touch me not." '
Possibly Chesterton is right; and Francis was inspired. But he certainly does not seem to have been inspired by the commandment 'Honour Thy Father and Thy Mother.' The quarrel, as Chesterton implies, was in itself gratuitous, could easily have been settled without going to law, and both sides were in the wrong. But that was surely no excuse for Francis to scandalize everybody by exposing himself in public – and stark naked he most certainly was, 'not even retaining his breeches,' as Thomas of Celano specifies. Not even Chesterton suggests that in this he was imitating his great model.
Furthermore I would say that this *was* 'the mere continuation of the quarrel' in so far as, despite those fine phrases about his new and heavenly Father, Francis was not really turning towards religion so much as, if the modernism can be forgiven, publicly choosing a new life-style, dropping out. He was making his own personal, individual protest against the bourgeoisie and bourgeois values. The moment marks a break and an ending; but not yet did he put on the new man in the Christian sense.

❧ Building Mania ❧

5: Building Mania

Vague Vagabond

Francis left Assisi. He had nowhere to stay and nowhere to go, and so he took to the road. Before he left the bishop's palace, as if to give his grandiose words some sense and his aimless steps some purpose, he traced a cross in chalk upon the farmhand's tunic. By this rather pathetic gesture he was trying to make himself out as, still, a crusader.[1] Last time he had set out for Apulia to join the Pope's knights, complete with warhorse, arms, armour and shield-bearer. This time he set out – and it must have been a deliberate choice – in the other direction, towards the North, as if to turn his back on his princess – and indeed on San Damiano.

It never does to underestimate the importance of money. For the first time in his life Francis had none; and not only had none for the moment but had no hopes of obtaining any. This is a most disconcerting state of affairs for a man in his late twenties who has always been used to having plenty of largesse to scatter about. In particular it was exceedingly embarrassing for Francis, who had been patronizing the poor priest with talk of how he would have his church restored, to find that, in fact, he had come out of the lawsuit with not enough to pay for bricks and stones, still less for builders and masons. In strictly practical terms he had lost a lawsuit involving a considerable sum of money and as a result was unable to take up the new career of church-restorer, for which he had enthusiastically decided that he was fitted. No wonder that he left Assisi by the gate almost diametrically opposite to the gate leading down to his 'home' at San Damiano. The situation was aggravated by the fact that, having failed in his third attempt at a career, he had not the least idea of what to do next – nor indeed the slightest qualifications for doing anything at all.

So Francis traced the Cross on his tunic, turned his face to the North, and took to the road. Perhaps he had some vague idea of making his way to Venice and from there joining a ship to the Holy Land. At any rate the road meant adventure: knights, merchants, princes, pilgrims, students, clerks, *belles dames*, fellow crusaders – there was no telling whom one might fall in with. His spirits rose as he left Assisi further and further behind, and on joyful impulse he chose his own role among the many suited to the confraternity of the road: that of a *jongleur*, a wandering singer of the troubadours' songs.

Although we do not know which of the many famous songs he sang, we are told that he went on his way singing gaily in the French language; and this, if not the actual song, at least is the sort of song, as he went further and further away from his never-seen princess, his '*amor de lonh*', that he might have chosen.

'Lanquan li jorn son Lonc en Mai
M'es bels doucs chans d'auze ls de Lonh
E quan mi soy partitz de lay
Rememba. M d'un amor de lonh
Vau de talan embroncx e clis
Si que chans ni flors d'albespis
No. M platz plus que l'yverns gelatz.'[2]

At least the last two words would have been apposite; for it was certainly a
'*yverns gelatz*', with heavy falls of snow.[3] Unfortunately there was yet another
group of the confraternity of the road, not mentioned above: and it was this
group that gave Francis his first and nearly final adventure on the way. As he
was walking through the forest singing gaily, a group of robbers closed in upon
him. It is easy enough to picture the scene: Francis was small and frail in
physique, and always rather delicate; when he had travelled before, he had
travelled in company or on horseback, without fear or need for fear. And now,
suddenly, he was on his own, confronted for the first time by the hostile prole-
tariat and very likely to be contemptuously killed when they found that he had
no money. They surrounded the quavering young man and asked him who he
was. Fortunately for Francis his reply seems to have appealed to their sense of
humour: 'I am the herald of the great king,' he said.[4] And so they let him off
comparatively lightly, merely beating him up and throwing him into a ditch
full of snow and telling him to 'Lie there, you peasant herald!' 'With that,' says
the *Legenda Major*, 'they made off and Francis jumped from the ditch full of
joy and made the woods re-echo with his praise to the Creator of all.' I wonder?
I doubt whether St. Bonaventure ever tried to jump from a ditch full of snow;
it is not an easy manoeuvre, even when one has not been beaten black and blue.
I suspect that Francis lay very low till the robbers were well away and then
crawled out of the ditch extremely shaken, and full of joy only in the sense that
he was thankful to find himself still alive and in one piece. He may have sung a
quavering note or two to keep his spirits up; he must have been very tempted
to turn tail and scuttle back to Assisi. Life as a wandering minstrel did not, as
evening drew in, appear to be as rosy and promising a prospect as it had earlier
in the day. He was cold, wet, ragged, and bruised both literally and in his hopes.
Also, he was hungry. Also, he had no money.

Fortunately for such wayfarers as Francis, there were monasteries. Probably
the monastery at which he begged hospitality that night was the Benedictine
priory of Valfabbrica, a small town on the northern borders of the territory of
Assisi.[5] If this indeed was the monastery, it was impoverished at the time and
its prior, Ugo, can hardly have welcomed his duty to provide for such rag-tag
and bob-tail of the road as might knock up his doorkeepers with tales of being

beaten by robbers or try to impress him with their basic holiness by tracing chalk crosses on dirty tunics. Francis got some bread and a blanket to sleep in.

He stayed there for at least a few days, working as a kitchen-hand. He may have been very tempted to stay there for ever. Monastic life even as a lay-brother would have solved his difficulties. But Francis, even if he had been attracted by the religious life and by the direct service of God (which he certainly was not at this time, whatever he may have declared at the bishop's judgement) could never have taken the last of the monastic vows: poverty, obedience and chastity, yes: but stability, no. He was a wanderer; his feet were itchy by nature; and all his life, though he was drawn back and back again to the surroundings of his childhood, by that longing for security that affects all wanderers, he was never really happy if he was forced to stay longer than a few weeks in the same place.

Perhaps he wisely waited till the weather was better and there were several people going that way before he set out for Gubbio, that great crusading town that had sent, in the old days, a thousand crossbowmen to join Peter the Hermit in the Holy Land. But at Gubbio his own 'crusade' came to a full stop. He had got about as far north this time as he had got south on his journey to Apulia. This time, as before, it was as if the frontiers of Umbria, of the Duchy of Spoleto, acted as a psychological barrier: up to this point Francis was in territory he knew. Beyond lay *terra incognita*, and once again his spirit of adventure failed him. Gubbio had been Assisi's ally in the war against Perugia, and Francis had at least one friend there, a nobleman, Count Spadalunga, who presumably knew nothing of the disgraceful scenes in Assisi. Heaven knows what story Francis spun him, but at any rate he obtained some rather better clothes and stayed at Gubbio some time, looking after the lepers of the town. Quite possibly he was considering joining the Order of St. Lazarus; this would have been one way of getting to the Holy Land. But more probably he was just filling in time, drifting along between vague aspirations, as he had done since leaving Assisi. For in a sense he had tried out three possible vocations – *jongleur*, monastic lay-brother and lazarist. None of them satisfied him. He decided once again – this time without benefit of voices or visions – to go back to Assisi.

What is amazing about this drifting period in Francis' life is that he should have drifted home again. He could so easily have fallen in with a group of goliards; and their wandering bohemian life, with the companionship, songs, and satirical attacks on the merchants and the rich, would in a way have suited him, the rebel and outcast, ideally. He, as well as any wanderer and better than most, could have echoed the famous verses of the archpoet:

'*Factus de materia levis elementi*
Similis sum folio de quo ludunt venti.'[6]

For indeed he was a leaf, lightly constructed and the wind's plaything. But the wind blew him back to Assisi rather than out into the wide world and adventure; and so, for the second time, he came ignominiously back. However, he was now a changed man.

Resourceful Restorer

It would be conventional to say that it needed more courage to come back than to go on. That is not true. It would have needed great boldness and resolution to go on alone out into a world where he knew no-one; to come back to Assisi was, as the French put it, *une solution de facilité*. But at least Francis came back with a positive idea. For once he knew exactly what he was going to do, odd idea though it was. To quote Chesterton once again: 'There had dawned on him one of those great paradoxes that are also platitudes. He realized that the way to build a church . . . is not to pay for it, certainly not with somebody else's money. The way to build a church is not even to pay for it with your own money. The way to build a church is to build it.'

What Francis had learnt on his journey was that he was perfectly capable, like all human beings if forced to do so (though the sons of the bourgeoisie, not being forced, often do not realize it, particularly not in Italy), of working with his hands. He had washed dishes and washed lepers. If he had carried plates and basins, he was capable of carrying stones. And so at long last Francis found the occupation that suited him and was to keep him occupied and happy for many months to come. He set about repairing ruined churches.

There was, I think, nothing particularly holy or devout about this. If he had been a nobleman's son, he would probably have set about repairing ruined towers; for there was a fever of reconstruction in the countryside of Assisi. As it was he repaired one after the other, beginning with San Damiano, three little ruined churches, chapels really rather than churches, lying in the open country below Assisi, all within a radius of a mile or two of the town.

Those who have suffered from it will know the sort of fanatical bug that bites restorers and renovators. First you see a ruined or half-demolished or empty building and say to yourself: 'What a shame.' Then, indignantly, you turn to others: 'Why doesn't someone do something about it?' From there it is only a step, though a big one, to trying to raise the money and get something done about it yourself. But raising money, as Francis found, is difficult, however worthy the cause. And in the end you realize that the only thing to do is to do the work with your own hands, to set to physically with a paint brush or a sack of bricks, or a few nails and planks, and to hope that support and money will be forthcoming. It usually is in the end, once people see physical effort.

Of course Francis' position was particularly difficult and his efforts needed to be particularly impressive if he was to convince anyone at all that this was not just another whim. It says much for the charity of the poor priest that he accepted his eccentric young lodger back at San Damiano and allowed himself to be persuaded to give Francis another chance. Pietro Bernardone's heart must have sunk when he heard that his worthless son was back again. It sank even further as the weeks and the months went by and it became obvious that Francis was determined to go on with his own 'career'. In a way it was a deliberate affront and provocation, the latest of a long series, for Francis to insist on living and working in and around Assisi. If he had decided to become a sort of lay stonemason-cum-labourer in Gubbio, or further away still, his father might have forgiven him and eventually have become reconciled. As it was, there was never any chance of a family reconciliation, and there never could be with Francis' way of life so obviously and definitely contrasted to that of his family and the merchant class in general.

Even if he had wished to avoid his father, it would have been difficult to do so in as small a town as Assisi. As it was, he made no attempt to spare anyone embarrassment. He started coming back to the streets and squares of Assisi, wearing a kind of hermit's dress as if to mark himself out from the crowd and in particular from the merchant class, and begging for stones with which to restore the church. 'Whoever gives me one stone will have one reward; two stones, two rewards; three stones, a treble reward,' he would call out to the passers-by, all of whom of course knew him or of him. Naturally enough he collected more insults than stones. But gradually, as people saw that he was literally putting his back into it and carrying loads of stones down the very steep path that leads to San Damiano, their jeers and taunts died away. At least he was doing no harm. As for the priest, he appears to have been agreeably surprised and impressed by his hard-working handyman and, poor though he was, he did his best to get Francis the sort of food that he had been used to in his parents' house. He was well enough repaid. Francis gradually overcame what shyness he had left and begged for whatever the church needed – not only stones for restoring the building but also for oil for keeping the lamps alight. There was one occasion on which he was too timid to break up a gambling party at which, probably, some of his former drinking companions were playing. But he thought better of it, hurried back to the house, went in, explained to the gamblers that he had been ashamed to interrupt their gaming and begged them in French for oil. And occasionally when he was working at San Damiano, he would call out 'loudly and joyfully in French'[2] to the passers-by to ask them to come and lend a hand.

Why on earth *in French*, one wonders? Certainly he used to enjoy talking it, though, the *Three Companions* tell us, he could not in fact speak it very well and probably his hearers could understand it even less well than he spoke it. Perhaps it was simply to cover his embarrassment that he preferred to do his begging in a foreign language; perhaps, as Thomas of Celano implies, it was a fairly harmless form of snobbery designed to impress on his listeners that he might be ragged and dependent but for all that he was *au fond* a more cultivated person than any of them. But, more likely I think, it was his way of showing, both to himself and others, that he was still on crusade, even if he was merely rebuilding chapels instead of slaying Saracens; and that heavy and hot though the labour might be, it was still the sort of thing that a French knight would gaily undertake in the service of chivalry.

It seems that Pietro Bernardone could just tolerate his son begging for stones and for oil for the church; but that when Francis started begging for scraps of food for himself, the disgrace was too much for his strictly limited patience. It is a sad little story, a sort of tail-end to their relationship; for after this we hear no more of Pietro Bernardone or indeed of any of Francis' family, though heaven knows he must have seen them often enough. But after this last clash he does not seem to have cared whether they lived or died; as far as we know, he did not even attend his mother's funeral, let alone his father's. After this, his family was to all intents and purposes dead for him, and he was at last free from the need to shock and outrage his dominating father. Yet, though they held no further interest for him, he must for all the rest of their lives have been an object of fascination and amazement for them. It is all the sadder that their last encounters should have been so unpleasant; and the story does no credit to Francis.

It happened like this. Francis decided that he could not go on living at the poor priest's expense and in particular could not go on being fed by him. There was an element of mere commonsense in this; for the repairs to San Damiano were almost finished and Francis had his eye on a couple of other chapels lower down in the plain which were not only in ruins but deserted. He never seems to have considered cooking for himself; it was not, naturally enough, one of the skills he had learnt as a merchant's son. So he acted, as he usually did, with a literal sort of commonsense that verged on the exaggerated; he simply took one of the priest's bowls and went begging for scraps of cooked food from door to door in Assisi, 'And knowing what his former life had been,' says the *Three Companions*, 'many were exceedingly astonished at such degradation and at seeing him so completely changed. When it came to eating the contents of the bowl Francis' stomach turned, for he had never seen such a mess, let alone tried to eat it. At last, making a great effort, he started to gulp it down, and it seemed to him the most delicious food in the world.' Which was all very well; but

Pietro Bernardone would have been less than human if he had not been more aware of the degradation of his son than of the turns of his stomach. Yet it was not just family pride and outraged feelings that dominated him, as even the chronicler acknowledges. Probably regular meals were waiting every day for Francis in the family house – if only an apology had been forthcoming, or perhaps if he had merely deigned to put in an appearance. 'When his father saw him in this pitiful plight, he was filled with sorrow, for he had loved him very dearly; he was both grieved and ashamed to see his son half dead from penance and hardships; and whenever they met he cursed Francis.'

His brother was more venomous. Sneering ironically at Francis when winter came round and he noticed him shivering with the cold, Angelo turned to his fellow-townsmen and said: 'Ask Francis to sell you a pennyworth of his sweat,' – to which Francis made a suitably high-minded retort about preferring to sell his sweat to God. But it was on his father that he played a last humiliating trick. He found a poor old man of Assisi called Albert, promised him a share of the food he would obtain, and had the man follow him around like a tame parrot.[8] Whenever he passed his father and heard his curses, he would turn to this man and say 'Bless me, father,' and the man's duty was to make the sign of the Cross and bless him as his father should have done. A little of this was obviously enough to put an end to Pietro Bernardone's behaviour; though humiliating, it was sufficiently ingenious to put the people of the town on Francis' side. And Francis had the last word. Indeed the very last words that are recorded in the life-long dialogue between father and son are the words with which Francis finally turned on his father, and, as it were, adopted a superior moral attitude to declare their relationship at an end: 'Do you not realize that God can give me a father whose blessings will counter your curses?'

Philip of Swabia

The war with Perugia might have ended in the year that Francis set off for Apulia if the Germans had not reappeared in Italy and attempted to re-establish the imperial power. They acted with greater tact and discretion than usual because they were in a weaker position; but they succeeded in stirring up central Italy. Little towns like Assisi that had tasted freedom and revolution were not prepared meekly to accept the Pope and his legates as masters in place of the Emperor and his dukes. Most of the citizens of Assisi may have welcomed the results of Cardinal Leo of Santa Croce's intervention in the autumn of 1204, but they could hardly have welcomed the methods that led up to these results – the interdict, and the exceedingly dictatorial visitations. So when the Pope's champion, Walter of Brienne, was killed the following June in Apulia by

Dipold, they – like the citizens of many other towns – turned back to the Emperor as a counter-weight.

Although Francis took no part in the political life of Assisi, it inevitably affected him. He had been, in spirit at least, Walter of Brienne's man; he was never a lover of the Germans or the imperialists and even less so after Walter was slain. His emotional loyalty therefore went very strongly to Walter's master and the Germans' antagonist, the Pope.

Innocent III had made a nearly fatal mistake in the second year of his pontificate. It had been naive to hope that the Empire would be held together and administered in the name of his ward, the baby emperor in Palermo. Within nine months of the death of the Emperor Henry VI, a pretender had been elected and crowned at Aix in Germany: Otto of Brunswick, born in Normandy to Matilda of England, nephew to Richard the Lion Heart, brought up in England, the Plantagenet candidate, young, proud, and stupid. Two months later a rival candidate, backed by Philippe Auguste, was crowned at Mainz. This was Philip of Swabia, brother of the dead Emperor, uncle therefore of the Pope's ward, former governor of Tuscany, equally young – both Emperors were under twenty-five – small and frail in physique, but nobler in character and greater in repute.

Faced with two, or rather with three candidates, Pope Innocent had to choose which Emperor to accept and which to crown. Towards the end of the year 1200 he published his famous *Deliberatio*, an open weighing-up of the pros and cons of the rival Emperors. Most unwisely, as it so happened, he decided that Otto of Brunswick had the best claim; a decision which said more for his sense of equity than for his statecraft. Otto had less support in Germany and, with the death of Richard the Lion Heart, inadequate support in Europe. But it was only after the killing of Walter of Brienne that Philip of Swabia felt confident enough to turn some of his efforts aside from the struggle against his rival in Germany and attempt to re-establish his influence south of the Alps. His legates toured the cities and towns of northern and central Italy offering generous pacts of alliance provided Philip's sovereignty was recognized. The imperial Curia guaranteed Assisi, by a diploma of 29 July 1205, that the Emperor would make no pact with the Perugians except by mutual consent, would recognize the consuls provided they swore fealty, would not reconstruct the imperial castle on the Rocca and would revoke the privileges of the self-exiled nobles if they remained in Perugia. This last clause was highly effective; the imperialists had always been the natural supporters of the nobles in the countryside; and, threatened by imperial disfavour, not realizing that in any case their power as a caste was doomed, the nobles came trickling back to Assisi. The lords of Coriano, the five brothers, returned with their children, the eleven-year-old

Clare, her two sisters Agnes and Beatrice, her first cousin the delicate Rufino, and her kinswoman Bona di Guelfuccio. A month later the *Podestà* of Perugia attempted to react by imposing an *Ordinanza della Pace*[9] which the Assisians were summoned to obey; under pain of dire punitive expeditions they were ordered to restore to all exiles all their possessions both inside and outside the walls, to rebuild demolished town houses and country towers and in particular to restore the castle of Sassorosso, plus a hundred Lucchese *denarii* by way of compensation, to the brothers Leonardo and Fortebraccio, the two lords of Sassorosso who had survived the battle of Collestrada. Of this ordinance the citizens of Assisi took no notice whatsoever; and, having sworn their loyalty to a distant and unprovocative Emperor, reinforced by all but the hard core of their dissident nobles, they kept up a desultory sort of warfare against the Perugians and, more importantly, kept out the importunate representatives of the Pope.

By 1206 Philip's rival Otto of Brunswick had lost his last stronghold of Cologne, and was forced to take refuge in England with his uncle King John – who, equally unsuccessful in the field, had lost his duchy of Normandy to Philippe Auguste and the French. They made a sad pair of allies. The Pope decided that central Italy must be disciplined before Philip of Swabia in person should descend from the North. He moved up to Viterbo in June of 1207, eradicated the heretics and Cathars there[10] – more by the destruction of their property than of their lives – and in September summoned to a great Diet at Viterbo all the notables in the land – all the abbots, counts, barons, *Podestà* and consuls of the Patrimony of St. Peter, the Duchy of Spoleto and Le Marche of Ancona, in order to re-establish papal authority. Innocent's prestige was at its height; and it would have been unthinkable for the consuls of Assisi to have refused his summons or to have rejected his authority. As the Pope's man Francis must have been delighted at the news, and have turned with even greater enthusiasm to his church-restoring. Perhaps he did now begin to see it as symbolic; the time of his real conversion was drawing near.

Santa Maria degli Angeli

Francis had finished his work at San Damiano, and went on to restore the dilapidated chapel of San Pietro della Spina, further down the hillside.[11] By now he seems to have been well into his stride as a mason and competent enough technically to have developed an appetite for his work. No sooner had he finished with one chapel than he set his sights on the next. The third chapel he tackled was to become the most famous of all. In the woods down on the plain below Assisi, not far from the *leprosarium* and close to land owned by his father, stood the ruins of a very old church that had been named Santa Maria degli Angeli but at the time was generally known as the Portiuncula. It belonged to the monks of St. Benedict up on the mountain, but in fact was deserted and cared for by no-one. Having restored San Pietro, Francis turned to the ruins of Santa Maria.

He might have gone on in this rather feverish way, restoring chapel after chapel after chapel for many years. When a mania of this sort grips a man, he hardly stops to consider the point of his activity; he generally prefers to go on and on without a pause for reflection. As far as we know Francis made no plans for the chapels he rebuilt. If it benefited an occupant, as at San Damiano, so much the better. If it remained empty, as at San Pietro, very good all the same – better a reconstructed chapel that might be of use to somebody some day than a blot on the landscape. And yet there comes a moment, for everyone who becomes totally immersed in the passion for restoring buildings, when an irritating question rears its irritating head and distracts the restorer from what he feels to be his real task of getting on with the job. Usually this irritating question – 'what or who am I doing this for?' – is forced upon the restorer by outside circumstances. And in Francis' case outside circumstances seem to have taken the form of a sudden interest by the monks of St. Benedict's abbey in the chapel which the son of Pietro Bernardone had so kindly reconstructed on their land. It seems that they sent a monk down to celebrate Mass in the restored chapel. This was of course a compliment and a gesture of gratitude and appreciation; yet at the same time it was a delicate way of reminding Francis that the monks owned Santa Maria degli Angeli, and that indirectly Francis had been working for the invisible Abbey up on the mountain.

Francis was not offended; it was not in his character to be possessive. But this quiet claim to the benefit of his work clearly set him thinking. He had found something useful and satisfying to do with his life; he had been restoring buildings and thereby improving the appearance of the countryside. But it so happened that the buildings were churches; and churches were for the service and worship of God. Therefore he, Francis, was indirectly serving God and indeed directly helping the clergy, both regular and secular. But if this was what he was in fact doing, was he doing it in the best and most effective way?

One feast day in February 1208, a priest came down to celebrate Mass at the chapel. Francis had certainly heard the day's gospel (Matthew 10, 5ff.) often before: it is the famous passage where Christ tells his disciples to go out into the world without money or possessions and preach penance and the Kingdom of God. After Mass Francis humbly asked the priest to explain the gospel more fully to him. In a way this was a rather puzzling request, for the words of the gospel are fairly self-explanatory: but presumably the monk could quote other similar passages from the other gospels and expound ideas which were very much in the air in Italy at that moment. 'This is what I want,' cried Francis. 'This is what I long for with all my heart.'

His immediate reaction might strike us as trivial; he simply changed his style of dress – a change which in the circumstances was equivalent to a tramp shedding a few accoutrements. In fact, however, it was more than a change of style, it was a change of uniform. In the Middle Ages more than in most epochs external appearance marked out the man, and not only the man's class but his vocation and therefore his loyalties. Tonsured, a clerk; armoured, a knight; richly robed, a merchant – these were only the most obvious of the distinctions. Scallop-shells signified a pilgrim, a lyre a *jongleur* – and of course the mark of the Cross a crusader. Francis appears to have abandoned his Cross and therefore his claim to be a crusader on his return to Assisi. Instead, he adopted what the chroniclers rather delicately described as 'a kind of hermit's dress', with a leather girdle and pouch, shoes, and – significant detail – a staff in his hands.

This sort of dress was certainly not the uniform of a mere mason: it indicated higher aspirations. In fact it was noticeably similar to the dress that the Perfect wore when they walked the roads going from community of Believers to community of Believers. They would be familiar enough figures on the plains of Italy and France, as they strode along two by two, halting to preach penitence and the true Kingdom of God, leaning on their long staffs. Their distinctive leather girdles, from which hung a leather pouch containing the New Testament, are often mentioned in the chronicles of the time.

This was the sort of uniform that Francis cast off. He discarded his leather girdle, his shoes and his staff. As his new dress he chose a very rough tunic, worn over breeches, which he fastened round his middle with a small cord: one tunic and one only. Although we are not told so, we may imagine that unlike the black of the Perfect's tunic he chose a different colour, undyed grey.

By changing his outward appearance Francis was proclaiming to all who might see him that he was changing his vocation. He had become a penitent.

The Penitent

It seems that Francis' way of life changed almost immediately. He went on living at or around the Portiuncula but he repaired no more ruined chapels. He learnt by heart the words of the gospel that had so impressed him and determined to put them into practice. The easiest part was the renouncing of gold and silver – which had already been forced upon him by circumstances. Secondly, the disciples had been enjoined to have neither haversack, nor staff, bread nor shoes, nor second garment: that involved a comparatively minor, though symbolic, change of style; and he accepted it. The third part was the real crux: to go forth and preach penance and the kingdom of heaven.

Francis began mildly enough, he did not exactly go forth and he did not exactly preach penance. He simply went back to Assisi and preached peace. In precise terms what he appears to have done was to have walked along the roads in the countryside and the streets in Assisi and to have greeted every passer-by with the greeting: 'God give you peace.'[12] This showed an unusual degree of tact on his part. It was not the sort of greeting that could offend anyone individually[13] and, politically, it probably echoed the wishes of most of the people of Assisi. For in this early spring of the year 1208 the warfare with Perugia was still dragging on; and after ten years of upheaval, internal disturbance and sporadic bloodshed, the ordinary inhabitants of Assisi were ready for peace at almost any price.

Many months had passed since the scandal at the bishop's judgement, and many more since the expedition to Apulia. No-one in Assisi could forget who Francis was or what he had done; and inevitably there were people in Assisi who all his life would treat him with contempt. But even they were uneasily aware that in a sense they were playing into his hands by doing so; for once Francis had chosen the role of penitent, he threw himself into the part with his usual wholeheartedness. And taunts, and jeers and hardship were what a penitent, in theory at least, welcomed.

But most people in Assisi began to accept him. A penitent had a recognized place in the scheme of things; and just as it was right that every court should have its jester, so it was right that every town should have its penitent: both fulfilled the same role, that of keeping the dominant class faintly and often deliciously uneasy, and both were expected to speak out where others kept silent.

The mark of a penitent was, of course, penance. Penitents were expected to lead a life of physical hardship: to own no property, to beg scraps for their food, to have no fixed address, to wear poor or ragged clothes and in particular to go without shoes. As the purpose of their way of life was to do penance not only for their own sins but for the sins of mankind, it was understood that they should spend a great deal of their time in prayer and vigils, and that, though gnashing of teeth and flagellation were excessive except in times of universal crisis, such as the imminent end of the world, moaning, groaning and weeping were suitable and indeed essential activities.

There was, however, a distinction between what we might call voluntary and involuntary penitents. The second category had their penances imposed by their confessors – priests, bishops or, in extreme cases, the Pope – as temporal punishment and atonement for their sins; their aim was to fulfil the penance as quickly and as discreetly as possible and thereafter to return to normal life.[14] But the voluntary penitents, those who had chosen of their own free will this harsh way of life for the benefit not only of themselves but of the community, were allowed by the community a rather higher status. In particular, they were not expected to be discreet. Rather, they were expected to proclaim loudly and openly the need for penance and for leading a life of perfection according to the teachings of the gospel, taken literally. Rather like twentieth-century economists, they were expected to be serious, gloomy, and statistical; and they had just about as little influence on the ordinary life or understanding of those who would make the gesture of listening with apparent attentiveness and would then pass by.

Francis, however, was an unusually attractive penitent. Although, as has been noted, he threw himself into this new role with his usual wholeheartedness and accepted not only the conventions but the spirit of the pact, his natural gaiety and high good humour would keep breaking through. It is impossible to be sure what his actual day-to-day routine was at this time, and in particular where he lived and where he slept. Probably, as he was always to do all through his life, he lived as a sort of outlying raider, making lightning descents on the town from a rough base in the countryside. But it seems that if ever he was invited in to stay the night inside Assisi, he would accept – it being understood that he was invited in his role as a penitent and not of course merely as a friend or a former friend who might need a break and a rest and a good meal and a comfortable bed. Not that he invariably or on principle refused these comforts, but he took his duties as a penitent seriously, and these duties involved talking to his hosts about penance and the life of perfection. This was the price that they had to pay for what was undoubtedly the pleasure of his company.

In one way, however, Francis' way of life did change completely. When he had been rebuilding the chapels he had begged for stones; but if people had no stones to give him – and not every citizen of Assisi had building materials ready to hand – he naturally enough accepted money instead, it being understood that he would use the money given him to buy stones and so forth, and not for his own personal needs. But after hearing the gospel of St. Matthew in February at the Portiuncula, he gave up money entirely. 'Take neither gold nor silver,' Christ had told his disciples, and Francis took this literally. From that day onwards he never touched a coin nor accepted a piece of money either for a good cause or in lieu of a meal.

It was both Francis' strength and weakness that he took the gospel so literally. In one sense there is something magnificent about this total rejection of money, whatever the circumstances. But in another sense it is puerile and ridiculous. If you are begging for a meal and the householder says, 'I have no food to spare in the house at the moment but take this, my man, and buy yourself something to eat,' surely it is mere quibbling to refuse, for after all the householder would have had to spend the money on your food in any case. So, at any rate, many of Francis' later followers decided. But he himself always stuck hard and fast to the principle; indeed to see coins handled by anyone who claimed to have accepted his ideas was about the only thing that could make him lose his temper. From this time on he (often literally) treated money as dung.

It would be naive to suppose that this was entirely because of the words of the gospel. Like all Christians at all times, Francis only chose those particular passages that fitted in with his own ideas. It was admitted with much greater frankness at this period of Christianity than it is now that the gospels are contradictory; indeed the whole basis of theology in the Middle Ages and in particular of university education consisted in openly confronting contradictory passages in the scriptures and in the writings of the Fathers of the Church. The eventual aim, of course, was to harmonize the differences and thereby to produce an exposition of the Christian doctrine. But there was no attempt to pretend that contradictory passages did not exist or that the words of Christ were automatically consistent.

I am not suggesting for a moment that Francis had studied, or indeed even heard of, the *Sentences* of Peter Lombard, the immense text-book which was used everywhere as the basis of theological education and in which all these contradictory passages were expounded on the principles of '*Sic et Non.*' What I am suggesting is that he, like all Christians of that time, knew very well that even the New Testament was often contradictory and that this was a fact that he, like his contemporaries, accepted without difficulty. It was therefore not by grace of God or inspiration of the Holy Ghost but by deliberate (if instinctive) choice that he latched on to the passage outlawing, for Christ's disciples, the use of money, made it the central principle of his life and imposed it with such obstinate determination upon his followers. Yet it is obvious that it is not coinage as such that Christ condemns but riches and the love of riches. But Francis fastened on to a general rule, reduced it to one particular point, and on that particular point, fanatically observed, built a whole way of life. Why?

It is possible to imagine a psychological background to this obsession. Merchants love money; Francis loathed merchants; therefore Francis detested even the sight of money. But this mental picture of Pietro Bernardone sitting like a Shylock greedily counting up his piles of coins is too much of a caricature to be convincing. What was perhaps behind Francis' attitude was a longing for a more idyllic past. Money, in the sense of coinage, was a comparatively recent invention, or rather re-invention, in the Italy of that time; indeed, the first florin was not struck at Florence till 1252, over a quarter of a century after Francis' death. And in so far as the use of coinage coincided with, and to some extent was the outward symbol of, the rise of a world of trade dominated by the middle-classes and the disappearance of a simple feudal world of knights and peasants, it was in Francis' character to hate money. It is unlikely that he felt attracted to barter as an economic principle of society; but it was certain that he was attracted to that more primitive and clear-cut way of life that had existed in the very recent past. Money, trade, heresy, the ruin of chivalry based on a knighthood in the service of the Church, were all, as Francis instinctively knew, linked; and he may well have felt that if only the first link in the chain, coinage, disappeared, the whole constricting system that he disliked so much would collapse. And so, as with the rebuilding of the chapels, he set out on a one-man crusade to put his ideas into practice. He himself, he decided, would on no account use or circulate money; and though his own efforts might not be enough to break the system and bring back the sort of world in which he would have liked to have lived, others might follow his example. And if enough people followed his example, why then, the world would change. This is to sum up in a few words a process of thought and daydreaming that must have been slow, instinctive, confused and often itself contradictory. But I believe that it alone explains why Francis clung like a leech to the basic principle of no use of coinage, not in any circumstances whatsoever; and how at this time he began to feel that he had something to teach; and quite rapidly began to impose his ideas upon others whereas before he had simply attempted to follow the ideas imposed, by life and by literature, upon him.

NOTES

1 'To take the Cross' was both the physical and the spiritual sign of the crusaders. So by tracing a Cross on his tunic Francis was signifying symbolically a vow to go to Jerusalem. It was not however quite as simple as that; for the Popes had gradually extended the right to wear the symbolic Cross, with all the spiritual and material privileges it signified, first to the knights and princes fighting the Saracens in Spain, and eventually to any knights – such as Walter of Brienne – fighting for the Church against heretics or the excommunicated. So the symbol had at the same time become wider and more precise: those seeing Francis would have known only that he had dedicated himself to the Pope's service.

2 'When the days grow long in May,
It is sweet to hear the songs of birds in the distance,
And when I go away from there,
remembering a far-away love,
I go bowed by such chagrin that neither songs nor flowers
please me more than a freezing winter.'

3 About 2,500 songs of the troubadours survive, about a tenth with not only words but melodies, too, like the song quoted here. It was composed by one of the most famous of the troubadours, Geoffroi Rudel, who had fallen desperately in love, for the fame of her beauty, with the Countess of Tripoli in Outremer, a lady he had never seen. It was one of the conventions of courtly love that the lover could love at a distance and by repute. More fortunate than Francis, Geoffroi Rudel finally saw his most noble and beautiful beloved – though only to die in her arms.

Not all the troubadours' songs were as pastoral in spirit. Bertrand de Born with his '*Trompas, Tabors, Senheras e Penos*' was the poet of feudal warfare who would have appealed to Francis in the days of his expedition to Apulia; less, in this case, the last line of the same song in praise of highway robbery: '*Anz sera rics qui tolra voloniters*'.

For the original of many of these songs, and a fine study of the troubadours, see *Les Troubadours* by Henri Davenson, Editions Seuil, in the series *Le Temps Qui Court*.

It is Henri d'Avranches who tells us that Francis was intending to live as a *joculator*, or *jongleur*. The *jongleur* (*joglar/joglador* in the *langue d'oc*) was the minstrel who accompanied the *troubadour* and sang his songs; when a troubadour sang his own songs, he was filling a double role. *Joculatores* were much condemned in papal Bulls of this whole epoch.

4 One theory (Fortini's) is that the 'robbers' were an armed band of marauders from Perugia. When therefore they asked Francis who he was, their purpose was to find out whose side he was on; in which case his answer was tactful, if not particularly courageous.

5 Alternatively the monastery may have been the Abbey of St. Verecondo, only six miles from Gubbio. In any case Francis appears to have been turned out after a few days and treated so harshly that later on, when he had become famous, the monks apologized for the 'misunderstanding'.

6 Francis was perhaps too naive and basically too optimistic to become a goliard; also too unintellectual. He wrote and spoke Latin, as Thomas of Eccleston tells us, badly; and Latin was both the mark and the means of communication of the wandering scholars.

For the archpoet's lament, and for many others, see Helen Waddell's affectionate and scholarly book *The Wandering Scholars: the life and art of the lyric poets of the Latin Middle Ages* (Constable, 1927).

7 When Francis spoke or sang in French, what language did he in fact use, the *langue d'oc* or the *langue d'oil*? The texts show a slight confusion: e.g. '*cum laudes Domino lingua francigena decantaret*' (*First Life*, I, c. 8, no. 16), on the road to Gubbio; but '*audientibus cunctis, gallice loquens clara voce prophetat*' (*Second Life*, II, c. 8, no. 13) when rebuilding San Damiano.

Yet *gallice* is not the adverbial form of *francigenus*, for we also find '*quasi spiritu ebrius lingua* gallica *petit oleum et acquerit*' (*Second Life*, ibid.) on approaching the gamblers. Nor does it seem, as I was tempted to believe, that he sang in the *lingua francigena* (i.e. *langue d'oc*) and talked in the *lingua gallica*, for in another passage (and by the same author) we find: '*Dulcissima melodia spiritus intra ipsum ebulliens, exterius* gallice *dabat sonum, et vena divini susurrii, quem auris eius suscipiebat furtive gallicum erumpebat in jubulum*' (*Second Life*, II, c. 90, no. 127), describing a later episode when Francis played a mock harp to accompany himself. See also the *Three Companions*, IX, c. 32, where Francis again sings the praises of God '*voce alta et clara decantatus* gallice.'

It would seem therefore that the two adjectives, *gallicus* and *francigenus*, are interchangeable. Francis would certainly have sung in the *langue d'oc*, the literary language of southern France and northern Italy; for that is the language in which the songs were written. When, however, he had to find words rather than memorize words already written, in other words when he begged, did he use *francien*, the northern French dialect of Paris and Champagne which was at this time beginning to oust the rival dialects of *Picard* and *Anglo-Normand*? He would perhaps have been more likely to have known merchants' jargon in this language. It seems that his biographers did not know, though they must have been aware of the distinction.

8 It is the *Anonymous of Perugia*, very good on local inhabitants, that gives us the name of the poor old man of Assisi, Albert. According to the same source this trick did not in fact win Francis any credit, on the contrary the townsfolk thought him insane:

'*Nudibus pedibus ambulans, contemptibili habitu indutus erat, zona quoque vilissima cingebatur. Et ubicumqe pater eius inveniebat eum, vehementi dolore repletus maledicebat eidem. At beatus vir quendam senem pauperem, nomine Albertum, assumebat, postulans benedictionem ab eo. Multi quoque alii deridebant eum et verba ei iniuriosa dicebant, et pro insano quasi ab omnibus habebatur.*'

(He walked around barefoot and in rags, though with a loin-cloth in place. And wherever his father came across him, filled with sorrow, he would curse him. But the blessed Francis took on a poor old man, Albert by name, whom he would ask for *his* blessing instead. Many other people, too, used to mock him and insult him and he was considered a madman by nearly everyone.)

9 The fact that the phrase '*bona et firma pax*' is used in the archives to describe the negotiations of August 1205 has led some historians to give this failed attempt an importance it does not merit. It was in fact an *Ordinanza* of the *Podestà* of Perugia, Giovanni di Guidone di Papa.

10 It appears that the Cathars of Viterbo fled from the city before the Pope's arrival in June 1207; and that their houses inside the walls were on his orders demolished – the same form of retaliation that the burghers of Assisi had inflicted on the nobles. It was not till the following year, after the murder of the papal legate, Peter of Castelnau, near Toulouse that repression and physical persecution began on any scale; and even then it was limited to France. There was never a sustained attempt to persecute the Cathars in Italy.

11 San Pietro della Spina was about two miles outside Assisi. The chapel no longer exists. At that distance it is hard to imagine Francis toiling up to Assisi and down again with a load of stones; he must have hired helpers or beasts of burden. We know that he paid for stones from a canon named Sylvester; so the deduction is that he had begged money as well as materials.

12 According to the *Three Companions* Francis' preaching of peace was not original. He had had a predecessor – a man who had appeared, greeted everyone with the phrase '*pax et bonum*', and then eventually moved on. It sounds as if this may have been Assisi's first sight of a wandering penitent.

13 Or hardly anyone. But, a hundred and fifty years later, when on the same roads of Umbria some Franciscans greeted Sir John Hawkwood of the White Company with the same greeting, he retorted 'God take from you your alms!' The friars said they meant no offence. 'How,' asked the famous English captain, 'When you pass me by and pray that God will make me die of hunger? Do you not know that I live by war and that peace would ruin me?'

Quoted in the present author's book *Mercenaries* (Macdonalds, 1970).

14 The following letter from Pope Innocent written at about this period gives a very good notion of how 'involuntary' penitents had to live, dress, eat and behave. I quote it in full, for its weird appeal.

'To the archbishops, bishops, abbots and friars to whom this letter shall come.

The bearer of this letter, Robert by name, came to the compassionate Apostolic See and tearfully confessed his sin, a great one indeed and a grave one.

For when he had been captured with his wife and daughter by the Saracens, their chief whom they call the Admiral issued an order that since a famine was imminent all those prisoners who had children should kill them; and by reason of this order the wretched man, urged on by pangs of hunger, killed and ate his daughter. And when on a second occasion another order went out, he killed his own wife; but when her flesh was cooked and served up before him, he could not bring himself to eat it.

Appalled by the horror of such a crime we have thought fit to enjoin upon him this penance: that he never hereafter on any account eat meat, and that he fast every Friday on bread and water and likewise on the Monday and Wednesday in the Lent of Christmas and the Lent of Easter; and on other days of each Lent he is to fast devoutly and remain content with one dish of pottage, observing the same on the vigils of the saints' days.

He is to go about unshod, in a woollen tunic with a very short scapular, carrying a penitent's staff a cubit in length. He is to accept no more food from anyone than suffices for a day, and he is never to spend above two nights in the same place unless driven by necessity and unable to proceed because of illness, war or weather.

In this way let him visit the shrines of the saints for three years; and when he comes to a church, let him prostrate himself and not even enter until he has received discipline with rod or whip.

He shall persist always without hope of marriage. He shall never attend public sports. He is to say the Lord's Prayer a hundred times every day and bow the knee each time.

At the end of three years let him return with this letter to the Apostolic See to seek mercy, and take pains to observe what shall then be enjoined on him.

You, therefore, brethren and children, show pity to the pitiful and in the time of his need reveal to him the fulness of your love.

Dated at the monastery of Subiaco, the 3rd of September, in the fifth year of our pontificate.'

Quoted in Chena, C. R., *Mediaeval Texts and Studies* (Oxford, 1973).

❧ Wild Men of the Woods ❧

6: Wild Men of the Woods

The First Followers

Francis was not a natural leader; hence many of his future troubles and disappointments. He was not a natural follower, either; hence many of his past troubles and disappointments. But at this point in his life he found just the right role, and the next few years were to be the happiest and best of his life. He was the sort of person who inspires other people to follow his example; and who is at his happy best provided they follow his example unquestioningly.

Francis did not deliberately set out to form a group. But he had a burning idea, thought about it, talked about it, practised it; and being totally convinced was in his turn convincing. Such people, provided they are naturally friendly and sociable, attract followers. Francis was never a hermit by character; he liked his fellow-men too much. And, though often extraordinarily obstinate, he was never repellently extravagant. He liked to shock and surprise, particularly by taking things literally – which is a habit the conventional invariably find both surprising and shocking. He could be distinctly exhibitionistic. But even the worst of his exhibitionism – for instance, the stripping naked in front of the bishop's palace, or the ostentatious humility later on – had a purpose. It was nothing like that totally inhuman desire for sanctity that put St. Simon Stylites up on top of his pillar. St. Simon attracted only rivals; Francis attracted followers.

He had almost certainly had people helping him sporadically while he was rebuilding the churches. Perhaps they came for an hour or two, possibly they stayed for the day or even overnight. Francis had always been used to having people of the lower-class at his beck and call – whether it was the person from his father's household who brought him meals in the pit or the old man whom he had hired to follow him around. Probably it was one of these, a helper in the building days, who first tried to keep up with Francis when he changed from reconstruction to repentance. Only Thomas of Celano mentions him: 'a certain man from Assisi, of pious and humble spirit' – and then never to mention him again. So the first, anonymous follower dropped away, unable to keep up with the strain of 'devoutly following the man of God.' Francis must have been very disheartened. He was not a loner; in all his schemes – even the search for treasure on the mountain, let alone his normal gay life in Assisi – he had always had someone to share his ideas with. It is difficult to keep going entirely by oneself; and I think that if Francis had been forced to keep going without support for longer than a few weeks – or months at the most – he would have given up.

Fortunately a supporter appeared; and even more fortunately it was not just another 'certain man' but a man whose conversion to Francis' way of life made an absolutely decisive impact on Assisi. Messer Bernard of Assisi, Bernard of Quintavalle di Berandello, was not, apparently, a nobleman; but he was rich and respected and of established position, and therefore probably a member of the merchant class. He had been observing Francis' behaviour and was impressed by his patience and firmness. 'Of a truth,' he said to himself, 'it is impossible that this Francis hath not great grace from God.' So Messer Bernard invited Francis to supper and to spend the night. And 'Francis joyfully gave thanks to God because so far he had had no companions and Messer Bernard was a virtuous and godly man.'

Bernard of Quintavalle died in July 1246; when he invited Francis to spend the night, it was mid-April of the year 1208. Therefore if he died at the age of seventy, he would have been thirty-two at this time. It seems about right – a good few years older than Francis, but not yet middle-aged and set in his ideas. It was an enormous decision that he was thinking of taking. 'If a man receives from God few or many possessions and having enjoyed them for a number of years now no longer wishes to retain them, what would be the best thing to do?' he asked Francis over supper, being very careful to frame the question hypothetically.

It was of course obvious both to Francis and to himself that it was not a hypothetical question. It was very important, perhaps decisive for his whole future, for Francis to get the answer right. Only seven weeks had passed since his own 'conversion' – and eight weeks earlier he would probably have had no hesitation in replying that the man in question should finance the rebuilding of churches. Eight weeks later it still must have been a tempting thought. Here was the chance to found a new Order for rebuilding churches – a perfectly respectable and holy objective – or perhaps for improving the conditions of lepers or indeed for almost anything at all, for money opens all sorts of possibilities. Francis seems to have hesitated: he told Messer Bernard that it was better for a man to give back to God what he had received. This really begged the question: there are many ways of 'giving to God'; and most of these involve giving directly to the clergy or would-be representatives of God on earth. It was Messer Bernard, not Francis, who interpreted the answer and resolved the question. 'Then, brother,' he said, 'I will give all my worldly goods to the poor for love of God who gave them to me.' But he added – and this showed the question had after all not entirely been resolved – 'according as you may think best.'

The two went up to bed to sleep on it. Would it be iniquitous to picture them both as very exalted – and slightly drunk? Messer Bernard had had a bed made up for Francis in his own bedroom; Francis went up first, laid down and pretended to go to sleep. His mind must have been ticking over with excitement: did Messer Bernard really mean it? Would morning bring second thoughts? If he did mean it, how to distribute the money, who to and where? What about the relatives? What about the house? What about this, that and the other?

Messer Bernard finished his wine and came up a little later. His thoughts must have been running on much the same lines as he looked down at Francis, apparently sound asleep. Or was he? Perhaps an eyelid flickered. Bernard in his turn got into bed and, to convince Francis that he at any rate was really and genuinely asleep, began to snore at once and loudly – a convincing sign of a well washed-down supper.

Soon Francis, assuming that Messer Bernard was completely deaf to this world, got out of bed and began praying. 'Praying and weeping continually,' says the chronicler, 'and always repeating "My God, my God," and nothing else.' And so he went on till the darkness faded and day began breaking – a day that meant for him either new disappointment or the beginning of great and impressive things.

Messer Bernard always kept a night-light burning in his bedroom; and so was able not only to hear but to see Francis' vigil. Dozing off and waking up again to find Francis still on his knees, still muttering 'My God, my God', he passed the night. By the morning he was convinced that this was a true penitent, and the cold light of day only strengthened his decision.

'Francis,' he said, 'brother, I am altogether disposed in my heart to leave the world and to follow you in whatever you order me to do.'

On hearing this Francis, in the words of the chronicler, 'rejoiced in spirit'. Of course he did; he had not only a companion ready to take up his own way of life but a follower: for Bernard had promised not only evangelical poverty but also obedience to Francis. He reacted with great tact.

'Messer Bernard,' he said, 'this which you speak of is so great and difficult a work that we ought to seek the advice of Our Lord Jesus Christ about it, so that he himself may deign to show us his will regarding it and teach us how we should carry it out.' In a sense this was totally unnecessary; all Bernard had to do was to join Francis and imitate his way of life. Everybody knew what a penitent's way of life was meant to be, and there was no need to seek divine advice on the subject; nor had Francis done so in the case of his first temporary follower.

But where large sums of money are involved – and in particular the renunciation of large sums of money – men are always inclined to become rather solemn. And it is quite understandable that Francis did not want to take the whole responsibility for the disposal of Messer Bernard's fortune upon himself. Should things go wrong, it would be too late for Messer Bernard to change his mind. The decision to give all your possessions to the poor is not particularly important when you have no possessions to give. This had been Francis' case. He had never had anything of his own to give up bar his prospects – and it is much easier to sacrifice prospects than hard cash. In any case he had drifted into poverty by gradual and almost enforced stages. But Messer Bernard was making a conscious and voluntary decision of a sort that Francis had never had to face. It would be a really heroic and self-sacrificing gesture, with immediate and drastic effects. It was worth taking advice about it. A little hesitation was only fitting.

They might have gone to the bishop, but they did not. Francis always believed in going directly to the top where possible – and, besides, he possibly feared Bishop Guido's reaction. Nor was it the moment for dreams or voices, the truth of which only he could guarantee. The advice must be not only objective but be seen to be objective. It was the sort of challenge that inspired his fantasy.

The pair of them went down to the bishop's palace, found a good priest whom Francis knew, and persuaded him to say Mass for them. After this they went on praying. Then the priest on Francis' request took the missal, made the sign of the Cross over it, and opened it three times at three different places. 'Lord God, glorious Father,' prayed the priest, 'we ask you by your mercy to show us what we ought to do.'

The first opening was the most satisfactory imaginable; it was a complete and indeed miraculous confirmation of Bernard's decision – and really one thinks they would have been prudent to stop there. The missal fell open at the passage in St. Matthew where Christ advises the young man who has inquired about the way of perfection: 'If thou wilt be perfect, go, sell what thou hast, and give it to the poor, and thou shalt have treasure in heaven; and come, follow me.'

The second time the missal fell open at the passage which Francis had already heard in the previous February at the Portiuncula: 'Take nothing for your journey, neither staff nor wallet nor bread nor money.'

And if the first piece of advice was addressed clearly to Messer Bernard and the immediate problem, and the second passage was a confirmation of Francis' own way of life for both of them, the third opening seemed to foretell Francis' end. It was again Christ's spoken words which they found: 'If any man will come after me, let him deny himself and take up his Cross and follow me.'

Poverty, travelling and penance – as Francis cried to Bernard, 'This is what we wanted, this is what we were looking for. This is our life, this is our Rule, and anyone else who wants to join us will have to do this.'[1] And in fact they were joined almost immediately by a certain Peter, and a week later by a peasant called Giles who came down on St. George's feastday, 23 April, to find them at the Portiuncula. Giles went down early in the morning, after praying, suitably enough, at the Church of San Giorgio; he knew that Francis and his two followers were living in a little hut they had made somewhere near the *leprosarium* but he got rather lost in the woods on his way. Fortunately Francis bumped into him; whereupon Giles, who had only wanted to come and see, promptly fell on his knees and asked Francis, for the love of God, to accept him as a new member of the group.

Francis' reply must have astonished the poor man. He had been expecting to meet a penitent, and received instead the benefit of a high-flown discourse about knights, lords and emperors.

'Dearest brother,' said Francis, 'God has done you singular grace. If the Emperor should come to Assisi and should desire to make a certain citizen his knight or his lord of the bedchamber, should not such a one rejoice exceedingly? How much more then ought you to be glad that God has chosen you for his knight and well beloved servitor, to observe the perfection of the holy gospel. And therefore be firm and constant in the vocation to which God has called you.'

And taking the astonished and speechless new recruit by the hand, without letting him get a word in edgeways even had he been capable of doing so, Francis almost manhandled him to the hut before sitting him down at his new Round Table. 'Messer the Lord God,' he called out exultantly to Bernard as he displayed his captive, 'has sent us a good brother, so let us all rejoice in the Lord. Let us eat to celebrate.'[2]

It had been the best week in Francis' life. However hard, difficult and distasteful it may be to make money, nothing is easier and quicker and more relaxing than to give it away. Immediately after hearing the three passages from the gospels Messer Bernard had set about selling all he had – 'and he was very rich,' adds the chronicler respectfully. Nothing was left in reserve, nothing (apparently) went to his family, it all went directly or indirectly to the poor. He went round Assisi carrying the money as it came in, and giving it out generously to widows, orphans and pilgrims. It must have been the greatest sensation in Assisi since the pulling down of the Rocca. Then it was up to the monasteries and down to the hospitals. Whatever his objections to handling coins, Francis gaily assisted his new companion in this flinging around of largesse, a gesture on a far grander scale than he had ever made himself in his revelling days. The populace were thrilled, the clergy amazed, the nobles amused, the merchants aghast – the young madman's madness seemed to be contagious, the world was indeed turning topsy-turvy when respected and apparently sane citizens like Messer Bernard took the words of the gospel quite literally.[3]

Francis' triumph was the beginning of Francis' problems. As long as he was isolated, he was acceptable: he did no harm. But as soon as he started attracting followers, he started creating problems for the Commune. First, of course, there was the simple question of food: scraps to feed a single penitent were no difficulty, and one man begging was no real bother. But when it was first four, and then six, and then a dozen, murmurings began to arise. But this was a superficial question that Francis dealt with, when it cropped up seriously, on a superficial level. More profoundly, Messer Bernard's example had an unsettling effect on the community – and, no doubt, in particular upon his relatives. It was one thing for the rich, or their sons or daughters, to enter a monastic order: if money or property went with them, it was at least contributing to maintain a decent and indeed influential way of life for them. If it did not go with them, it was handed back to their families, not redistributed with wild gaiety in the streets. But the dominant classes were reassured by Francis' next two followers, for Peter, though apparently respectable, was not a man of property, and Giles, the peasant, had nothing.

Nothing, that is to say, except the clothes he was wearing, and even these were too much for Francis. As soon as the four of them had finished eating, Francis hurried the new brother up to Assisi to beg cloth with which to make him a tunic. On the way they met a beggar woman who asked them for alms; Francis and Bernard must have been known, by this week's end, to all the beggars, pilgrims, widows, orphans in the territory as fountains of apparently unending gifts. But the fountain had dried up. And the begging woman was begging off would-be beggars. This was the sort of situation that Francis loved. He turned to Giles 'with a face like an angel' and said: 'For the love of God, dearest brother, give your coat to the poor woman.' And Giles did this so readily that, as Francis told the story later, he saw Giles' coat flying straight up to heaven and Giles flying up with it, 'whereby he felt within himself unspeakable joy, with new stirrings of spirit.' Everything was going right for Francis, and he had never been so justifiably elated in all his life.

And so he set off for another journey. This time (and from this time onwards) there was never any journeying alone; Francis had learnt at least one practical lesson from the journey towards Gubbio. He took 'neither staff nor wallet nor bread nor money' but he took Giles, and the two of them headed north-east over the mountains towards Nocera and Ancona in Le Marche while the other two, Bernard and Peter, remained behind. Strangely enough, Francis always seems to have felt more at his ease with Giles than with Messer Bernard, or Fra Bernard as he should now be called, possibly because Giles was a simple soul – and also his social inferior. It was springtime, there were no robbers, they strode along in a very good humour and Francis sang his French songs, in a very clear voice, praising and blessing God.

But that was all that remained of the wandering *jongleur*, and the songs he sang had a different theme. When they passed through towns and castles, Francis did not exactly preach, but he would go up to men and women and beg them to fear and love God and do penance for their sins. And Giles would add, 'Do what my spiritual father here tells you, for what he says is very right.'

It was good practice, but it was very little more than this. The normal reaction was simply to ask, 'Who are these people and what are they talking about?' The general opinion was that they were either stupid or drunk. And even those who defended them said that the pair must be either perfect or mad – with an obvious inclination to accept the latter solution, 'since their way of life seems a desperate one, with little food, going about barefoot and clad in rags.' As for the girls, when they saw them coming, they ran away in panic – which must have been the hardest blow of all for Christ's knight and minstrel to bear, and none too encouraging even for his new squire, a peasant perhaps but a peasant of pithy sayings and well defined opinions. Nevertheless Francis managed to keep Giles' spirits up – and probably his own too – by prophesying brighter days to come. 'Our brotherhood will be like a fisherman who throws his net into the sea and draws out a great number of fishes, and he leaves the small ones in the water and keeps the large ones in a jar.' At which, as the chronicle not surprisingly says, Fra Giles marvelled because as yet there were only three brothers and Francis himself. And none of them, except in Francis' romantic imaginings, could be considered particularly big fish at that.

It cannot have been a long journey, for they were back at Santa Maria degli Angeli before the summer. They probably never reached Ancona or the sea, but at least Francis had ventured outside Umbria and the Duchy, although their tour had hardly been a great success and they had picked up no further followers on the way.[4] On the other hand they found three new companions in the woods when they got back: Fra Sabbatino, Fra Morico the Small and Fra Giovanni di Capella. None of these were 'big fishes', either then or later – but that made seven in all, a real brotherhood – and from that time on Francis knew that there was no going back. He had set out as an individualist, he had started a movement. When that happens to individualists it confronts them with nasty problems of what they find most distasteful, formal organization.

Things were not at that stage yet; but Francis and his companions were faced with the first of the difficulties. The people of Assisi turned sour: 'You have got rid of your own property,' they said, 'and now you want to live off other people.' In simple commonsense terms it was a true and unanswerable observation. Behind it lay all the wisdom of the monastic life: give away your own property, St. Benedict had ordered his novices, but give it to your new community, so that the community may have enough to live off and be self-supporting. But on this particular principle Francis was adamant. Although he was always on good terms with the monks, he – like all his contemporaries in Christian Europe – could see the abuses to which these correct and common-sensical principles had led. He explained it to Bishop Guido, his one supporter in the town, whom he would often go and see and ask for advice.

'Your way of life seems overharsh and difficult to me,' the bishop said, 'possessing nothing and not even having the use of anything.'

'My Lord,' Francis replied, 'if we had any possessions, we would also be forced to have arms to protect them, since possessions are a cause of disputes and strife, and in many ways we should be hindered from loving God and our neighbour. Therefore we do not want to have any temporal possessions at all.' This argument, though a barely veiled reproach to the bishop's own way of life, convinced Guido. But it did not convince the people of Assisi, who derided 'the brothers' as madmen and fools, and it almost did not convince the new brothers themselves, who, for all their enthusiasm, did not like being persecuted by their friends and relatives or going totally hungry for penance' sake. But Francis was fanatical; and as he alone knew what he really wanted, he managed at this stage to impose his will. One day a would-be benefactor placed some money by the crucifix at Santa Maria degli Angeli, and one of the new brothers, sensibly enough one might think, put the money safely away in a cupboard. This was enough to drive Francis into a rage. When he heard what had happened and that coins had been touched, he ordered the culprit to pick up the money in his mouth, carry it out of the chapel, and drop it with his teeth into the nearest dung heap he could find. But no-one yet among his followers resented his ways or called his ideas wild or impractical. He had had more experience of the life of penance than they had, and he was their unquestioned leader.

Beggars and Vagrants

What he could not force them to do by words, he forced them to do by example. Begging for food had been the greatest difficulty; the brothers were embarrassed, and reluctant. 'They would blush, thought Francis, if they were to go out and beg alms. To spare them this shame, he went begging every day by himself.' But in this case the example was not enough. They found the whole idea so repugnant that they preferred to allow Francis, who admittedly by now had experience and practice in the art, to go begging for all of them. Apparently none volunteered to help him, so in the end he had had to call them all together and lecture them. In the lecture he expounded his philosophy of begging, and explained precisely and clearly why they should not be ashamed to beg. First of all, they were imitating Christ who had become poor for mankind's sake. Secondly – and this he added with great confidence – many nobles and scholars would join the fraternity and consider themselves honoured to beg. Thirdly they should beg with great cheerfulness and joy, for they were offering something much more precious than scraps of food in exchange. 'You will say "Give us alms for the love of God" and heaven and earth are nothing when compared to this love.' These arguments were a little too high-flown to be convincing in practice; begging is a very embarrassing business. But Francis backed up his philosophy with shrewder methods; instead of sending all the brothers to Assisi to beg, he pushed them out to the neighbouring villages, one by one, and encouraged the competitive spirit. When they all assembled after a day's begging, they would show Francis what they had collected. 'And they said to one another: "I brought back more than you did." Blessed Francis rejoiced to see them gay and happy. From that time on, each eagerly sought permission to go on begging quests.' As in all things, practice brings confidence.[5]

Evangelical poverty, in Francis' eyes, was a continual toughening-up process. He seems to have worked on this principle: look up the gospels, find a text that contains a simple and clear instruction from Christ to his disciples or followers, and apply it literally. The first text had been announced to him by the crucifix in San Damiano; then came the three chosen by hazard in the missal; the next he chose for himself: 'Do not worry about tomorrow.' He applied this to food; the brothers were told only to accept alms for whatever they needed for one day; and when the brother who was cooking started simmering vegetables the night before, as was the custom, he was told to wait till after Matins. For the life of the brothers did not simply revolve around begging and walking; they did spend a considerable time in the restored chapel at Santa Maria degli Angeli reciting the various offices of the day together: for, as regards prayer, Francis was a traditionalist, not an innovator. And the influence of the monks and monastic tradition on this side of the fraternity's life was very strong.

By the autumn, with the hot weather over, Francis could regard his little troop with satisfaction: their training had gone well, their morale was high, they were becoming near-professionals in the crafts of begging and blessing, it was time for a proper expedition. He called them all together in the woods by the Portiuncula and announced that they would all be taking to the road, splitting into pairs and teaching men and women throughout the world to repent, both by word and by example.

The brothers had known that something of the sort was in the air, but they had also heard, probably from Giles, of the rough treatment Francis and he had had on the spring expedition. There was no enthusiasm whatsoever at their leader's announcement of his ambitious programme; and, as often happens in such circumstances, everyone began to point out the difficulties and harp on the probability of failure. Their main formal objection was that they were untrained and uneducated and would not know how to preach. Francis retorted, quoting Christ's words to his disciples, that the Holy Spirit would inspire them, that all they needed was faith, and they would find humble and kind men who would welcome their words with joy and love. And then, rather unwisely, he went on to add: 'You will also find other people, without faith, blasphemous and full of pride, who will resist you and will cast scorn on what you say. Make up your minds to put up with all this with patience and humility.'

It is never wise, when attempting to prod reluctant followers forward, for a leader to emphasize obstacles of which they are already only too well aware. The brothers' faces fell still further. Francis never again made this particular mistake. And on this occasion he quickly corrected his error by emphasizing once again, with more conviction and greater detail than ever, how great and important a future this little group would have.

'Do not panic,' he said. 'For I assure you that it will not be long before many learned men, many respected men and many nobles will come to us and will be with us. They will preach to the nations and the peoples, and many will be converted to God. And the Lord will make this group of his increase and multiply throughout the whole world.' That was the stuff to give the troops; and, their morale boosted, with a quick blessing from Francis to set them off, away they went, two by two, to preach repentance throughout central Italy.

And a very unpleasant time indeed they had of it. Their worst fears had not been too bad. People thought they were wild men of the woods, and refused to allow them inside their homes for fear that they would be robbed. They were pelted with mud, they were teased and tormented, invited to debauchs, dragged along by their hoods, persecuted by children, and they even had their wretched garments filched from them. 'The brothers suffered all this,' the *Three Companions* nostalgically and perhaps a touch over-rosily tell us, 'hunger, thirst, cold, nakedness and many immense tribulations, firmly and patiently as St. Francis had bidden them. They were not dejected, they never cursed their tormentors; but like men whose faces are set to a great reward they exulted in tribulations and joyfully prayed to God for their persecutors.'

In addition to these more dramatic trials they were continually bothered with pinprick questions. People were always asking them to what Order they belonged; and they would reply, rather uneasily, that they were penitents and came from Assisi. But, as the chronicler noted, 'indeed their community was not yet organized as a religious Order.'

It is not certain how long the journeys took or how far the brothers went –

though Bernard at any rate, and his companion, reached Florence and had a very chilly time sleeping in doorways 'warmed only by the glow of divine love and covered with the blankets of Lady Poverty.' At any rate it seems that Francis, of whose journey nothing is recorded, was back at the Portiuncula first, after only 'a short while', and that, though no arrangements had been made or dates fixed, the brothers in answer to his anxious prayers began drifting back in to their base in the woods. Winters are cold in central Italy, and even though Santa Maria degli Angeli is down on the plain well below Assisi and the icy winds that sweep across from the mountain, you will find no campers out in these shivery months. Apart from the blankets of Lady Poverty and at most two tunics each, the followers of Francis were sheltered only by rough huts made of wood, rushes and clay. No doubt, though, Brother Fire, to whom Francis was so devoted, burned merrily. And though the great expedition had hardly been a success, except in the strictly self-centred penitential sense, at least the brothers were back in one piece, with plenty of stories to tell each other, not all discouraging. Fra Bernard, for instance, in the end had simultaneously been offered hospitality both by the woman whose husband had kicked them out of his house as tramps and by a citizen called Guido whose money he and his companion had, for love of poverty, refused to accept. Not all hearts were hard, nor all good examples unimitated. Furthermore the numbers had now risen to twelve – for five more men of Assisi joined them that winter, Philip the Long, Giovanni, Barbaro, Bernardo di Vigilante, and Angelo Tancredi. Including Francis, this now meant that the fraternity numbered a dozen, a band the size of Christ's own group and with at least two men of noble birth – Philip the Long and Angelo Tancredi – among them.

This wave of new recruits, at a time of year when even the most enthusiastic might have been tempted to wait till the spring, was symptomatic. The people of Assisi had changed their attitude once again, many even came down to the Portiuncula to beg the brothers' pardon for having previously insulted and injured them. And the brothers forgave them gladly 'saying, "The Lord forgive you," and gently admonishing them concerning their salvation.' Even the rich came down to see them and were kindly received and only mildly preached at. Partly this was, as the chroniclers record, genuine admiration; for Francis and his followers were gay and happy despite all their hardships, and lived in poverty, chastity and mutual obedience, dearly loving each other. The thorny question of begging Francis partly solved by a change in style; the brothers were encouraged to work with their hands, 'in order to banish idleness, the enemy of the soul' – and here too it is fairly obvious that the influence, direct or indirect, of St. Benedict and the monastic way of life was at work. As for prayers, they all rose at midnight and prayed with many sighs. They lived in such poverty that Francis would not allow any brother to have more than two habits, though as a special concession patches might be added, in such obedience that they never questioned an order, and in such chastity that should ever an offensive word be uttered, the brother who had spoken it would lie on the ground and only get up again when he had confessed his fault and asked those he had offended to stamp their feet on his mouth.

But though the citizens of Assisi were impressed by the holiness and resolution of 'their' penitents, there was a little more to their change of heart than that. In the early summer Philip of Swabia, the Emperor, had suddenly and unexpectedly disappeared – murdered in a private feud by Otto of Wittelsbach. This meant that the Commune of Assisi had lost its imperial protector; and this in turn meant that it would be wise, very wise, for the Commune to reconcile itself again with the Pope. The dominant class therefore realized that it would do them no harm at all to show an outward interest in, and open support for, holiness; and they may well have felt that, thanks to Pietro Bernardone's son and his unexpected perseverance, Assisi had a positive asset with which to placate the Roman Curia – a new and genuine fraternity of penitents. At any rate in the early months of the year 1209 Bishop Guido was in Rome, no doubt as a semi-official emissary of the town. And shortly afterwards, Francis and his band followed the bishop's footsteps and set out to see the Pope.

It was not of course as ambassadors of Assisi in any sense that the brothers approached Innocent. All Francis and his companions wanted was to receive some sort of official blessing for their vocation from the Church. The great expedition of the autumn had shown all of them how awkward it was to be merely an unofficial fraternity, liable to be taken for tramps and robbers or wild men of the woods rather than penitents proper. Before setting out again they needed some sort of status, and no doubt the men of the world, the richer visitors from Assisi who came down to the Portiuncula, knew of their problems and talked it all over with Francis and Bernard and the others. They pointed out that the fraternity was expanding and bound to grow in importance; and they suggested that therefore the group, which had managed very well on a small scale on the basis of mutual respect, did now need an official constitution. And Francis and all who were with him agreed.

Francis cannot have agreed with pleasure. Written rules and regulations, even the vaguest, were against all his instincts. But the same moment comes, alas, in all growing organizations. A group of friends gather round the founder, listen to him with respect, and follow all his ideas, even though they have to be hassled and bullied into the more extravagant. But then one of his schemes goes wrong in practice, and the myth of the founder's infallibility begins to crumble.

Someone calls for a precise definition of the aims of the group; someone else questions the way in which decisions are taken; and democracy rears its hydra-head. I have had some experience of this myself; and my feeling is that with about seven active members a group can function under a sort of dictatorship. But when there are over ten, discussions and arguments about both aims and methods are inevitable and grow and grow till a constitution must be put down in writing and either accepted by all or imposed on all who will accept it. And when this stage is reached, all that the rather disillusioned founder can do, if he wants to keep his own ideas and ideals pure and dominant, is to recognize the situation and write down a constitution himself before anyone else beats him to the mark. Described as starkly as this, the process sounds distasteful – unnecessary and almost underhand. In practice it happens slowly and almost automatically; and once it is over a group settles fairly happily back into its stride; for human beings feel much more contented when they have 'the rules' to refer back to – even though those rules may merely embody the founder's fantasies in written rather than in spoken form.

At any rate that is what Francis did. According to the *First Life*, 'he wrote for himself and his brothers, present and to come, simply and with few words, a form of life and Rule, using for the most part the words of the holy gospel, for the perfection of which he alone yearned.' The text of this, the primitive or *First Rule*, does not survive. But it is easy to guess which were the words of the gospel that Francis chose: the three passages which he and Bernard had found in the missal, plus the injunction to take no thought for the morrow. 'But,' Thomas of Celano adds, 'he did insert a few other things that were necessary to provide for a holy way of life.'

What exactly the *First Rule* contained is unknown, though several learned and imaginative attempts have been made to reconstruct it. We must guess at its tone from a story told in the *Fioretti*. When Francis was dying, Fra Riccardo of Le Marche came down to see him. 'Tell me, Father,' he said, 'what was your original intention when you began to have brothers? And what is it today? And do you intend to maintain it to the day of your death? For example, may we friars who are clergy and possess many books keep them, provided that we regard them as the property of the Order?'

'I assure you, brother,' Francis answered him, 'that it has been and remains my first and last intention and desire – had the brothers only trusted me – that no friar should possess anything but a habit, a cord and breeches, as our Rule allows.' And in his *Testament* he had written:

'When God gave me some friars, there was no one to tell me what I should do, but the Most High himself made it clear to me that I must live the life of the gospel. I had this written down briefly and simply and his holiness the Pope confirmed it for me. Those who embraced this life gave everything they had to the poor. They were satisfied with one habit which was patched inside and outside, and a cord, and breeches. We refused to have anything more.'

But the point about the *First Rule* is not just the remarkable consistency these two quotations show. It is this: that Francis himself drew up the *Rule*, without consulting any of the brothers or indeed anything but his own allegedly divine inspiration.[6] The founder imposed his own ideas; and, in my opinion, he was only able to do this because the group was still very small and because it had been in existence for less than a year. Had Francis delayed much longer, a more 'reasonable' leader would have emerged and a more 'reasonable' set of rules been drafted. But, as it was, Francis was spared the awful necessity of compromise.

Once again he gathered the fraternity together in the woods. 'I see, brothers,' he said, 'that God in his mercy means to increase our company. Let us therefore go to our holy mother the Roman Church and lay before the Supreme Pontiff what our Lord has begun to work through us, so that with his consent and direction we may continue what we have undertaken.'

To this rather formal proposal all the brothers formally agreed; and so for the first time the little band set out all together and joyfully. It was April once again, and fine weather; and all along the road they found hospitality.

There is one curious detail about their journey: on Francis' proposal they elected a guide and 'vicar of Jesus Christ' as a sort of leader of the expedition. And the brother they chose was not Francis himself but Bernard.[7] Perhaps to the later recruits Francis already seemed too impractical a person to be trusted with particular decisions (such as where to lodge) and incapable of the organization and administration that a journey involving a whole group rather than just himself and a companion inevitably needed. It was just a minor incident; but it was a straw in the wind that would one day become a gale.

And so the twelve penitents walked barefoot to Rome to see the Lord Pope.

NOTES

1 The story of Messer Bernardo's conversion is given at greatest length in chapter two of the *Fioretti*. I have here added details from the *Three Companions* and the other accounts. There are, invariably, certain inconsistencies and contradictions. The most serious of all is in the *First Life*, where the story is told as follows: 'He (i.e. Bernardo) noticed that Francis would pray all night, sleeping but rarely . . . and he wondered and he wondered and said: "In all truth, this man is from God." He hastened therefore to sell all his goods and give the money to the poor, though not to his parents; and laying hold of the title to the way of perfection, he carried out the counsel of the holy gospel: If thou wilt be perfect . . .' If this simplified

version is accurate it means of course that the whole charming story of the opening of the missal at three places is a mere embroidery.

There are, incidentally, two references – to Perfection and becoming Perfect – in this passage alone. And *all* the earlier accounts of Bernard's conversion are littered with the adjective. Mere coincidence? Or did he, too, come of a merchant family of Cathar sympathies? A Perfect would always travel in company of a Believer who prepared his food and handled alms for him; as Giles did for Francis. And the way in which Giles referred to Francis as 'my spiritual father' was the way in which Believers referred to the Perfect. Furthermore at the ceremony of the *Convenenza* the new Believer would prostrate himself before his Perfect master and vow obedience – to be welcomed by a sort of ritual feast, with the blessing of bread – as Francis welcomed Giles, when he advised him to observe 'the perfection of the holy gospel.' Without going any further than these hints seem to warrant, I would suggest that Francis and Bernard, who knew the Cathars' way of life, took this way of life – which, we must remember, was genuinely admired even by those who detested their doctrines – as a model; and that their early fraternity of four bore a very marked resemblance to a group of two Cathar Perfects attended by two Cathar Believers.

2 There is a continuous controversy about the names, social status and precise occasions of conversion of Francis' earlier companions. The accounts are inextricably confused. But there is no doubt at all that the first three were called Bernard, Peter and Giles; nor that Bernard was rich and Giles was poor.

It is Peter that has caused the greatest head-scratching. The *First Life* does not even name him; it simply says: 'But immediately another man of the town of Assisi followed him: he deserves to be greatly praised for his conduct, and what he began in a holy way, he finished after a short time in a more holy way.' This remark is obscure and unexplained – and why no name, seeing that Thomas of Celano names 'Brother Bernard' in the section before and 'Brother Giles' in the sentence immediately afterwards?

In the *Second Life* only the story of Bernard is told, with – this time – the full details of the opening of the missal. St. Bonaventure in the *Legenda Major* follows the *First Life* in mentioning only Bernard and Giles by name.

The *Anonymous of Perugia* is the first of the early sources to give a name, and then the writer simply tells us that Bernard was rich but '*Ille vero frater Petrus pauper fuerat temporalibus*' – which is confirmed and more or less repeated by the *Three Companions*.

According to the *Three Companions*, when Francis and Bernard woke up and decided to consult the gospel, they went not to the bishop's church (Santa Maria Maggiore) but to San Nicola in the *mercato* – 'with another man, named Peter, who also wished to join them.' There is no explanation of Peter's presence at all. The chronicle simply states that 'they rose early.' I would suggest, then, that Peter was a servant of Bernard, or at least a member of his household. This would explain (a) his accompanying the two of them (b) his being there at all (c) his decision to join the pair. For if he was Bernard's personal servant, he would be all the more inclined to follow his master – particularly as, with the distribution of Bernard's riches, his job would, otherwise, have disappeared. This would also account for the fact that Peter's presence at the examining of the gospel is *not* mentioned in some accounts – e.g. that given by the *Fioretti* – for the presence of a servant hardly counted.

It *is*, however, mentioned by the *Anonymous of Perugia*, and for a very good reason. The story here is that Francis asked the priest to open the missal and read out the texts '*quia ipsi adhuc bene legere nesciebant*' – because none of them knew at that time how to read well. As regards Francis and Bernard, this merely confirms that the merchant class in small towns were only semi-literate; they were not clerks, nor expected to be clerks. But it is Peter in whom we are interested here. And this passage seems to prove conclusively that Peter was *not* Peter of Catania, with whom he is usually identified. For Peter of Catania, whom Fra Giordano of Giano identified mistakenly with the second follower, and who later played an important part in the Order was described by Fra Giordano as '*curiae perito et domino legum*' (i.e. a legal expert and certainly literate) and has in his turn been identified with a canon of the cathedral. [The only early passage that seems to favour this identification is in the *Life of Fra Giles*; possibly – I have not studied the manuscripts – a textual interpolation. But, significantly, Peter is not mentioned in the *Fioretti*, to which the *Life of Giles* is by tradition attached.]

My conclusion therefore is (1) that Peter, the third convert, is *not* Peter of Catania; (2) that he was probably Bernard's servant; and (3) that quite possibly he died fairly soon after his conversion. This would explain why there are few references to him, why confusion with a later and more important Peter developed – and, above all, Thomas of Celano's mysterious phrase 'and what he began in a holy way, he finished after a short time in a more holy way' – i.e. a holy death rounding off a holy conversion.

3 By giving his goods to the poor but not to his own parents or relatives Bernard set a precedent that created great trouble, Francis was always very strict, indeed severe, on this point. At a later time in Le Marche, a would-be convert on his instructions distributed his goods to the poor. 'Brother, I have done what you told me to do: I divested myself of all my possessions,' he told Francis. 'How did you do it?' asked Francis. 'Brother,' he replied, 'I gave all my goods to certain members of my family who needed them.' 'Go your way, Brother Fly,' said Francis. 'After having given your goods to your family, do you expect to live among your brothers on alms?' (*The Legend of Perugia*, chapter 20.)

'Go your way, Brother Fly.' This retort of Francis' became famous. But I find it hard to see the reasoning behind Francis' attitude. For if the man's family were needy, surely they were just as much the deserving poor as complete strangers. Of course it might be taken as a form of insurance – 'look after my goods, in case one day I change my mind and leave the Order' – but surely Francis, with his own experience of family life, must have realized that members of a family are no more likely to return possessions given to them than non-members; in fact often rather the opposite.

On the only occasion when Francis did make an exception and allowed a convert to give his ox to his poor family, he made it very clear that he was breaking his own rules. A peasant, John the Simple, eager to join the Order, gave his ox to Francis to give to the poor – at which his family began 'to cry bitterly and to groan out aloud.' They were, they felt, the poor. And Francis as a special exception allowed them to keep the ox, 'although according to the holy gospel,' he added severely, 'John should rather give it to other poor people.'

4 The earlier journeyings are also very confused. The *Anonymous of Perugia* has Messer Bernard and Peter staying at the Portiuncula while Francis and Giles went off to Le Marche; but according to the *Three Companions* they too set out 'in another direction.' And then on the second expedition it is by no means sure whether seven or eight (i.e. including Philip the Long) took to the road; indeed there may possibly have been two expeditions, an autumn one and a winter one.

All this is most obscure, as, too, are the precise names of several of the early companions. What is striking however is that none of these first members played an important part in the Order, with the exception of the first two, Bernard and Giles. It is possible, of course, that they left the fraternity: new groups usually have a fairly high casualty rate in the early stages, and there was no desire to imitate the monastic system of perpetual vows.

5 Nothing disgusted the public in later medieval times with the friars so much as their habit of begging. But by then the Orders of Mendicants had become as rich and as powerful as the monasteries had been, and were far removed from the days of service to Lady Poverty.

Begging is degrading for the beggar, undignified for everyone involved – even the mere spectator – and liable to cause insults to fly on both sides. Yet, the *Legenda Antiqua* tells us, 'Blessed Francis believed that asking for alms for the love of God was an act of the greatest nobility, dignity and courtesy before God and even before the world.' That whining phrase 'God bless you, sir' – if uttered with sincerity, Francis thought, made all the difference. 'Blessed Francis used to say that the servant of Christ who goes and asks for alms for the love of God should do it more confidently and joyfully than a man who, wanting to buy something, would say in proof of his courtesy and generosity "For something worth a penny, I offer a hundred silver marks!" The servant of God offers a thousand times more; in exchange for alms, he offers the love of God in comparison with which all the things of heaven and even of earth are nothing.'

A chasm separates Francis from conventional modern thought. It is now considered that poverty is degrading in itself and dehumanizing in its effects. And nothing is considered more degrading and dehumanizing than begging (there is, I suspect, a hangover here from the Victorian concept of 'dignified poverty'). But for Francis it was not begging that was the mark of an unhealthy society but the absence of begging.

One day he explained to the Lord Bishop of Ostia, his host, why he had brought his scraps back to the bishop's table to eat ostentatiously in front of all. It was in order to set an example to some of the brothers 'who, held back by shame and by conventional attitudes, disdain and will disdain to humble themselves and to demean themselves to beg and perform servile work.'

But note the last four words. For in his *Testament*, in the last days of his life, Francis all the same reduced begging to a sort of auxiliary level. 'I worked with my own hands,' he dictated, 'and I am still determined to work; and with all my heart I want all the other friars to be busy with some kind of work that can be carried on without scandal. Those who do not know how to work shall learn, not because they want to get something for their efforts, but to give good example and avoid idleness. When we receive no reward-in-hand for our work, we can turn to God's table and beg alms from door to door. God revealed a form of greeting to me, telling me that we should say "God give you peace." '

While preparing this book, much in the company of Franciscans in England and Italy, I have never seen or heard of one single friar who begged for food from door to door – held back as no doubt they now are by 'shame and conventional attitudes.' Have they utterly forgotten that 'Blessed Francis often said that no brother should spend a long time without going out to beg'?

6 A convention ought to be established in all Franciscan writings (I am not alone in suggesting it) that the term *First Rule* should apply to the written but lost Rule of 1209; *Second Rule* to the *Regula non Bollata* of 1221, and *Third Rule* to the *Regula* confirmed by the papal Bull of 29 November 1223. This would avoid immense and unnecessary confusion, and the use of terms which are almost designed to confuse non-specialists, such as 'The Primitive Rule.' It is at any rate the system to which I will stick.

Probably the most imaginative attempt to reconstruct the *First Rule* is contained in Dr. Moorman's very erudite *Sources for the Life of St. Francis* (Gregg International, 1967).

The references to those passages in the New Testament that were read when the missal was opened are Mark, 19, 21; Luke 9, 3; and Matthew 16, 24. As the reader will probably have gathered, my view is that they are so apposite that it was *either* a genuinely miraculous intervention *or* a later embroidery. Nevertheless, whichever of these two solutions is true, I am convinced that these texts, plus more precise rules and regulations, particularly about clothes, formed the basis of the *First Rule*.

7 Bernard in fact was no great organizer. He developed into a great solitary with more of a mystic bent than Fra Giles, and took little active part in the Order's later affairs; though right at the end Francis virtually chose him as his successor.

That, however, was nearly twenty years later, when any rivalries that might have existed between the two founders of the fraternity had long since disappeared.

❧ The Roads to Rome ❧

7: The Roads to Rome

A Stink at the Lateran

The Popes were weary of penitents. They had seen so many. It is important to realize that there was nothing, literally nothing, of a bright new dawn about Francis and his ideas; he was not the herald of salvation for whom the Church had eagerly been crying out. The roads to Rome had long been crowded with reformers of all sorts and conditions. Francis of Assisi was treading, metaphorically and even literally, in the footsteps of multitudes that had trod the same way before him – Berno, Odo, Aymard, Maieul, Odilo, Romualdo, Bernard, Norbert, Alberic, Stephen, Bruno and Robert to name only the canonized saints. And if on that journey towards Rome, the *Penitentiales* of Assisi could have been joined by their predecessors, they would have been swamped in the vast ghostly crowds of *Passagieni, Humiliati, Arnaldisti, Pauperes Spiritu Fratres Italici, Apostoli, Pauperes Lombardi, Sandalati* and the rest – most of whom, in the accepted view, were languishing in hell. For, basically, the saints had been monks, and the non-monastic reformers, however great their zeal and admirable their aims, had veered away into error and heresy. In every generation, if not in every year, new enthusiasts appeared at Rome demanding advice, support and approval. The Popes listened, usually, with benevolence: but it is understandable if a flash of weary cynicism or abrupt impatience from time to time coloured their pastoral care. Evangelical poverty, a life lived according to the gospels, the end of simony and abuses – they had heard it all before.

Yet it would be as wrong to portray the Popes as world-weary and disillusioned as it would be to imagine them naively ingenuous. Innocent III and his predecessors and successors were not Renaissance prelates. They genuinely believed in God and they hopefully believed in God's Church; they pictured that Church as the Church Militant rather than the Church Triumphant; and they did not reject *a priori* the possibility of reforming that Church or the probability of God's direct aid in doing so.

The Popes had faith in their role, yet they knew that at times they needed help and that that help might well come from the humble. Experience had taught them to be sceptical; but experience had also taught them to be sceptical of their own scepticism. It would be ridiculous to picture Innocent III as a Hamlet; but it would be true to say of him that he was symbolic of the Church he ruled: though he was drastic he was never inflexible – and he always considered the possibility that both he and the voice of experience might have made a mistake. Hence his bad manners and his troubled tolerance.

Francis had been in Rome once before as a pilgrim. It is not surprising, then, that he knew his way about; and given his direct character (and the non-existence of the Swiss Guard) it is not surprising either, that no sooner had he arrived than he should have managed to make his way directly into the Lateran.

Innocent was in the Lateran, walking in a gallery known as the Hall of Mirrors, lost in thought, when the penitent from Assisi was announced. The sight appears to have shaken him. As Francis babbled on rapidly about penance and evangelical poverty and preaching and a Rule, Innocent studied his visitor's appearance: his clothes were ragged, his beard too long, his hair uncut, his eyebrows black and heavy, his face – what could be seen of it – unattractive. He waited till Francis had ground to a halt. 'Go, brother,' he said, 'and find some pigs, share their life in the pigsty, let them live by your Rule and listen to your preaching. For you are more like a pig than a human being yourself.' Francis followed his usual habit and took the Pope's words literally. He went off, found a pigsty, wallowed in it till he was covered from head to foot in muck, and then returned to the Lateran Palace – where, according to the story, he simply told the Pope: 'Lord, I have done as you commanded: please, now, hear my petition,' at which the Pope, abashed, granted him all that he requested.[1]

Personally I cannot quite see Francis being readmitted to the presence of the Vicar of Christ, stinking as he must have stunk with an odour that was very far from the odour of sanctity. In medieval times access to the great was, we know, open and easy, but there must have been some limits and some protection. That is perhaps how the episode ought ideally to have ended; but in fact from other sources it is clear that it did not end so happily, or so conclusively. Let us imagine Francis rejected at the entrance to the Lateran despite his indignant demands to see the Lord Pope again and his protests that he had only done exactly as he had been told to do, and trudging back through yelling, nose-holding Roman children to find his comrades and explain that he had failed. The group decided on a more orthodox method of approach; they knew their bishop was in Rome and they knew, apparently, where and how to find him.

Bishop Guido, however, had not expected them and was, Thomas of Celano tells us, 'grievously annoyed at their coming.' The reason Thomas gives is that he was very attached to the brothers and feared that they might be planning to leave his diocese. It seems more likely, though, that he was engaged in fairly delicate negotiations with the Curia over Assisi's status and alliances and must have been horrified at Francis repeating, in front of the Pope, the sort of shock tactics which he had practised in Assisi. At least – small mercy – he had kept his clothes on!

But if the name of Assisi was not to stink for ever in papal nostrils, any new approach would have to be very, very tactfully handled. The bishop arranged for the brothers to see his friend, Cardinal Giovanni of San Paolo, Cardinal-Bishop of Santa Sabina.[2]

Indeed it is more than doubtful whether the bishop had the slightest desire for his embarrassing protégé and the Pope ever to come face to face again; but knowing Francis' character he knew that Francis would stay in Rome till he had had a proper interview with someone – and, not to put too fine a point on it, he attempted to fob Francis off with an amiable cardinal.

The amiable cardinal sent for Francis and some of the brothers and spent several days with them. He seems to have understood his role very well; after listening to all that Francis had to say, he began to urge him, gently and tactfully, to turn to the life of a monk or hermit; in other words, to return to Umbria and join an already established Order. No doubt this was partly at Bishop Guido's prompting. But no doubt also the cardinal was genuinely impressed with Francis' enthusiasm and sincerity; he knew, however, how forty years before, a similar enthusiast, Pierre de Vaux,[3] had come to Rome with a few followers – and how his movement had subsequently developed.

The Poor Men of Lyons

Lyons on the Rhone was one of the great trading centres of the Empire, as the titles of the five highways that converged on it indicated: the *Route de l'Allemagne*, the *Route de Paris*, the *Chemin d'Auvergne*, the *Chemin du Dauphiné* and the *Chemin du Languedoc*. It was also a great ecclesiastical city, ruled – despite the pretensions of the Counts of Forez – by its archbishops. In or about the year 1176, a year of famine, a rich merchant of Lyons, a man in his thirties, Pierre de Vaux, heard the Lay of St. Alexis – so the legend goes – and deeply touched by this saint's charity, put his two daughters in a convent, sold all his goods and distributed the proceeds to the poor and starving, and determined to live a life of evangelical poverty and imitate the apostles by preaching repentance and charity. Very quickly – far more quickly than Francis, it seems – he attracted followers from the richer classes of Lyons, the *majores*, and by 1178 he and a band of these followers calling themselves 'the Poor Men of Lyons'[5] were on the road to Rome, where Pope Alexander III had called 302 bishops together for the Third Lateran Council.

Pierre de Vaux was received by the Pope, to whom he presented his '*propositum vitae*', his proposed way of life. The Pope not only welcomed the enthusiasm of these non-clerics – '*laici sine litteris*', as he rather condescendingly described them – but kissed Pierre warmly and approved all his proposals but one. It was on this one point that enthusiasm turned to bitterness and co-operation foundered, to such an extent that a brief five years later the same men who had been so warmly welcomed by one Pope at one council were being condemned as heretics at the next and subjected to examination and the rigours of the secular arm – exile, confiscation of property, demolition of houses, loss of civil rights. Yet to us nowadays it appears a very minor dispute; it concerned, simply, the right to preach – a right as Cardinal Giovanni could not fail to note, Francis was also set on claiming.

It is hard to understand the desire of the medieval Church to restrict preaching, for to present-day Christians, used to an immense diversity of sects all free to preach and all more keen to extend than to restrict that freedom, it must inevitably seem that the more preachers of Christianity there are, the better. This was not the attitude in the Middle Ages; and the reason was that the Church had to deal with a society that was basically Christian and therefore needed instructing, not with a society that was, as nowadays, basically agnostic and therefore needed converting. The distinction is important. When Christians are in a minority, then ideally all should be preachers, for it is the general ideas that need to be put across. But when all are Christians, the general ideas are accepted; it is the details of doctrine and practice that need to be defined. Hence only the professionals should preach. Indeed so far was this theory applied that only bishops were considered professionals; the ordinary priest, usually an unlettered man, could only give his views and exhortations in private. It was therefore even more unthinkable in theory that laymen should be allowed to step in where ordained clerics were forbidden to tread.

In practice, even in the twelfth century, the Church had grown more tolerant, for the situation had grown more complex. The spread of the Cathar doctrines, with their mere veneer of Christianity, meant that it was more difficult to hold that society was entirely Christian; indeed, at its edges, in Sicily and Outremer and Spain, society had fallen under the influence of the pagans. And so Pope Alexander granted Pierre de Vaux and the Poor Men of Lyons the right to preach, provided only that they first obtained the permission of the bishop.

'Go ye and teach all nations,' Christ had told his apostles. The difficulty was that the bishops, all 302 of them who had assembled at the Lateran, saw themselves and themselves alone as the legitimate successors of the apostles; and they were not ready to surrender their rights or extend their privileges. On the other hand the reformers – and by 1179 Pierre de Vaux was merely the latest of a long line – in their heart of hearts considered the bishops, and indeed the clergy in general, to be the illegitimate successors of the apostles in the sense that they claimed the apostles' privileges (e.g. the prerogative of preaching) but were not prepared to live a really apostolic life. Clearly however those who were prepared to live a really apostolic life (e.g. the Poor Men) ought to have the right to exercise the apostles' privileges. The injustice rankled. Ignoring the Pope's proviso, Pierre de Vaux and his followers began to preach: and as true sons of the Church they preached most vigorously against the Cathars and against Cathar doctrine, to such good effect that the merchant class of Lyons remained orthodox in belief and the *Chemin de Languedoc* saw Catholic preachers striding out rather than Cathar preachers striding in.

Their success did not endear them to the local authorities. The clash followed quickly upon the accession of a new archbishop, Jean Bellesmains. The Poor Men of Lyons, by this time a numerous fraternity, were expelled from Lyons. As penitents, pilgrims and above all as wandering merchants they took to the road, spreading south through Provence and Languedoc and north up to Lorraine and Flanders, always preaching, and always on the move, so much so, that they became popularly known as the *Passagieni*, the Passers-By. Inevitably they adopted their own form of distinctive dress, a simple costume with sandals of wood or leather laced in the form of a cross; hence another name, that of *Sandalati*, and indeed another practice, for they too were inevitably influenced by the Cathars with whom they were so often in contact: to each *Sandalatus* was attached a *Novellanus*, or novice, bound by vows of obedience to serve and obey his comrade on the road, as the Believers were bound to the Perfect.

Looking at the bare feet of the penitents of Assisi, Cardinal Giovanni must have shaken his head to himself. Here was a fraternity more fanatical even than the Poor Men of Lyons. Like the Poor Men, they had given all their goods to the poor and wished to lead a life of apostolic poverty, preaching the gospel on the roads. Like the Poor Men, they claimed to be true and loyal sons of the Holy Church; and like the Poor Men, they had come to Rome to see the Pope and obtain his approval for their way of life. On the surface they seemed to be submissive to their bishop; but was it likely, if the same situation recurred and the same qualified right to preach were granted, that Bishop Guido would give his permission? And, if he did not, would the penitents of Assisi ignore his refusal? Their leader Francis came from the same social class as Pierre de Vaux, and the cardinal knew how anti-clerical that class had become. Would it not all end with at best a local quarrel between the penitents and the bishop, and their expulsion from Assisi? And at worst with immense confusion and the spread of revived heresies. Cardinal Giovanni was only too well aware how Pierre de Vaux' movement had ended.

The quarrel between the two men, Pierre de Vaux their founder, and Jean Bellesmains, the local bishop, on what was basically a legalistic issue had had the most ruinous consequences. Expelled from their city and understandably embittered by such treatment, the Poor Men of Lyons had been led step by logical step into doctrinal opposition. They went on preaching despite being forbidden to do so by the bishops. In order to justify their attitude they began to explain that there was no duty to obey bishops who were unworthy. What bishops were unworthy? All those bishops who failed to lead apostolic lives. As there was virtually no bishop who led an apostolic life, it followed that virtually all bishops were unworthy. A Church whose bishops were unworthy could not be the true Church of Christ. Furthermore, unworthy bishops – and unworthy priests for that matter – could not worthily administer the sacraments; indeed, better a Host consecrated by a worthy layman than by an unworthy priest. And who were the worthy laymen? Why, the Poor Men of Lyons.

Furthermore, Pierre de Vaux had obtained permission from the Pope to translate the scriptures from Latin into Provençal. The Poor Men of Lyons concentrated on the New Testament, which many of them knew almost by heart. After all, had not the Acts of the Apostles (4, 19) told them that 'It is better to obey God than man'? Like all Christian enthusiasts – like, as Cardinal Giovanni must have noted, Francis and his followers – they chose texts and tried to apply them literally. 'Thou shalt not kill,' stated the commandment. The Poor Men of Lyons preached against feudal war; they went further, they said that no real Christian could ever kill a fellow man, that the authorities had no power to order executions. They preached against indulgences, against prayers for the dead, and indeed against the taking of oaths, the practice that bound feudal society together; and they found texts in the gospel (as many have done after them) to support all these themes. By this time the quarrel had extended far outside the diocese of Lyons; but it was Jean Bellesmains who had officially denounced them to the new Pope, Lucius III. And Lucius III at the Synod of Verona had published the Bull *Ad Abolendam*, dated 4 November 1184, which condemned all heretics and in particular the Poor Men of Lyons and placed them outside the pale of the Church and lawful society.

Persecution, which had been mild at first, began to grow. The Poor Men spoke out against the priesthood and the sacrament of ordination. They were never allowed to stay or to settle; and in particular they were prevented from holding the Chapters that should have reassembled them all once or twice a year. In these conditions any sort of coherence became impossible; and the movement split into half a dozen different strands. Some groups held that not only men but also women had the right to preach the word of God, and women began travelling with these Poor Men on the roads. In the year 1205 an old man from Piacenza led a breakaway movement, the 'Poor Lombards', who held that the Church of Rome had deviated from the true path at the time of St. Silvester and the Emperor Constantine. Soon the Poor Lombards could boast their own splinter group, the even more extreme 'Brothers of Prato'; and so on and so forth. By the year 1209 it was clear that a fine idea had degenerated, and though Pierre de Vaux himself was not only still alive but was to live for almost ten years more, no-one could have pretended that even the founder of the movement was happy with the way his inspiration had turned out. Cardinal Giovanni may well have looked at Francis with sympathy and pity – sympathy for his spring-like enthusiasm, pity for the quarrels and difficulties that inevitably lay ahead.

The Humiliati of Verona

Not that there was any real risk of the sad history of the Poor Men of Lyons repeating itself, with awesome inevitability, step by step. For the Church had learnt its lesson too, and had realized that concessions, though only careful concessions, must be made to enthusiastic non-clerics. Innocent III had, right at the beginning of his papacy, been faced with the same problem once again: another group of laymen had come to Rome to ask for a Rule and by the Bull *Omnis Boni* of 7 June 1201 he had granted their request. Eighteen months earlier he had already been thinking it all over and decided on a policy of cautious tolerance. He had written to the Bishop of Verona to advise him not to be too severe against 'men who are called by the people *Humiliati* and who, it is said, are not heretics but orthodox, and strive to serve God in humility of heart and body.'

The *Humiliati* of Verona were a group that had originated about the same time as the Poor Men of Lyons. They too wished to live simply, in apostolic poverty, but they differed from the Poor Men in one vital point. They did not intend to break away from their families but to go on living at home and working. The old saying of St. Benedict, 'Leisure is as poisonous to the soul as the air to fish' was their inspiration. They appear to have had no individual leader but to have grown up and spread among one particular class, the town-dwelling wool-workers, who were employed at very low piece-work rates by the merchants.[5]

From an economic and social point of view the *Humiliati* were certainly the most cohesive and probably the most interesting of all the gropus who set out to live a life of voluntary poverty in the name of Christ. They wore, in striking and deliberate contrast to what they produced, grey and undyed clothes.[6] They disapproved of begging: 'He who will not work neither shall he eat' was *their* biblical text *par excellence*. Before starting work they would repeat three times the appeal for help: '*Deus in adjutorium meum intende.*' During work they would recite the Offices and otherwise avoid speaking. At the end of a job they would repeat three times a phrase of thanks, '*Benedictus es, Domine, qui adjuvisti me.*' They lived, in every sense, a grey and humble life.

Their fraternity spread more slowly than that of the Poor Men of Lyons, for the obvious reason that they did not travel. Yet, by the end of the century, when they came to Rome to seek approval from the Pope, their influence had reached both Milan and Florence. Innocent considered their petition with great care before granting them a Rule. He approved their voluntary poverty and permitted, exceptionally, the absence of chastity which their desire to continue living a normal family and working life implied. He laid down regulations for their prayers and Offices. He allowed the refusal of oath-taking (though in this they were dangerously close to the Poor Men of Lyons), which they based on the gospel texts, despite the rejection it implied of the feudal system. He even more temerariously allowed them exemption from feudal military service, to which both the preceding objections applied. But he was very, very careful indeed when it came to preaching. The *Humiliati* were forbidden to preach in public or to the public. But they were authorized to meet every Sunday to listen among themselves to the words of a brother 'of proved faith and prudent piety' on condition that their hearers should not thereafter discuss among themselves questions of doctrine or the sacraments of the Church. On the other hand, bishops were expressly forbidden by the Pope's Bull to oppose or query any of these semi-private sermons, for 'the spirit must not be stifled.'

It is in this sense that one can talk of Innocent's 'troubled tolerance.' This tolerance was relative but it was real. The Church was not blindly reactionary or repressive. The Popes learnt from their predecessors' mistakes. Bishops and priests were a structual necessity; yet, if unworthy, they discredited the Church; and Innocent in his thunderbolts was no less harsh to such as the 'dumb dogs and simoniacs' of Languedoc, 'who sell justice, absolving the rich and condemning the poor' than the most anti-clerical of the reformers. There must be a place in the Church, Innocent realized, for enthusiastic and organized laymen, but that place, if the disaster of the Poor Men of Lyons was to be avoided, must be very carefully defined. All in all, it was infinitely preferable if new enthusiasts would agree to join one of the established organizations.

And heavens knows, as Cardinal Giovanni must have pointed out to Francis, it was not as if there was a lack of choice. There were Orders catering for the most immense diversity of aims and tastes. If it was a life of fasting and penitence that the brothers from Assisi wanted, why did they not look a little north towards Arezzo, where the white hermits of the Camaldolese lived a life of fasting, silence and prayer in little cells on the hillside? If it were singing that apaealed to them, there were always the monasteries of the black monks of Cluny; if manual labour and an isolated life, the monasteries of the piebald monks of Cîteaux. For strict enclosure, the Order of Vallombrosa; for pastoral work, the White Canons of Prémontré. Should they desire to help their Bishop Guido, they might adopt the Rule of St. Augustine and live as canons sharing all in common at the bishop's household. Or if, as it seemed, they were vowed to Santa Maria, let them follow the 'Customs' of the Carthusians, and retire like Bruno, Archbishop of Calabria, to a remote valley and live there a life of hermits and cenobites, in a spirit of prayer, mortification and devotion to the Mother of God. Or even follow the new Rule of St. Bruno's successor in Calabria, the saintly Abbot Joachim, but recently dead.

Abbot Joachim of Calabria

'We have seen,' Sabatier writes, 'that the return to evangelical simplicity had become a necessity. All the heretical sects were on this point in accord with pious Catholics, but no-one spoke in a manner so Franciscan as Joachim of Flora. Not only does he make voluntary poverty one of the characteristics of the age of lilies but he speaks of it in his pages with so profound, so living an emotion that St. Francis could do little more than repeat his words.'

Perhaps it was from Cardinal Giovanni that Francis learnt the words he would repeat. For, after great uneasiness, the Church had accepted Joachim; the Calabrian Abbot had been summoned to explain himself to at least four Popes – Lucius III in 1184, Urban III two years later, Clement III two years later still, and finally Celestine III in 1196. Each time he had confounded his accusers and convinced the Popes of his sanctity and orthodoxy. Despite Cistercian disapproval Celestine III had accepted his proposals and his Rule for a new and more austere Order, the *Florenses*. Yet the uneasiness persisted. When Pope Innocent succeeded to the Holy See, Joachim had been summoned once again to make complete submission. He had forwarded all his works to Rome, but he had died, on 30 March 1202, before they had been thoroughly examined or approved.

In his handling of Abbot Joachim, Innocent had shown even more skill and finesse than he had used towards the *Humiliati*. He had needed to; it was a much more difficult case. For the lay wool-workers of Lombardy were of only limited importance; their ideas were traditional, and the scope for the practice and spread of their ideas confined. But the Abbot Joachim was a seer; and his vision was unbounded.

In a way the Abbot Joachim was less important alive than after his death; it was his writings, not his person that could become – and did become – so influential. This Innocent realized: a saintly hermit living in the vast mountain forest of La Sila in Calabria with his followers posed no threat to Christendom; but his writings might travel, though he himself was static. And so the Pope insisted on control of those books; and, wisely, he made no attempt to censor them, for, as he himself had said, 'the spirit must not be stifled.'[7]

Yet in this case he must have been very tempted to stifle the spirit, for the Abbot Joachim foresaw a world in which the Papacy would play at best an obscure part subordinated to a sort of monastic theocracy. In the lyrical and rhetorical writings that poured out from his pen, he was concerned with two major themes: first, the nature of the Trinity; secondly, the meaning of history. It was the second theme that so impressed his contemporaries and successors. For Joachim accepted the general view that the age, and the Church, were corrupt and imperfect and full of abuses; but instead of merley proposing a reformed way of life within the system (which was what basically all other reformers, heretical and Catholic, were doing) and general structure of society, he announced a New Age and a new society; and furthermore he announced that both would begin in the year 1260.

It is as easy, with hindsight, to dismiss Abbot Joachim's ideas as to sneer at his arithmetic; and that is precisely what Fra Salimbene, who had been an ardent Joachimite did, when the year 1260, with its apprehensions and its flagellants parading everywhere, came and went and no New Age dawned. But men have always felt something unsatisfactory in the idea that the world must plod on to the end of time in much the same way; and every century has in its own way and its own language looked forward to a sudden and spectacular bound that would mark a break with the past and the introduction of the millennium. In a sense Abbot Joachim had a modern approach to progress; he believed in a New Age and a break but he did not believe in an absolute change. Each Age developed out of the preceding one, and each followed patterns that were already apparent.

'The First Age was that of knowledge,' he wrote, 'the second that of wisdom, the third will be that of full intelligence. The first was trial, the second action, the third will be contemplation. The first was fear, the second faith, the third will be love. The first was the age of old men, the second that of sons, the third will be that of children. The First Age corresponds to the Father who therefore is the author of all things, the second to the Son who deigned to wear our clay, the third will be the Age of the Holy Ghost of whom the apostle said: "Where there is the Spirit of the Lord, there is liberty." ' And, in the finest and most gentle phrase of all, he summed it up. 'The First Age bore thistles, the second roses, the third will bear lilies.'

From Joachim's often tortuous and indeed turgid prose, the pattern of his theory of history emerged. His First Age corresponded to the period of the Old Testament; it was the time of the Married, its three great men were Abraham, Isaac and Jacob, and it had lasted for 42 generations, divided into 7 smaller epochs, that is to say for 1,260 years. The Initiator of the Second Age, the period of the New Testament, the time of the celibate priesthood, had been

Zachariah; and the three great men of this Age were Zachariah, John the Baptist and Christ, who was True Man as well as True God. The Third Age would be the period of the Eternal Gospel, the Age of the Holy Spirit, a time of contemplation and of the monastic way of life; its three great men would be the man clad in a linen robe foretold by the prophet Daniel, the Angel with the sickle and the Angel with the seal of the Living God, both seen by the seer of the Apocalypse. After a thousand years of peace, the Greater Antichrist, a great prelate, Gog or the Seventh Head of the Dragon, would arise and rule the world till its destruction and the Day of Judgement.

Such, briefly and oversimplified, was the structure of Abbot Joachim's theory. It would not do to be too cynical about reactions to it; all the evidence shows that even the most learned, perhaps particularly the most learned, were gripped by its fascination. The Popes themselves, Innocent included, though dubious about Joachim's teachings on the Trinity, were struck by his vision of a purified bishop of Rome and a thousand years of monastic peace stretching ahead after the convulsions that would mark the seventh and final period of the Second Age. For in this seventh stage of the Second Age a great ruler, Antichrist, would be born, to be vanquished in his turn by the rider on the white horse.

All this was looming in the year 1209; and though there is no knowing how much, if any, of Abbot Joachim's visions Cardinal Giovanni expounded to Francis and his brothers, yet we may assume that he spoke of the saintly Abbot and his new Order of monks and hermits, and gently insisted on the thousand years that lay ahead and on Joachim's picture, so appealing to Francis, of the ideal monk whose only possession was a lyre.[8] Neither of them could have foreseen that the time would come when Francis himself would be hailed as the man clad in a linen robe, the Initiator of the Third Age;[9] or for that matter that Frederick Roger, the fifteen-year-old ward of Pope Innocent in Sicily, would be condemned and persecuted by Francis' future protector as the Antichrist whose birth Joachim had announced.[10]

All Cardinal Giovanni's urgings were in vain. Francis would not be convinced. He would not become a monk or hermit. He would not join any existing Order. He would not listen to good advice, he had his own ideas and he wanted to put his own ideas into practice in his own way. He was most extraordinarily obstinate: he had been prepared, then or later, to give up everything but he was never prepared, then or later, to give up his dreams. People like Francis, as Cardinal Giovanni appears to have realized, are the sort of people who can change history: all depends on how they are handled by the more conventional powers-that-be. Despite his misgivings, Cardinal Giovanni went to the Pope.

Before the Lord Pope

Cardinal Giovanni went to the Curia and spoke to Innocent III. 'I have found a most excellent man,' he told the Pope, 'who desires to live according to the gospel and in everything to observe evangelical perfection. I am convinced that through this man Our Lord works to renew the faith of the Holy Church in the whole world.' The Pope, the *Legend of the Three Companions* rather naively continues, was very astonished at these words and bade the cardinal bring Francis to him.

He may have been astonished at the cardinal's convictions; but he can hardly have been astonished at the ambitions of the 'excellent man' the cardinal had found. At that time Prior Burchard of the Order of Prémontré was at Rome and busy recording his impressions. From these we can see that Francis was by no means the only visitor to Rome at that time who desired to live according to the gospel.[11]

'At that time,' the prior noted down, 'we saw a certain group of those who are called the Poor Men of Lyons with their leader, whose name was, I think, Bernhard: and they were petitioning that their sect should be approved of and granted privileges by the Apostolic See.[12] They claimed that they led a truly apostolic life, and wished to possess nothing and to have no fixed abode; they were always on the move through towns and castles. But the Lord Pope found something excessive and objectionable about them, no doubt because they cut their shoes away above the feet and walked about almost barefoot, but especially because they wore habits that looked like those of a religious Order but yet did not cut or shave their hair in a clerical style; there also seemed to be a cause for scandal in their case in so far as men and women would travel together and would mostly stay in the same house, and it was said that they would sometimes sleep in the same beds – all of which however they themselves claimed were practices that had been handed down by the apostles.'

So Innocent had rejected the petition for a Rule that this particular splinter-group of the Poor Men presented. No doubt he disliked an outward appearance which both was and was not clerical in style, with all the legal and jurisdictional muddles that that implied. Either Bernhard and his followers were to be clerics and exempt from civil courts, in which case they should have adopted the tonsure that even university students wore as a matter of course, or else they were still fully laymen, and should not have dressed confusingly. But this was a comparatively minor point. The reason for the Pope's intolerance in this case was quite clear: there could be no question of men and women living together, however chastely and apostolically, with the blessing of the Holy Church. There had been too many scandals in the past. It was not a question of whether fornication was committed; it was a question of whether the people believed fornication to be committed.

The Pope had already had to deal with a similar issue in the case of the *Humiliati*. There were those among them who had opted for community rather than family life; and for these the Pope had approved a Rule (by the Bull *Diligentiam* of 12 June 1201) which gave rise to their Second Order; under this Rule men and women were permitted to live a community life of work, poverty and chastity (and obedience to their superior – always a male), but with this proviso: that they lived in separate houses, side by side. It had been a slightly risky experiment; but in fact successful, because the community was both fixed and working. To grant a similar sort of concession to wandering penitents and preachers, virtually free from the pressures of local public opinion, with more time to spend walking and talking than working, was a very different proposition. So Bernhard was turned down; and when the leader of the next group, Francis, appeared, the Pope was at any rate relieved to find that he had to deal with only one sex.

Possibly he did not recognize the penitent whom he had brushed aside so abruptly a few days before. Possibly he recognized him but listened with greater sympathy to a petitioner who had been introduced through the proper channels. Possibly Cardinal Giovanni had persuaded Francis to allow a barber to do something about his appearance, trim his eyebrows and his beard, and at least trace an outline of a tonsure; possibly the rags had been laundered; and possibly the Pope was amused.

Or perhaps indeed Innocent had had the dream which so many of the accounts recall. He had dreamt that the Church of the Lateran was falling and that it was only saved from total collapse by the shoulders of a small, insignificant man. He had woken up depressed and surprised, to think over his dream. And when a few days later Francis appeared, and began to explain his Rule and his aim, Innocent had remembered the dream and wondered whether this could be the little man by whom the Church of God would be supported and upheld.

Be that as it may, dream or no dream, Innocent did not rush into any decision. It seems that the twelve penitents of Assisi were all admitted to the Lateran; and that Innocent and his cardinals listened as Francis explained their aims. 'My sons,' said the Pope, 'your plan of life seems too hard and rough. We are convinced of your fervour but we have to consider those who will follow you in the future and who may find this path too harsh.' This was the sort of crisis that brought out the best in Francis; besides, he had certainly been used to pleading against the same arguments from Cardinal Giovanni. He spoke out. Half convinced by his plans, Innocent wavered: 'My son,' he said, 'go and pray to God that he may reveal whether what you ask proceeds indeed from his most holy will: and this in order that we may be assured that in granting your desire we shall be following the will of God.'

Dismissed from the presence, the penitents from Assisi retired to pray, hopefully, for inspiration; the Pope talked their petition over with the cardinals, while they were out of the audience hall.

They were worried. They felt that the Rule Francis was preparing was too severe, and in particular that his insistence on living without money and without fixed abode would lead to trouble. 'Probably,' as Chesterton wrote, 'they meant, especially when they said it was unduly hard, that it was unduly dangerous. For a certain element that can only be called danger is what marks the innovation as compared with older institutions of the kind. In one sense indeed the friar was almost the opposite of the monk . . . The whole point of a monk was that his economic affairs were settled for good: he knew where he would get his supper, though it was a very plain supper. But the whole point of a friar was that he did not know where he would get his supper. There was always the possibility that he might get no supper. There was an element of what would be called romance, as of the gipsy or adventurer. But there was also an element of potential tragedy, as of the tramp or casual labourer.'

Cardinal Giovanni alone supported Francis. 'We must be careful,' he said. 'If we refuse this mendicant's request because it is new or too difficult, we may be sinning against Christ's gospel, because he is only asking us to approve a form of gospel life. Anyone who says that a vow to live according to the gospel contains something new or unreasonable or too difficult to be observed is guilty of blasphemy against Christ, the author of the gospel.'

These were, on both sides, arguments that must have been heard time and time again. Where Chesterton is mistaken is in implying that there was something new or original about Francis' request. But where he is right is in insisting on the risks that a life such as Francis proposed necessarily involved. The cardinals were compassionate. But the cardinals were also confused. Indeed at the time the whole Church was confused; and the Lord Pope himself was perhaps the most confused of all. Was it or was it not a good thing for the sons of the Church to lead a life of wandering poverty according to the gospel?

The Lesson of Dominic

Five years earlier the question had arisen in an acute form. Two Spanish clerics from Osma Cathedral, Bishop Diego and Canon Dominic, had set out towards the Marches of Germany to convert the pagans but had found that there was more converting needed closer at hand. They had stopped off in Cathar country; and Dominic had stayed on. At this stage it was the Cathars (and, further east, the Poor Men), in other words the heretics, who were leading a life of wandering poverty according to the gospel; and the Church that was trying to combat them – unsuccessfully – by intellectual arguments. Indeed Cardinal Giovanni had just retired from his position as papal legate in Languedoc when Dominic appeared; and it was probably on his advice that the Pope agreed to the change of strategy that Dominic proposed. For Cardinal Giovanni had seen how useless it was to attempt to overawe a popular movement with the might and prestige of Holy Church, as the abbots and monks dispatched by Rome had been trying to do. What Dominic proposed was that he, and others like him, should try and combat the Cathars on their own ground, by going among the people in apostolic poverty and by preaching humbly to them.

At first Dominic's methods seem to have been successful; in open public debates he and his handful of imitators would argue against the Perfect in front of the populace. And after converting a group of Cathars, he founded a fraternity at Prouille near Toulouse that was later to grow into the Order of Brothers Preacher.

But the initial success of these new methods soon failed and faded. By the end of the year 1208 it was clear that no more than a little dent had been made on Cathar influence in Languedoc. Therefore the Pope and cardinals who, a few years earlier, had been prepared to see in these new methods the way of combating heresy successfully on its own ground, were now less sure. Admittedly the new methods had been more successful than the old methods; but they had not been successful enough.

Yet Innocent might have considered continuing with them, had it not been for the murder of his legate, Peter of Castelnau, Cardinal Giovanni's successor. That murder occurred on 15 January 1208 and was generally believed to have been arranged by Count Raymond of Toulouse, the protector of the Cathars, who had had a stormy interview with Peter of Castelnau the evening before.

Political murders have unpredictable consequences; it is never, never, never wise, however tempting, to take the risk of ridding oneself of an immediate encumbrance. This particular political murder led to thirty-five years of bloodshed, the virtual extinction of Catharism as a religion and of the county of Toulouse as a political entity; to the establishment of the inquisition and the perversion of Dominic's methods; to hatreds north and south of the Loire which centuries have not totally extinguished and which are now being somewhat artificially revived. All this stemmed from the needless murder of one man.

Murder of a papal legate marked the limit of Innocent's tolerance. It would be unfair to say that he threw aside the mask of comparative courtesy under which the great debate with the Cathars had hitherto been conducted. Rather, from the Church's point of view, and from the point of view of the whole Christian community, it was the Cathars who had thrown aside their mask. Innocent thundered. It is impossible to imagine that any Pope could have reacted in any other way. But Innocent's thunder was followed by bitter lightning. He called on the barons and prelates of France north of the Loire to come to the aid of the Church; and the barons, led by Simon of Montfort, only too eagerly struck.

This was the background against which the Pope and his cardinals considered Francis' request. The attempt to stem heresy by Christians leading a life of evangelical poverty had failed in southern France. That was a reason for refusing his request. It had not failed absolutely; that was perhaps a reason for accepting it. As Cardinal Giovanni had pointed out, there ought to be no objections in principle. But in practice was it wiser to allow the penitents of Assisi a free rein at the risk of possible future quarrels between them and the bishops, or to turn them down flat and perhaps drive them into the camp of the Poor Men of Lyons or the Poor Lombards? No wonder the cardinals hesitated.

In the end it came down to a judgement of personalities. Were Francis and his followers submissive, and likely to remain submissive, both to the authority of the Pope and to the teachings of the Church? There the impression that the men of Assisi created was favourable, particularly when compared to that of Bernhard and his group of the Poor Men, as Prior Burchard went on to report. 'However the Lord Pope welcomed some others who rose up in the place of those men [i.e. Bernhard and his followers] who called themselves the Lesser Poor Men[13] . . . in all things obedient to the Holy See.'[14]

This is important outside evidence. Times being what they were, 'obedient to the Holy See' implied two fundamental answers to two fundamental questions. First, would the brothers recognize the authority even of unworthy priests? Secondly, would they totally accept the sacraments and in particular the holy eucharist? If the Pope and the cardinals had judged that the answer to both or either of these questions was no, then there could be no question: permission must be refused, for these laymen were potential heretics like the Cathars and the Poor Men.

But the answer was yes; yes to both questions and a very definite and fervent yes. And here I must quote again from Francis' last wishes, the best inside evidence we have: the third paragraph of his *Testament*, which shows how totally he rejected Cathar doctrine and accepted the teaching of the Church. And these are the two points on which undoubtedly both Pope and cardinals questioned him most closely.

'God inspired me, also,' Francis dictated as he lay dying in Assisi, 'and still inspires me with such great faith in priests who live according to the law of the holy Church of Rome, because of their dignity, that if they persecuted me, I should still be ready to turn to them for aid. And if I were as wise as Solomon and met the poorest priests of the world, I would still refuse to preach against their will in the parishes in which they live. *I am determined to reverence, love and honour priests and all others as my superiors. I refuse to consider their sins*, because I can see the Son of God in them and they are better than I. I do this because in this world I cannot see the most high Son of God with my own eyes, except for his most holy Body and Blood which they receive and *they alone* administer to others. *Above everything else, I want this most Holy Sacrament to be honoured and venerated* and reserved in places which are richly ornamental.' [My italics.]

Nothing could have been more satisfactory, nothing could have been less Catharist, than a declaration of this sort.[15] From the Church's point of view the penitents of Assisi were, in intent at least, very much on the side of the angels. Yet still the Pope hesitated. And he was right to hesitate. For the experience of recent years had proved that only trained and tried clerics, like Dominic or Joachim, could be trusted not to diverge from the straight and very narrow path of submission. Laymen, however admirable their intentions and however orthodox their declarations, had an almost irresistible tendency to veer. And God alone knows what stories Bishop Guido had told the Pope about these particular laymen.

The Decision of Innocent

Innocent III was a man of nearly fifty at this time; and Francis was still under thirty, young enough – just – to be his son. I suspect that they rather took to each other; and that behind Innocent's stern exterior Francis could detect a paternal twinkle. At any rate he seems to have decided to appeal to the Pope's sense of humour; and it was as if the two of them, and the two of them alone, shared the joke.

Francis came back into the papal presence and announced solemnly that in response to his prayers (and therefore, by implication, at the Lord Pope's intercession) God had spoken to him by spirit in a parable. Whereupon he proceeded in front of the Pope and the assembled first to recount and then to interpret this parable. There was an element of cheek about this; it is not usually young men who expound parables to Popes but Popes who expound parables to young men. But there was an even greater element of tongue-in-cheek. The parable had a heroine, a poor but beautiful maiden, a hero, an enamoured king, and a result: a bevy of splendid and legitimate sons. When the story had been told, Francis interpreted the details: 'I am that poor but beautiful maiden,' he explained; and his sons would be honoured by the King of Kings.

'On hearing this,' the chronicler says, 'the Pope was "greatly amazed".' No wonder. Francis was small, dark and ugly: his ears stuck out, his face was a very odd shape; and even if he had had his beard trimmed since his first appearance in the Lateran, by no stretch of the imagination could he be described as the beautiful maiden of legend.[16] And despite the reverential interpretation he had given to the other main character, it was fairly obvious that the king who was so impressed with the beautiful maiden that he immediately signed the marriage contract was meant to be the Pope himself, who had before him a Rule that he was being asked to approve – from which many splendid sons would be born to the pair of them.

In any case, Francis' outrageous parable appealed to the Pope. He made up his mind there and then; he embraced Francis, approved the Rule, and gave him permission to preach penance to all.[17] And Francis, in a ceremony that must have appealed to all his romantic notions, knelt before Innocent and swore obedience and reverence to the Lord Pope and the Lord Pope's successors. And then Innocent ordered all the other eleven brothers to kneel and swear obedience and reverence to Francis. He was now in the full knightly sense the Pope's man; and his brothers were his men. A dream had been achieved.

The Pope gave his blessing, and they left the Lateran to pay a visit, *en masse*, to the tomb of the apostles. One important formality remained. Cardinal Giovanni arranged for them all to receive the clerical tonsure.[18] There was no question of allowing them to remain ambiguously devout, like Bernhard's followers. They were henceforward the Church's men, under the protection of the Church and the jurisdiction of canon law, to be recognized as such wherever they went and therefore expected to behave as such. The days of long-haired vagabonds, of the wild men of the woods, were over.

NOTES

1 The story of Francis' first encounter with the Pope is told only in the chronicle of Roger of Wendover, as copied by Matthew Paris. Yet though these are late sources, there is nothing very improbable in the tale. It is the sort of way Francis would have behaved; and Innocent too. Yet it is the sort of tale that most biographers, even the more open-minded, would tend to leave out, for it is not particularly flattering either to Francis or to the Pope. Strangely enough, the *Legenda Major* has the only early hint of it: 'He [the Pope],' wrote St. Bonaventure, 'knew nothing about the saint, and so he sent him away indignantly.' This bowdlerized version is repeated by Fra Mariano of Lisbon.

2 Bishop Guido's whole attitude towards Francis' arrival is of course a matter for speculation. In my view he had known that the penitents were coming and was prepared to welcome their presence as proof of Assisi's new holiness – till Francis by-passed him and shocked the Pope, after which his one desire was to get rid of them. Sabatier holds that their arrival came as a complete and most unwelcome shock.

3 Or Valdo or Valdès. Hence he is often known as Peter Waldo and his followers as the Waldenses.

4 For Lyons and the Poor Men, the original sources are Innocent's *Letters* and the *Chronicon Universum Anonymi Laudanensis*, in M.G.H., *Scriptores*, XXVI. See also J. Jalla's *Histoire des Vaudois* (Pinerolo, 1922). Their name, and beliefs, passed on to the sect now known as the Vaudois or Waldenses, about 30,000 strong, in the mountains of northern Italy and southern Switzerland. See also Preger's *Beiträge zur Geschichte der Waldensier* (Munich, 1875), and J. J. Dollinger's *Beiträge zur Sekten Geschichte des Mittelalters* (1890) for a more general picture. I know of no good work in English.

5 Again Innocent's *Letters* (and of course Bulls) are one of the main sources for the *Humiliati*. The best modern study appears to be L. Zanoni's *Gli Umiliati* (Milan, 1911).

Rather confusingly, the First Order of the *Humiliati* (i.e. the lay workers living a more or less normal life) became eventually the Third Order when priests and nuns were admitted and, under a more severe rule, usurped the title of First Order. Thus the Three Orders of the *Humiliati* preceded, though they did not resemble, the Three Orders of the Franciscans.

It is interesting to compare the history of the two movements. The *Humiliati* spread with greater rapidity, and by 1216 there were 150 houses within the archbishopric of Milan alone. They were much loved – and so much admired for their honesty that they were eventually put in charge of tax-gathering in most of the Communes of northern Italy. Perhaps it was this position of official authority that led to their eventual decline. In 1569 they were suppressed, after an attempt by members of the Order to murder the Protector of the Order, St. Charles Borromeo.

There is a striking resemblance between the aims and the way of life of the first *Humiliati* and the way of life of members of the *Opus Dei*, the lay Order that has become so influential in Spain and elsewhere.

6 Like the *Humiliati*, the penitents of Assisi wore undyed grey robes. It was not till long after Francis' death that brown became the colour of the Friars Minor; the ideas that the artists have so firmly implanted is false.

The symbolic importance of clothes in the Middle Ages was enormous. Clothes were, to use a tiresome phrase, the great example of conspicuous consumption.

'*Aissi Guerpise Joi e Deport*': Farewell, sang Guillaume of Poitiers in a melancholy mood, to joy and sport; '*E Vair e Gris e Sembel*' – and to three types of fur. That was what death meant to a noble and a troubadour, the end of fine clothes.

7 The three major works of Abbot Joachim of Flora, the *Concordia Novi ac Veteris Testamenti*, the *Expositio in Apocalypsim*, and the *Psalterium Decem Cordarum* were last published in 1517 and 1527 in Venice; and despite the revival of interest in his ideas and his movement there has been, as yet, no modern critical edition of these books – a great gap in medieval scholarship.

The handiest and best short study was written by M. W. Bloomfield and is called *Joachim of Flora: A Critical Survey of his Canon, Teachings, Sources, Biography and Influence*. It was published in 1957 by the Fordham University Press of New York in Volume XIII of their learned magazine '*Traditio – Studies in Acient and Mediaeval History, Thought and Religion*.' This contains a full bibliography.

Of Felice Tocco's *Eresia nel Medio Evo* (Florence, 1884) which concentrates largely on Joachim, Sabatier wrote 'I know nothing more learned or more luminous.' His own master, Renan, published his views of the Abbot in *Nouvelles Etudes de L'Histoire Religieuse* (Paris, 1884). Dr. Marjorie Reeves published a thesis entitled *Studies in the Reputation and Influence of the Abbot Joachim of Flora* in 1932 (University of London Press). And, more recently, in

1969, the Oxford University Press issued her book, *The Influence of Prophecy in the Later Middle Ages: A Study of Joachimism.*

It is interesting that Joachim's influence is still not dead. Now that myth and magic are becoming so popular, pages on him can be found in such works as *After Nostradamus – Great Prophecies for the Future of Mankind*, recently published in paperback (Granada Mayflower, 1973).

8 What in fact was Joachim's influence on Francis? This is a matter of great doubt; but, *pace* Sabatier, the general opinion is that there was little or no direct influence. It seems a reasonable assumption therefore that Francis first heard about him in any detail from Cardinal Giovanni when, as the *First Life* says, he 'urged him to turn to the life of a monk or hermit.' There were certainly both motive and opportunity, for the *Three Companions* state that the brothers 'spent several days' with the cardinal – time enough for him to have discussed with them all the Orders available, and in particular to have explained all about the Order of Florenses, which was (a) much in favour at the time (b) the obvious choice for one of Francis' inclinations.

There is a rather suspect series of coincidences between Abbot Joachim's early life and Francis'. Like Francis, Joachim was converted after a life of dissipation, and, like Francis, once converted he began to preach as a layman. It seems probable that many of the incidents of Francis' early life were incorporated into the shadowy accounts of his great predecessor; at least one hopes it was that way around. But the resemblances between the accounts of the lives of the three of them, Francis, Joachim and Pierre de Vaux – are embarrassing.

9 What there can be no doubt about at all is the immense influence that Joachim's writings had upon the Franciscan movement after the death of Francis. Unfortunately no copy survives of Fra Gerald di Borgo San Donnino's notorious book *The Introduction to the Eternal Gospel* (*Introductorius da Evangelium Aeternum*), which held that Joachim's three major works were in fact the eternal gospel of the Third Age: and hence the continuation and to some extent the replacement of the Old and New Testaments. This was published in 1254, less than thirty years after Francis' death, in Paris; it was condemned as heretical in three successive Bulls; and directly or indirectly, its publication led to the perpetual imprisonment of the author, the ruin of his protector the Minister-General of the Friars Minor, incessant and embittered disputes at the University of Paris which spread all over intellectual Christendom, vast popular apprehension as the year 1260 approached, and a whole legacy of trouble for the Franciscan Order. Even St. Bonaventure, though appointed by the Pope precisely to damp down the tendency to regard Francis as a second and more modern Christ, was not immune to Joachimite ideas. See Joseph Ratzinger's *The Theology of History in St. Bonaventure* (translated by Zachary Hayes, Chicago, 1971); and also Bernard McGill's *The Abbot and the Doctors: Scholastic Reactions to the Radical Eschatology of Joachim of Flora* (in 'Church History', No. 40, 1871). See also Bonaventure's own *Collationes in Hexaëmeron*, where he adapts and develops the schema of two series of seven stages. At the General Chapter held in Paris at Pentecost 1266 he preached on the text of the apocalypse: 'I saw another Angel, ascending from the rising of the Sun, having the sign of the Living God' – that Angel being Francis. But it was the 'Spirituals' who came closest to insisting on Francis' divinity – Fra Angelo Clareno, Fra Ubertino da Casale and the great poet Fra Jacopone da Todi. See also D. Douie's *The Nature and the Effect of the Theory of the Fratricelli* (Manchester, 1932).

10 Two apocryphal works attributed to Abbot Joachim, the *Expositio in Jeremiam* and the *Expositio in Isaiam*, were directed against the 'Antichrist' of the Second Age, the Emperor Frederick II.

Among the other writings of Joachim, probably the most fascinating is the illustrated *Liber Figurarum*, discovered only this century, in which he (or his pupils) draw figures illustrating his theories. There is a manuscript in Corpus Christi College, Oxford.

11 It is now generally agreed that Francis and his companions were in Rome in the spring of 1209 rather than 1210. Yet Prior Burchard appears to be writing of the year 1210; see the papal Bull of 14 June 1210 *Cum inaestimabile pretium*, which refers to Bernhard. This is a difficulty. Personally I disagree with the general agreement (see the next chapter), though conscious of my temerity.

12 Prior Burchard also noted that the Friars Minor did *not*, unlike the Poor Men, seek any privileges from the Pope whatsoever. This again is most valuable outside evidence of a principle that Francis thereafter always practised: no privileges for the brothers. As he wrote in his *Testament*:

'In virtue of obedience, I strictly forbid the friars, wherever they may be, to petition the Roman Curia, either personally or through an intermediary, for a papal privilege, whether it concerns a church or any other place, or even in order to preach, or because they are being persecuted. If they are not welcome somewhere, they should flee to another country where they can lead a life of penance, with God's blessing.'

13 *Pauperes Minores*. He goes on '*Maluerunt appellari Minores Fratres quam Minores Pauperes*' – and this proves, though he does not mention either Francis or Assisi by name, that it was the Friars Minor whom he had seen at the Curia. It is more than probable that they used a variety of names, and continued to do so till the *Second Rule* laid down in writing (chapter VI): 'No one is to be called Prior. They are all to be known as Friars Minor (Lesser Brothers) without distinction, and they should be prepared to wash one another's feet.'

14 The *Legenda Major* gives yet another name that the fraternity used after the visit to Rome, the 'Order of the Brothers of Penance.' (This is generally held, without in my view sufficient reason, to refer simply to the Third Order.)

The fact that Prior Burchard described them as '*Pauperes Minores*' indicates how closely they were linked, at least in public opinion if not in their own, with the established (though heretical) Poor Men. Perhaps it was for this reason that Francis rejected the name of '*Pauperes*', which otherwise must have appealed to him.

As for *Minores*, Buonacuti (in *Ricerche Religiose*, No. IV, 1928) suggests that the choice of this term was a precise proof of Abbot Joachim's influence. He had described the monks that would dominate the Third Age as '*parvuli*', or 'Little Ones'. Hence Francis, aware of this, defined his own followers as the future millennarians: '*minores*' or 'Lesser Ones'. This view is now generally rejected – as is the view that there was something political in the choice of name: '*minores*' as opposed to '*majores*', i.e. *populo minuto* as opposed to *populo grasso*.

It seems simpler, however, to suppose that Francis was merely following the text of the gospel of St. Matthew (18,3), '*Nisi conversi fueritis et efficiamini sicut parvuli*', etc. In the *Legenda Antiqua* Francis explains to his brothers that the Son of God had asked the Father to raise a new and humble people; a request immediately granted. 'That is why,' blessed Francis added, 'the Lord has willed that the brothers be called "lesser" because they are this people whom the Son of God asked of his Father and of whom he said in the Gospel "There is no need to be afraid, little flock, for it has pleased your Father to give you the kingdom" and again "In so far as you did this to one of the least (*minomus*) of these brothers of mine, you did it to me."'

It would be extremely in character for Francis to have chosen the title from the New

Testament. (The two passages quoted are from Luke, 12, 32 and Matthew, 25, 40.) In any case what is certain is that he hesitated about the title of his group; for, like all imaginative people, he knew very well the enormous importance of choosing a name that was not merely descriptive but that appealed to the imagination.

15 Around the year 1210 Pope Innocent ruled that converts should make the following pro-fession of faith:

'We can find no fault with the sacraments that are celebrated in the Church with the co-operation of the inestimable and invisible virtue of the Holy Spirit, even if they are adminis-tered by a priest who is a sinner, provided that he is authorized by the Church. We do not reject any of the ecclesiastical offices or blessings given by such a priest, but we accept them as if they were those of a very holy priest, with sincere heart; for the evilness of a bishop or of a priest does not invalidate the baptism of a child or the consecration of the eucharist or the celebration of the other ecclesiastical offices.' (Quoted by Denz, V, 424.) This is extra-ordinarily like Francis' profession of faith in his *Testament*. It indicates how, at this time, the real test was the attitude of laymen towards unworthy priests and bishops.

16 Most people derive their idea of St. Francis from Giotto's paintings and frescoes – including all later artists. In fact his features were neither so charming nor so symmetrical; and in any case Giotto was drawing from imagination, not from life. Cimabue's portrait (in the Basilica di S. Franceso, Assisi) is much more like the Francis who once explained to his brothers a more natural parable, that of the hen and her innumerable chickens: 'The hen is I, small as I am in stature and naturally dark.'

But probably the only genuinely contemporary portrait of Francis is that of the '*Sacro Speco*.' The fact that there is no halo indicates that it was painted at any rate before his canonization which occurred only two years after his death. (See page 250.) It is less idealized (particularly as to the ears) than Thomas of Celano's pen-portrait: 'He was a man of cheerful countenance, of kindly aspect. He was of medium height, closer to shortness, his head was moderate in size and round, his face a bit long and prominent, his forehead smooth and low, his eyes were black and sound, his hair black, his eyebrows straight, his nose symmetrical, thin and straight, his ears sticking out but small, his temples smooth. His teeth were set close together, even and white. His neck was slender, his shoulders straight, his arms short, his hands slender, his fingers long, his nails extended; his legs were thin, his feet small, his skin was delicate, his flesh very spare.'

17 The Pope did *not* in fact 'sign the marriage contract.' He very carefully confined himself to giving merely verbal and to some extent conditional approval to Francis' written Rule. His actual words (as reported by the *First Life*) were these:

'Go with the Lord, brothers, and as the Lord will deign to inspire you, preach penance to all. Then, when the almighty God shall give you increase in number and in grace, return to me with joy, and I will add many more things to these and entrust greater things to you with greater confidence.' In other words, even after visions, dreams, parables, the Pope hesitated. In the circumstances can one deny that hesitation and a merely conditional approval was wise?

On the vital question of preaching, there is this to be said. (1) Francis and his brothers did not get blanket permission to preach on any subject: they were limited to preaching peni-tence. The Pope's own words indicate that they were not to discuss matters of faith or doctrine. (2) From other indications it is clear, however, that they were allowed to preach without first obtaining the bishop's authorization (unlike the Poor Men). However, if the bishop should object (and Francis in his zeal extended this even to the local priest – see page 147), then the objection over-ruled the permission. In other words the onus was not on the brothers to seek permission but on the bishops to refuse it: an important and very tactful advance.

How well this worked out in practice is shown by the following story, from the *Second Life*. (Francis of course was especially scrupulous.)

'Once when St. Francis came to Imola, a city of Romagna, he presented himself to the bishop of that region, asking his permission to preach. The bishop said to him: "It is enough, Brother, that I preach to my people." Bowing his head, St. Francis humbly went outside, and after a short time, he came back in. The bishop said to him: "What do you want, Brother? What are you seeking now?" And the blessed Francis said: "Lord, if a father drives his son out of one door, he must come back in by another." Subdued by this humility, the bishop embraced him with a happy countenance and said: "You and all your brothers may preach in my diocese in the future with my general permission, for your holy humility has merited this." '

18 The clerical tonsure did not necessarily mean that the brothers were admitted into Minor Orders. It simply identified them as being legally subject to canon law. The whole question of what exactly was meant by the term '*clericus*' is extremely complex. On occasions it was used in a narrow sense – a cleric; on other occasions (as this) in a broad sense; and on yet other occasions it simply indicated the ability to read and write.

❧ The Fellowship of Francis ❧

8: The Fellowship of Francis

The next ten years were the happy, sunlit years, the legendary years of the
Franciscan movement. Peace returned to central Italy; the brotherhood expanded; men of all social classes 'left the world' and followed the founders.
The learned and the noble joined, side by side with the poor and the illiterate.
Under the guidance of Francis and the watchful eye of the Church, heresy was
avoided; indeed heretics were absorbed. One explanation of this phenomenal
swelling of numbers is that the new Order attracted all those in central Italy
who had felt the tug towards the life of apostolic poverty; and all the different
currents flowed together towards Assisi.

Why? Partly it was Francis and his personality. He was wildly eccentric but
never exclusive; and that is a very attractive combination. He practised what
he preached, but though he was penitent, he was gay: and that, too, is a very
attractive combination. Above all, he never condemned. Often he pitied, sometimes he regretted, occasionally he scolded, once or twice he expelled. But he
never never condemned any class of people as a class, and that shows a rare
tolerance in any century, and perhaps especially in those centuries of the Middle
Ages which were so free with their exchanges of erudite insults. To put it in a
word, Francis alone of the great men of his time never condemned anyone else
as an Antichrist. And within his own Order he hated above all backbiting and
malicious gossip, as countless stories relate.

No doubt the brotherhood would have expanded even if it had not been under
the protection of the Church. But no doubt also it would have grown more slowly and more hesitantly. For the years that followed were the triumphant years of
Innocent's pontificate. Inside Christendom the heretics were dispersed; outside
Christendom the infidels were defeated. Everywhere the power and influence
of the Pope was felt. This was no doing of Francis or his followers, but, as the
Pope's men, they benefited from the glory that Innocent reflected and from
their loyalty to a Church that had been weak and shaky but was now once again
surging ahead. Had this not been so, the background would have been different;
and if the background had been different, the conditions in which Francis'
movement drew so many followers would not have existed. It is for this reason
that I would place the great expansion, which we know occurred between the
years 1209 and 1219, in the years 1212, 1213, and 1214. For these were the
decisive years of the three decisive battles; first, the battle in Spain at Las Navas
de Tolosa (16 July 1212), which ended Saracen expansion and gave Christianity
the confidence that the fall of Jerusalem had undermined; secondly, the battle

in Languedoc at Muret (12 September 1213), where the Cathars, or rather the noble protectors that made them so dangerous, were humbled and King Pedro of Aragon killed; and thirdly the great battle of Bouvines in northern France (27 July 1214) that effectively eliminated an Emperor, Otto, who had become a rival to the Pope, and established Innocent's nominee and ward, the youthful Frederick Roger from Sicily as the Emperor Frederick II in fact as well as in name. Had any of these battles been lost, the Church's influence would have wobbled. Had all of them been lost, it is doubtful whether there would ever have been a Franciscan movement to speak of – but merely a group of hermits hiding in the woods of a Europe bloody with civil war and torn by raids and invaders.

Knights and Hermits

When the twelve brothers left Rome, that was in any case their first temptation. The journey back was so pleasant that they took it very slowly, and once they had safely crossed the Tiber and were in Umbria, they stayed for two weeks outside Orte, one of the most agreeable hill-top towns in the world, living in a remote spot by a cemetery and sending out occasional foragers to beg for food in the town. Despite all the trouble they had gone to in Rome, despite even the Pope's permission for them to preach penance, they thought they might become hermits and live apart from, rather than in, the world.

This was obviously a moment of considerable and genuine doubt. To be a hermit is possibly a holier vocation than to be a preacher; it is certainly less involved and less embarrassing. Francis himself was always attracted to a hermit's life; and indeed always returned to it. And very possibly all that he and his followers had heard in Rome of the Abbot Joachim influenced them more and more the longer they stayed by Orte. The abbot had tried preaching but had left the world to lead a hermit's life, and his Rule had been explained to them and pressed upon them. But I prefer to believe that Francis was more influenced by the legends of King Arthur.

'Behold my knights of the Round Table,' he used to say, later on, 'the brothers who hide in abandoned and secluded places to devote themselves with more fervour to prayer and meditation, to weep over their sins and those of others.'

Quite clearly, when he said this, he was not making a remote or fanciful comparison. He was thinking of the knights of the Round Table not in the heyday of their glory but in the days following the death of Arthur. According to the story the king's body had been taken to a hermitage where a solitary hermit, who had been the Archbishop of Canterbury, received and buried him. And there Sir Bedivere followed. 'Alas,' he had said, 'that was my lorde Kynge

Arthur which lyethe here gravyn in thys chapell. From hens will I never go be my wyll but all the days of my lyff to pray for my lorde Arthur.'

'And so he belaffte with the ermyte that was beforehande Bysshop of Caunturbyry. And there Sir Bedivere put uppon hym poure clothys . . . and so they lyved in prayers and fastynges and grete abstynaunce.' And there eventually they were joined first by Sir Lancelot, then by Sir Bors and within months by seven other knights, kinsmen of Bors and Lancelot; and there they lived 'in grete penaunce,' sharing a hut, 'for they alle laye in one chambre,' and 'toke no regarde of no worldly rychesses.'[1]

In that famous hermitage there had been ten brothers in all; in his group Francis had twelve, only a couple more. They too could live in great penance, in prayers, fasting and great abstinence, lying in one chamber, taking no regard of worldly riches. This had been how a famous bishop and the most famous knights of all the world had ended; and among them he who had been 'hede of al Crysten Knyghtes, the curtest knyght that ever bare shelde, the kyndest man that ever strake wyth sworde.' There can be no doubt that Francis knew the tale and knew, if not the precise words, others very like them. If the noble fellowship of the Round Table had ended in a hermitage, was it not tempting for one who had also borne shield and struck with sword, who had probably dreamt of becoming in his day the head of all Christian knights, to avoid all the intervening disasters and to begin with his fellowship where that fellowship had ended?

It must have been; but to avoid all the intervening disasters meant equally to miss all the intervening glories. The life of the hermit settles like the dust; and for somebody as passionately attached to knightly legend as Francis his fellowship needed adventures before it deserved its repose.

I think that from this time onwards at the back of his mind, and very often at its forefront, Francis saw his company as a renewed fellowship of the Round Table, and his Order more as an Order of Knighthood than as an Order of Religious. Consciously or unconsciously he modelled the practices of this novel Order of his upon that of the knights of King Arthur. The brothers had sworn an oath of obedience and loyalty to him; new brothers continued to do so, and thus Francis became an unheard of phenomenon in the history of religious Orders: a leader to whom all the members of the Order owed a personal loyalty, just as the knights had owed a personal loyalty to King Arthur. Exactly how novel this was the most superficial study of other Orders shows: in all of them obedience was given to an office, and to the member elected to that office, rather than to a person, even if that person was the founder. Francis alone was in the position of a miniature Pope – with this difference, that he had chosen himself – and the Pope, though in office for life, was elected by others. Beneath Francis, all, whatever their social background, however long they had been in the Order, were equal: all sat side by side around an imaginary table where, at least in the early years, precedence was given to none and there was, unlike other Orders, no hierarchy, no grades at all. And I think that Francis saw himself as an Arthur; as a knight who had to show greater prowess than his fellows and undergo great hardships; but yet as one who could impose commands 'under obedience' and who had a right to expect instant and unquestioning submission, just as his fellows had a right to expect courteous words, courteous treatment and that streak of inspiration that would entice even the most staid to adventure.[2]

And just as Arthur, once the Round Table has been founded, has less adventures himself and indeed becomes less interesting than his knights, so Francis too in the next ten years fades a little into the background as Fra Juniper and Fra Pacificus and Fra Masseo and others of the fraternity cavort upon the stage. Yet much less so than Arthur; for even if in the accounts of his life a certain air of pious convention muffles the saint and miracle-worker, the real man cavorts too, and indiscreetly leaps into eccentric prominence.

An Insult to Otto the Emperor

So at Orte the brothers conferred together; and decided to lead an active life of preaching, intermingled with a retired life in hermitages. They left Orte and retraced their footsteps, by Narni, by Terni, by Spoleto, by Foligno, towards Assisi. And there they stopped at a spot called Rivo Torto, which is probably (but not certainly) down in the plain a couple of miles from Assisi. There was an abandoned hovel there, in which they took shelter; and we know that, like Sir Bedivere and the other knights in the hermitage by Glastonbury, they all slept side by side, for 'Francis wrote the brothers' names on the beams of the hut so that each one, when he wished to sit or pray, should know his own place, and no unnecessary noise due to the close quarters should disturb the brothers' quiet of mind.' It was very cramped; and they lived on turnips which they begged in the plains. Possibly the citizens of Assisi were not overjoyed at having the mendicants back again; and Francis had deliberately chosen a spot a little further away from the city both in order to have a new begging-area and to give Assisi time to become used to the idea of having an authorized new group permanently attached. Or there could have been another reason why they stayed further away from Assisi, as a curious and never clearly explained incident indicates.

The incident was this: while the twelve were living in the hovel at Rivo Torto, which was close to the road, the Emperor came by 'with much clamour and pomp.' On Francis' orders none of the brothers were allowed out even to go and watch, except one. And this one was instructed to call out to the Emperor not once but continuously: 'Your glory will last but a short time.'

On the surface this appears a peculiarly pointless insult to the great, and a peculiarly dangerous 'obedience' for the wretched brother called upon to perform it – well below the level of the man-with-the-placard announcing 'The End of the World is at Hand,' nastier and more personal, though just as platitudinous, not like Francis at all.[3] The *First Life* adds that this was the Emperor Otto passing through 'to receive the crown of his earthly empire'; and this is even more confusing, first because those who have studied the question are unanimous in saying that Otto did not come within twenty miles of Assisi at that time, and secondly because, seeing that he was on his way to Rome to be crowned Emperor by the Pope, this gesture was therefore a gratuitous insult to Innocent. The incident undoubtedly occurred, but in my view it occurred *after* Otto had been crowned Emperor and not before – and this alone gives a *raison d'être* to an otherwise totally uncharacteristic gesture.

In the summer of 1208, after ten years of sporadic civil war in Germany, a settlement was in sight. Otto of Brunswick was pledged to marry the daughter of his successful rival Philip of Swabia, when Philip was assassinated. Almost immediately Otto, entirely innocent of the murder, was re-elected Emperor by the German princes. In the summer of 1209 he set out on the traditional 'Rome-journey' which would culminate in his crowning by his great supporter, the Pope. From Rimini, accompanied by his Italian adviser, the Patriarch Wolfger of Aquileia, he took the Via Flaminia towards Rome; by the end of September he was in Spoleto, having passed through Nocera and Foligno but leaving Assisi on the far side of a range of mountains, and on 4 October he was crowned Holy Roman Emperor with great splendour in Rome, where he swore the traditional oath to be protector of the Church. Innocent had every reason to be satisfied that his thirty-five-year-old protégé had at long last, by due process of law, obtained his rights.

Innocent's satisfaction did not last long. The almost inevitable riots and killings that occur whenever Germans in large numbers descend on Rome broke out immediately. On leaving Rome the new Emperor was joined by Dipold the German, and the innate Teutonic desire for power began to reassert itself. The embittered German host moved north to central Italy, and the shadow of imperial domination fell again over Umbria and Tuscany. On 3 December Otto was in Florence; sometime before early January he was in Assisi; from 5–8 January he was in Foligno; on 20 January he invested Azzo of Este with Le Marche, thereby breaking formally with the Pope and reclaiming imperial territory. And on 28 February 1210 Perugia swore loyalty to the Pope. This was a measure of retaliation arranged by the papal legate. It brings us back, inevitably, to the old, old question of the little local war that was still dragging on – though happily on its last legs.

Six months earlier the Perugians had attempted to settle it by another *diktat*. Their *Podestà* had appeared on the square in front of the bishop's palace in Assisi and had cited the Consuls of Assisi to appear on the following day at the hill of Collestrada to agree to the terms laid down by Perugia. This was a month before Otto's coronation, when the news of the impending approach of the Pope's faithful protégé with 6,000 German horsemen was abroad. It says much for the hatred of the Assisians against the Perugians that they once again rejected the humiliating ultimatum. By the time Otto returned to Umbria two months later, the situation was fluid. By the end of February 1210 the battle-lines were once again drawn: Perugia was papist; and so Assisi was the Emperor's.

Let us suppose that it was in the spring not of 1209 but of 1210 that Francis and his eleven companions went to Rome – as Prior Burchard's account seems to indicate – and that it was in the early summer that they reappeared. The Emperor Otto was elsewhere in Italy, fighting (or rather skirmishing) against papal supporters with moderate success. Francis and his companions were now, by oath, the Pope's men; so were the Perugians, Assisi's traditional enemies. Is it any wonder that the brothers kept a little distance from Assisi and were rather discreet in their appearances? Is it any wonder that they lay low at Rivo Torto?

In the autumn, on 18 October, after the usual fruitless negotiations the Pope announced that Otto would be formally excommunicated in a month's time. On 4 November, two weeks later, Otto reappeared and made a triumphant entry into Assisi. Dipold, his ally, the enemy who had been the death of Walter of Brienne, was proclaimed Duke of Spoleto, to hold the duchy 'on the same terms as once Conrad had held it'; the surviving lords of Sassorosso, Leonardo and Fortebraccio di Gislerio, returned to Assisi, abandoning their local protector Perugia for their natural protector, an Emperor from Germany apparently determined to restore the *status quo ante* but in fact without the power to do so. As Otto set out ot prepare to march south on the Kingdom, the ultimate affront to papal authority, there was the utmost confusion in Assisi.

But to Francis at least the issues were clear. An Emperor under threat of excommunication was setting off to invade a papal fief to which he had not the slightest legal claim; and riding by his side was another German duke imposed upon Umbria, the man furthermore against whom Francis would have fought had he gone to Apulia. He could hardly be expected not to make a gesture as the nefarious Germans jogged southwards; I would like to suppose that with a modicum of prudence he chose one of the brothers who did not come from Assisi to taunt Otto and Dipold as they rode by.

And indeed their glory did not last for long. On 18 November, as Otto entered the territory of the Kingdom at Sora, Pope Innocent solemnly pronounced his excommunication. Admittedly for the next sixteen months the German host dominated southern Italy from Capua; but never again did Otto appear north of Rome – except to scurry back to Germany when all his enterprises were failing.

Otto was 'a man who would promise everything but hardly perform anything,' as the chronicler Matthew Paris noted. When he left Assisi to march south, even his supporters doubted whether they would ever see this 'proud fool' or his newly appointed 'Duke' again. Nevertheless his swift and comparatively short intervention in central Italy – which, as we have seen, covered the span of one year, from autumn 1209 to autumn 1210 – brought one immense benefit to Assisi. With the return of the lords of Sassorosso, the first of the nobles who had chosen exile and the last to abandon the Perugian alliance, the civil war that had lasted for nearly a decade ended, and the war with Perugia fizzled out.

On 9 November, five days after Otto had entered Assisi and (probably) five days after he had left, a pact was proclaimed between the nobles and the people that ended, on a note of compromise, the period of violent class warfare.[4] Heaven knows, but history does not relate, what tortuous or frenetic negotiations filled those five days. Both the left and the right were in positions of potential dominance; the nobles had the support of an Emperor and could argue that when he returned triumphant, they had only to ask and the clock would be turned back. If he returns, their opponents retorted. In fact, however, both sides were tired of civil strife. The nobles recognized that the Commune had become a force that could not be simply abolished and was entitled to speak for all citizens, themselves included. The merchant class on their side admitted that the attempt to abolish feudalism root and branch had failed. The *Podestà*, Carsedonio, himself a noble, appointed a commission of seven to draw up the precise terms of what we might call 'a government of national unity' and this commission, which included at least two nobles, took the precaution of proclaiming their pact 'to the honour of Our Lord Jesus Christ, the Blessed Virgin Mary, the Lord Emperor Otto and the Lord Duke Dipold,' a nominal concession that must have infuriated the supporters of the Pope.

But even Francis could not have taken this too much to heart, for at long last God had answered his prayer and given Assisi peace – and, in the absence of the Emperor, it was inevitable that central Italy should slowly and gradually accept once again the hegemony of the Pope and the Church.

Francis' Camelot

Once Otto and the Germans had disappeared into the wild country south of Rome, Francis emerged from semi-hiding. He began to preach in Assisi, and the extraordinary thing is that he preached not at street corners or in the squares but in the churches. The first church he preached in was the church at which he had been educated, San Giorgio; but he also preached in the cathedral of San Rufino – indeed the *Legenda Major* implies that he preached there every Sunday.[5] And this occurred while he and his brothers were living at Rivo Torto. In other words his new official position as approved leader of an approved Order was immediately recognized by some at least of the local clergy; and in particular by the canons of the cathedral, those inveterate rivals of Bishop Guido. Whether this was the cause or the effect of a certain *froideur* that had arisen between Francis and the bishop is not clear. But that their relations were chilly at this period there can be little doubt.

For Bishop Guido flatly refused to help Francis and the brothers when they asked his help in finding a new base. All Francis wanted, now that the general situation in and around Assisi had settled down, was a place with room for a few simple huts and above all a little church where the brothers could recite their Office together. 'Brother,' said Bishop Guido, 'I have no church to give you.' This was a barefaced inexactitude; and Guido must have been feeling very prickly indeed to have come out with such a remark.[6]

Among the canons of San Rufino, Francis had a supporter, Silvester, who was ashamed of having treated both Francis and Bernard badly when they were persons of no significance. Even so the canons also refused to offer a church, perhaps because, unlike the bishop who was endowed with scores, they genuinely had none to offer. So Francis turned to the third and really the last possibility, the monks of St. Benedict on Monte Subasio.

It is extraordinary what good relations Francis had with the Benedictines. There would seem to have been every reason for mutual distaste, indeed antipathy both on the personal and on the general level. Instead, courtesy prevailed. Perhaps this was because the Benedictines were the noblemen of the religious world, and Francis almost invariably treated nobles with a respect that had become rather charmingly outdated. At any rate the abbot and his monks consulted; and they decided to give Francis a church. Not surprisingly it was the poorest church they had; and not surprisingly, either, it was the church that Francis himself had repaired during his church-restoring days, St. Mary of the Angels, the Portiuncula.

The courtesies were maintained. The abbot gave the new fraternity the little chapel with only one condition, which Francis was delighted to accept: that it should become the head of all the friaries that might be founded if the Order expanded. Francis in his turn refused to accept it as a free gift; every year, as a sign that his fraternity held is not in fee simple but from the abbey, he sent a basket full of loaches up to the monks. And every year, as a free gift, the monks sent down a vessel full of oil.

'The brothers,' Francis wrote in his *Last Wishes*, 'must be very careful not to accept churches or poor dwellings for themselves, or anything else built for them, unless they are in harmony with the poverty which we have promised in the *Rule*; and they should occupy these places only as strangers and pilgrims.'[7]

If there is one thing certain beyond a shadow of doubt, it is that Francis would be horrified if he could revisit the Portiuncula now. A vast, triumphant basilica rears up into the sky; inside it, like a tiny snail in an overgrown shell, stands the stone church of Santa Maria degli Angeli. The huts of branches and clay, that were all Francis allowed to be built for himself and his brothers, have been replaced by scores of buildings that the present-day Franciscans occupy as owners and masters.

But above all there is a tragic irony in the life that is led there. 'I wish,' said Francis, towards the end of his life, 'that at least this community be a beautiful mirror of the Order, a candelabra before the throne of God and the blessed Virgin.' It was Francis' Camelot.

In those early days, as the Order expanded and more and more brothers came down from Assisi to join the fraternity, they lived together a life of prayer and penance, and hard work. The brothers 'very often went and helped the poor in the fields, and these sometimes gave them bread for love of God.' Francis himself hardly ever ate cooked food and he would sleep with only a tunic between himself and the ground. Indeed he very often slept sitting up, with a piece of stone as a backrest. Silence and prayer was the rule; gossip was discouraged, as was news of the outside world. And to this inner sanctum the outer world was not admitted. Nowadays there is a mere travesty of the 'model of humility and highest poverty' that Francis desired. Incessant streams of tourists and visitors pour in, not a friar helps the poor in the fields or the factories, 'itching ears' stretch out, and above all there is the constant collection and jangle and rustle of coin and notes that would lead someone even as gentle as Francis to cast out the money-changers clad in brown from what he had seen as his temple. The odour that once was 'wonderfully fragrant' has become the odour of riches. And even the pledge to the Benedictines that their little church would be the head of the Order has been betrayed in letter as well as in spirit. So much for Francis' wishes. 'He wanted this friary always to be a model and a reminder to the present and to future brothers.'

Inevitably, among the first brothers, there were excesses. Francis himself had rather ostentatiously discarded a hair-shirt when he stripped before his father and the bishop. There were hair-shirts galore, but there were iron corselets, too, till Francis forbade them. As for the more usual penitential practices, even these Francis practised with moderation, not with that fanaticism that is so often repellent in ascetics. One night around midnight a brother began to cry out: 'I am dying, I am dying.' Francis got up and called: 'Get up, brothers, bring a light,' and when a torch was lit, he asked: 'Who cried out "I am dying?"'

'I did.'

'What ails you, brother? What are you dying from?'

'I am dying of hunger.'

Even the most mild mannered of men might be forgiven a certain just indignation at being woken up in the middle of the night by a fellow-penitent with, in the circumstances, an hysterically exaggerated gripe. Not Francis however. He had a meal prepared and made everyone eat. When they had eaten, he explained very politely that there were no hard and fast rules for penance, that some people could do with much less to eat than others, and that what had to be avoided was 'excessive mortification, for God desires loving kindness, not sacrifice.' Then he added: 'My dear brothers, it was my wish that out of love for my brother all of us should share a meal with him so that he would not blush: we did so out of love and because he greatly needed it. I warn you, I will not do this again, for it would be neither religious nor upright. Rather it is my desire and command that each and everyone, while respecting our poverty, give his body what it needs.' It is hard to see how anyone could have bettered this.

Brother Ass

Yet there were times when Francis treated his own body with total contempt and inflicted all the evil he could upon 'Brother Ass.' This is an extraordinarily difficult subject to discuss rationally, for it was almost always when Francis was contending with what Brother Giles[8] called 'the traitor carnal desire.'[9]

Once Fra Simon of Assisi, Fra Rufino and Fra Juniper were chatting together; and Fra Giles asked them how they dealt with temptations to carnal sin. Simon simply concentrated his thought on how abhorrent it was; Rufino more dramatically would fling himself flat on the ground and pray to God and Our Lady till the temptation disappeared. As for Fra Juniper, with his usual charming but devastating naivety, he ran away – the method which Fra Giles commended. But Francis was even more extreme than Rufino.

'If, as happens,' wrote Thomas of Celano, 'a temptation of the flesh at times assailed him, he would hurl himself into a ditch full of ice, when it was winter, and remain in it until every vestige of everything carnal had departed.' This is in the *First Life*; a far more famous episode is described in the *Second Life*: how, sorely tempted, Francis took off his tunic and beat himself with his cord, saying, 'See, Brother Ass, thus it is fitting for you to remain, thus it is fitting for you to bear the whip.' But when, even though he was marked all over, 'the most severe temptation of lust' still pestered him, he opened the cell, went out into the garden and threw himself into a deep pile of snow. And then perhaps the most pathetic and touching scene of all Francis' life occurred: it was night, but a moonlit night, and one brother who was there praying saw what happened. 'But when the saint found out later that the brother had seen him that night, he was greatly distressed and commanded him to tell the thing to no-one as long as he lived in the world.' What this eye-witness had seen was Father Francis shaping seven figures in snow, muttering to himself as he did so: 'Look, this larger one is your wife, these four are your two sons and your two daughters, the other two are your servant and your maid whom you must have to serve you. Hurry, and clothe them all, for they are dying of cold.' It needs no expert in psychology to deduce Francis' longing for a normal family life; though, as Chesterton says, 'he could only be tempted by a sacrament.' But this episode occurred at the hermitage of Sarteano near Siena, and so belongs to a later, probably much later, period of his life, when he would also say warningly and perhaps wistfully to those who thought him free from sin: 'I have no guarantee that I will never have sons or daughters,' – again, in Chesterton's words, 'almost as if it was of the children rather than the woman that he dreamed.' But the first episode, the plunging into an icy ditch, occurred, according to Thomas of Celano, while he was still at Rivo Torto.

If this is exact, it gives us an important clue to the chronology of the period, for it means that Francis and his companions were at Rivo Torto in the winter, or at least in icy weather, therefore certainly in November or probably later. It ties in very well with the taunting of Otto as he departed towards the Kingdom and excommunication, and it leads only too logically into the next great adventure of Francis' life. For it seems to show that he was tormented by sexual urges shortly before the time when he first started meeting Clare secretly in Assisi.

Enter a Lady

Inevitably a suggestion of this sort will give offence to many.[10] The relationship between Clare and Francis was so delicate that it seems almost sacrilegious to suggest that it was based on anything but purity; for most of their lives they lived separately in body though united in spirit, the woman closed up in her convent, the man wandering far and near, in mutual respect and affection.[11] So, less than a century earlier, had lived the most famous lovers in Europe, Héloise and Abelard, And though *their* love could only be heavenly in the end, no-one suggests that it was not mostly earthly in its beginnings. And even at the close all passion was not spent: there lingers about the pair a sense of peril that kept one or other of them always holding back, for fear that love might break out again. There was this same holding back, in the later years, with Francis and Clare.

Ten years later, when Francis, full of emotion, dictated the *Second Rule*, this is what he wrote about the relationship between 'his' men and women:

'No matter where they are or where they go, the brothers are bound to avoid the sight or company of women, when it is evil. No one should speak to them alone. Priests may speak to them in confession or when giving spiritual direction but only in such a way as not to give scandal. The brothers are absolutely forbidden to allow any woman to profess obedience to them. Once they have given her advice, they should let her go and lead a life of penance wherever she likes. We must keep a close watch over ourselves and let nothing tarnish the purity of our senses, because our Lord says: Anyone who so much as looks with lust at a woman has already committed adultery with her in his heart.'

No woman-hating Calvinist of the Reformation could have said more. This is not like the gentle and courteous Francis who prized chivalry. But it is not simply words, nor simply words for others. He himself in later years sternly obeyed his own rules, and in effect condemned one half of humanity as dangerous to the soul. He would never look a woman in the face, claimed that he could only recognize two by sight, asserted that all talk with women was frivolous and laid it down that a Friar Minor had no business with them. 'Rightly so, Father,' says Thomas of Celano bursting unusually into editorial *oratio directa*, 'rightly so, I say, for they provide no profit, but great loss, at least of time.'

Women – Guinevere and *la belle* Iseut and Héloise too, the more beautiful and beloved they were, the more they had ruined their men, and spelt the end of great ideals and noble fellowships.

'Through this same man,' said Guinevere to her ladies when Lancelot was brought before her, 'hath all this war been wrought, and the death of the most noblest knights of all the world; for through our love that we have loved together is my most noble lord slain. And therefore, Sir Lancelot, I require thee and beseech thee heartily, for all the love that ever was betwixt us, that thou never see me no more in the visage. And I command thee, on God's behalf, that thou forsake my company, for as well as I have loved thee heretofore my heart will not serve now to see thee: for through thee and me is the flower of kings and knights destroyed.' No, Thomas of Celano, you bustling worthy friar, it was not for the waste of time that your Father Francis averted his eyes from women but for the fear of passion and its absorbing, destructive consequences. In the later years he would not even share a meal with Clare, though she had 'very great longings to eat once with him and thereto besought him many times,' till Francis' own companions condemned him for lacking charity and he with good grace, but once only, consented. So close a watch was he keeping upon himself.

But in the year 1211 when Francis was thirty and she was seventeen, Clare fell in love with Francis. And Francis, I think, committed adultery with her in his heart, and never could forgive himself, or womanhood, thereafter.

Clare had spent years of her childhood in exile in Perugia. Possibly her father and his four brothers, the lords of Coriano, had fought, with their sons, against the men of Assisi at the battle of Collestrada. She may, as a young girl of nine, have peered down at Francis among the prisoners in the Perugian dungeons, but when she and her family came back from exile to Assisi and their fortress-house in the quarter of San Rufino by the cathedral where the nobles congregated, Francis was no longer the gay young man and the would-be knight that Assisi had once known but the ragged rebel whose outrageous behaviour shakes the middle-classes and the conventional in all ages. Such young men have been known to have a certain attraction in the eyes of well-brought-up but high-spirited girls.

Clare was fourteen and by all the standards of the time marriageable when Bernard of Quintavalle made his great gesture and Francis became, with Bernard, not an outcast but a talking-point, an influence and to some extent a force.

The nobles of Assisi inevitably at this period led the curiously closed life of a caste that had lost its political dominance, abandoned its traditional way of life, but retained its prestige, its property and its influence. Like all fading aristocracies, they despised, even if they envied, the middle-classes and the *nouveaux riches* that were rising; and the faster they faded, the more exclusive they became. Ortolana, Clare's mother, travelled widely: she even went as far as the Holy Land on pilgrimage; but she was always accompanied by a young kinswoman, Pacifica di Guelfuccio. Clare, her daughter, lived a social life: but the social life centred round her relatives – indeed in the Offreduccio household alone, besides her father, her mother and two sisters, there were her four uncles and at least three male cousins, and the former's children, Bernardino, Rufino and Paolo.

It seems that the head of the family, the violent Monaldo, died in 1209, before the great reconciliation that the pact of the following year marked. Rufino, who was small, delicate, and a man of thought rather than of action, was the first of the clan to be attracted to the way of life of the fellowship at the Portiuncula. It was probably in the winter of 1210, a month or two after the departure of Otto, that he abandoned the world and joined the new Order. And if it was through the weekly sermons preached at the cathedral that Clare first came to know Francis, it was almost certainly through her shy cousin Rufino that she first came to meet him.

Francis was inordinately proud of attracting a nobleman into the ranks of his Order. It was not mere snobbery; rather, he felt that his Order was noble and that all its members should be noble – in character certainly, but if possible by birth too. But he could never forget his own middling origins; it was this that kept crashing him down to earth again. Rufino di Scipione di Offreduccio swore obedience to him; and no doubt Francis persuaded himself that it was for Rufino's own good that, though shy, he should be forced to go and preach. Rufino, who spoke very little even in private, tried to beg off; whereupon Francis abused his authority. 'Because you did not obey me at once,' he said, 'I also command you under holy obedience to go to Assisi naked – wearing only your breeches – and to go into some church and preach to the people naked like that!' It is only too easy to imagine the agony of refined embarrassment with which Rufino obeyed and how he detested the humiliation and the insult not only to himself but to his caste. 'Look,' sneered the men and children when he stood near-naked to preach, they are doing so much penance they have gone crazy!'

But Francis had at least the quality of redeeming honesty. When Rufino had gone, he said to himself: 'How can you, the son of Pietro Bernardone – you low-born little wretch – order Fra Rufino, who is one of the noblest citizens of Assisi, to go naked and preach to the people like a madman? By God, I am going to see to it that you yourself experience what you order others to do.'

And the end result was that Francis, by humiliating himself too, saved Rufino from humiliation; and their preaching of penance was so moving and effective that when they put on their habits again and left the church the people who could touch the hem of their clothes considered themselves blessed.

If Francis was enthralled by Rufino, he could hardly avoid being even more enthralled by the admiration of Rufino's equally noble and far more beautiful cousin. 'The day will come,' he had told his noble fellow-prisoners in the dungeons of Perugia, 'when I shall be honoured by the whole world.' It seemed to be coming true; he was at least being honoured by his whole world, the local feudal families who, before, had accepted his money but sneered at his pretensions. Now they were swearing to be his liege-men; and even their daughters were asking to meet him and speak to him. Sexual desire or no desire, he would hardly have been human if the unexpected glory of his new position had not gone to his head. Finding himself attractive, he could hardly fail to be attracted. Admiration is the greatest of aphrodisiacs.

But any *jongleur* who knew and loved the French songs, as Francis did, knew that side by side with courtly love and its conventions there existed the grossest and equally enticing sexual urges.

'*Tant les Fotei com ausiretz,*' sang Guillaume of Poitiers, telling of his amatory exploits with two ladies over a period of eight days:

> *Cen e quatre vint e veit vetz*
> *Qu'a pauc no'i rompei mes coretz*
> > *E mes arnes.*

Indeed, had he not felt and nearly yielded to the temptation himself, can anyone believe that he would have become so hysterical about the possibility of a brother committing fornication that it was one of the only two reasons for which a member of the Order could be expelled?[12]

As for Clare, there is no greater sign of a woman's love for a man than the enthusiasm with which she accepts and follows all his ideals, however extravagant in themselves and however dramatic in their personal consequences. Clare, I think, loved Francis with all her heart; and for Francis' sake loved all his schemes and all his manoeuvres, even when eventually they excluded her. But for one year she and Francis shared a high adventure together, and during it they were both romantics, living romantically – clandestine meetings, growing but unspoken love, complicities, midnight escapades, ceremonial, armed men, clashes, their solitude. Without that year to remember, high-spirited Clare could never have accepted an enclosed life. Every woman of Clare's stamp needs her one year of romance.

Clare and Francis never met alone; she always came to their meetings with Bona di Guelfuccio, Pacifica's sister, and he with Philip the Long, who was at least of noble birth. But though they talked, presumably, of God and penance and evangelical poverty and of all the subjects about which Francis preached on Sundays, they met secretly, and they met often. That secrecy, perhaps unnecessary, gave their meetings the intriguing atmosphere of romance; in much the same way Tristram and *la belle* Iseut had met, with the complicity of his squire and her damsel, and taken a thousand precautions lest word of their meetings should reach King Mark. In a small place like Assisi Clare and Bona must have used stratagems learnt from the romances to keep these meetings concealed: scribbled and apparently innocent messages to each other, a system of look-outs, and rendezvous arranged obviously in the woods rather than in the town. There must have been near escapes and thumpings of hearts and sinking feelings in the pit of the stomach as each new meeting drew near. Clare and Bona could have lived only from one meeting to the next.

Francis of course was freer, and therefore much less involved. He would leave Assisi and wander, with a companion, through the nearby towns and villages, preaching: and he would, typically, usually take a broom with him and, whenever he had finished preaching in a church, would sweep it clean and remind the priests in charge of their duty to keep the altars beautifully decorated and their churches tidy. He cannot have gone far from the Portiuncula on any of these little trips; but he was, as it were, both practising and setting an example to the other brothers. Before going to Rome, he had merely talked to individuals in the squares or countryside on his journeys; now he was working out his own style of preaching, simple, spontaneous and effective. Sometimes, Thomas of Celano tells us, he had to admit to the people that he had thought of many things to say but could remember nothing at all of them. And then, without embarrassment he would just give a blessing and send the people away, 'feeling that from this alone they had received a great sermon.' However, when he was inspired, even learned men would be impressed by him. As his confidence grew, he developed the technique of fixing on one person in the crowd of listeners and speaking, as it were, to that person alone. Crowds would gather when he came to preach, 'for the inhabitants always enjoyed seeing and listening to him.'

So Francis was much on the road, very busy, and, being more and more successful, no doubt became more and more happy and more and more attractive. But whenever he came back to Assisi, there would be Clare waiting to see him and a quick flurry of messages to be sent and received. Clearly the secret meetings could not go on for ever, sooner or later there would be a slip-up and a scandal. Matters in any case were coming to a head; for Clare wanted to join Francis in his way of life.

This posed a problem: Francis had never imagined that women would be attracted to the life he had set out, as a sort of knight, to achieve. Clare could hardly become a brother. Yet he and Philip the Long both knew from their visit to Rome that groups and movements, like Bernhard's branch of the Poor Men, could and did exist in which men and women shared a common life of evangelical poverty, obedience and chastity based on gospel texts. It was difficult; but it was obviously not unthinkable. And in those heady days of the early spring of 1212, Francis in so far as he had thought of any solution at all, probably thought of this. But it was not in his nature to plan too far ahead; he preferred to act, and then see how things panned out.

The night of Palm Sunday was chosen for the great elopement. Clare had attended the High Mass in all her finery at San Rufino in the morning. Evening came, the last evening for her 'in the world'. When the house was quiet and all the household asleep, she slipped out, attended only by Pacifica di Guelfuccio, through a side door. Together they hurried through the deserted streets of Assisi, out into the fields and down into the woods. It takes a good half-an-hour, even by a moonlit night and on tarmacked roads to reach the Portiuncula. There, with lighted torches, Francis and Philip and the other brothers were waiting to greet her. And there Clare changed her beautiful dress and her jewels for a rough habit and a cord, and swore obedience, as the other brother's had sworn it, to Francis. And there, in that terribly erotic gesture of a woman who gives herself to her lover, she shook out her long hair – and let it fall, cut short for ever, to the ground.

Perhaps it was the finality of those tresses lying so pathetically on the dark stones of the chapel that brought the two lovers, exalted equally by the sensuality of the scene and the purity of their motives, to their senses. And I dare say it was the shocked, combined pleas of Pacifica and Rufino too, who knew how violently their kinsmen would react. Clare could not simply move into another hut; Clare could not stay, like another brother, at Santa Maria degli Angeli or set out on the road with Francis. No noble clan would permit a virgin of their blood to be involved in such a scandal. Clare, quite simply, could not stay.

But, obviously, she could not go back either. It is easy to picture Francis remembering, ten years later, how Clare pleaded and wept as they all, hurriedly, decided on the conventional solution; and with what emotion he dictated that no brother should ever allow a woman to swear obedience to him, as Clare had just done to himself. He was after all thirty and grown responsible; and I think he realized, as he stood there, not only what personal danger he was in, but, with far greater fear, how near he had come to creating a scandal that might rise up and ruin his whole fellowship. 'Give her advice if you must,' he wrote ten years later, 'but then let her go and lead a life of penance wherever she likes. Do not involve yourself.' Bitter words.

He was not as cold-hearted at the time. But, as he came to his senses, he acted swiftly and with decision. Before dawn came Clare had disappeared, and was safely and conventionally lodged at the convent of San Paolo on the banks of the Chiagio, under the care of the Abbess Sibilla, two miles away.

It took four days for her family to sniff out her whereabouts, decide to act, and track her down. On the morning of Good Friday a group of seven armed men rode down to San Paolo. At first their spokesman tried to reason with her, begging her to leave her foolishness and return; particularly they harped on her *vilitas*, the ignobleness of her behaviour, the sort of thing a member of the lower classes would do. But they were on difficult ground. For Clare had not spent the night with the brothers, she had been chaperoned throughout – and the convent of San Paolo was highly aristocratic in tone. When their plans failed and they tried to drag her away by force, she clung to the altar. The scandal that the nuns and abbess might cause was too great; and when Clare threw back her hood to show the men her shaven head, it was the perfect pretext for them to save their faces, and leave. For, tonsured, Clare was under the protection of canon law and the Church, and that day of all days was no day to use force.

But Clare refused to take the veil and become, easiest and best of solutions, a Benedictine nun. It seems that that night in the wood she had not only sworn obedience to Francis but to his Rule as well; and nothing would turn her from the vow of holy poverty, communal as well as personal, which certainly could not be observed among the aristocratic Benedictine nuns. It meant more trouble for Francis. He and Philip and Bernard went to fetch her and took her away from the offended Abbess Sibilla and the noble nuns, many of whom she must have known 'in the world', to a poorer, more rustic convent up on the slopes of Monte Subasio, the convent of Panzo. There the second drama occurred seven days later. Clare's younger sister, Agnes, only fourteen years old, ran away to join her. The fury of the Offreducci clan at the defiant disappearance of two of their nubile young females can be imagined. Twelve of the kinsmen rode out, like some avenging posse, to bring Agnes back. They manhandled her till she fainted; and then shame, Clare's reproaches, and, according to the legend, a miracle saved her; and perhaps also fear of how the pious and strong-minded Ortolana would react if a dozen men came back with her bleeding and bruised daughter.

At this stage all Assisi must have been abuzz; and Bishop Guido took a hand. Since Clare and her sister obstinately refused to accept the Benedictine Rule and neither could nor would return to their family, somewhere must be found for them to live. Probably Pacifica di Guelfuccio, who knew everyone involved and who was trusted by Ortolana, arranged it all. At any rate the bishop, who had had no church to give Francis, suddenly found when the noble ladies started to bring pressure to bear, that, after all, he did have San Damiano to dispose of. Francis was called in to dictate a written 'form of life'. And there at San Damiano, which he had rebuilt, perhaps two miles from Santa Maria degli Angeli, Clare and her sister and Pacifica, who joined them almost immediately, set up their little community that was, in the years to come, to attract many other noble ladies of Assisi and indeed not only the third of the sisters, Beatrice, but the mother, Ortolana, too. Three years later, by wish of Francis, Clare was to assume the title of abbess. It was all most respectable. They lived an enclosed life, with this difference only from the Benedictine nuns, that Clare, despite the pleas of successive Popes, refused any endowment of San Damiano with property. Strict poverty they observed; and Clare, with her basic sense of discipline and proportion, never again tried to break free. But it was a far cry from the free life of the road, in poverty and holiness and chastity, by the side of her beloved, for which she had yearned.[13]

NOTES

1 The Arthurian quotations are from Sir Thomas Malory's *Works* (O.U.P., 1954). He lived two hundred years after Francis had died, but all his material was 'drawyn oute of the Freynshe,' i.e. from the romances of Champagne and their successors.

2 Father Kapitan von Essen of the Friars Minor, in his most scholarly study, the *Origins of the Franciscan Order* (published in translation by the Franciscan Herald Press of America in 1970), demonstrates (1) that Francis intended to found a religious Order, not a group of Christians living in the world; (2) that his order was to be exclusively a *Fraternitas*, a brotherhood, open; to men of all classes but to men alone. He also insists on the novelty of the style; and in particular on the fact that the Order had one common superior but no community organization. The members were linked by personal bond to this superior, by the same style of clothing and of prayers, and by the institution of the General Chapter. Father von Essen does not take the further step and ask himself from where Francis derived his inspiration for an Order linked in these ways.

As far as I know, no-one has studied the similarities or differences between the structure of Francis' Order and those of the various Orders of knighthood existing in his day. This would be a fascinating field of research.

3 Francis always wanted his followers to welcome the rich and the noble '*alacriter et benigne*'. He told them to judge and despise no man 'not even those who find their delight in their eating and drinking and clothes. For our God is their God too and he who called us can also call them.' It was totally against his teaching then to taunt a noble or an Emperor, whether in public or in private, for ostentatious pomp.

4 The sequence of local events over this period is as follows:

1205, 29 July. Philip of Swabia's Imperial Diploma to Assisi – in effect a defensive and offensive alliance against Perugia, favourable to local autonomy. This led to the return of the first wave of nobles.

1205, 31 August. Ordinance of the *Podestà* of Perugia, Giovanni di Guidone di Papa; an attempted counter-measure which none took seriously.

1208, 21 June. Death of Philip of Swabia, followed by undisputed choice of Otto as Emperor.

1209, 1 September. Ordinance of the *Podestà* of Perugia, Uguccione di Guidone di Giovane, read out before the bishop's palace at Assisi; and followed next day by a Declaration of the Terms of Peace ('*Lodo*') at Collestrada – which the authorities of Assisi failed to attend.

1209, 4 October. Coronation of Otto by Pope Innocent in Rome.

1210, 28 February. '*Promissio Papae in Civitatem Perusii*' – papal alliance with Perugia.

1210, ? March. Otto, by way of retaliation, invests Azzo of Este with *Le Marche* and

Dipold with the Duchy of Spoleto – on terms that, if applied, would restore the *status quo* of pre-1198. This is a development as baffling for the exile nobles with the Perugians as it is for the middle-classes, who want freedom from the Church and from Perugian domination but also their local autonomy. It is the catalyst that leads to reconciliation.

1210, 4 November. Otto's triumphant entry into Perugia.

1210, 9 November. The '*Carta Pacis*' ending class warfare in Assisi.

It is of course possible that Otto remained in Assisi for several days; and that the '*Carta Pacis*' was his work or at any rate his inspiration rather than, as I have suggested, a natural reaction of all classes to future uncertainties after his departure. Fortini, the great expert on local affairs, glosses over this difficulty. He also rejects the theory, put forward by many Italian writers, that Francis was very influential in obtaining the settlement. The theory is based on the fact that the pact was made between the '*Majores*' and the '*Minores*'; therefore the use of the title '*Fratres Minores*' by Francis is highly significant of where his political sympathies lay. On the other hand (1) Francis *never* gives this in any account as a reason for choosing the title. (2) Although in this particular communal document, the pact, the nobles and the middle-classes are defined by the terms '*Majores*' and '*Minores*', in earlier documents other Latin terms are used. (3) If Francis' group by its title was obviously anti-noble within the framework of Assisi's politics, it is amazing to say the least that recruits of the noble families including even one of the two surviving lords of Sassorosso, Leonardo di Gislerio, were so ready to join him. I therefore agree in this instance with Fortini.

5 It is Fra Jordan in his *Chronicle* who tells us that Francis first preached at San Giorgio, and St. Bonaventure who mentions that while at Rivo Torto Francis went up to preach in the cathedral 'as usual.'

6 Why did Bishop Guido not give Francis San Damiano – seeing that it was available soon after for Clare? A proof of the *froideur* existing between himself and Francis is the story, told with great relish in most of the accounts, of how he came down to see Francis at the Portiuncula, pushed his way into the cell without knocking, and was immediately thrust out again violently 'by the will of God, because he was not worthy to see the saint.' Whereupon he left, trembling and stunned, after confessing his fault to the brothers. It would have been natural for Guido to feel pique at Francis' close relations with the canons of San Rufino, and some jealousy at the success of his new-fangled preaching. When one considers how the relations between Pierre de Vaux and the Bishop of Lyons had deteriorated in similar circumstances, it is amazing that it was only pique and only a passing phase. Perhaps this was because Francis always insisted on signs of outward reverence for the clergy. Not only did he order the brothers to prostrate themselves whenever they saw a church or a crucifix; but whenever they might meet a priest, they were to bow before him and kiss his hands – or, if he was riding, 'even the hooves of his horse.' One pictures Bishop Guido assuaging his wounded pride by gazing down from his saddle at a bevy of bent backs as the brothers scrabbled out of the woods and seized his, no doubt astonished, charger's fetlocks. I have myself had my hand kissed by a serf when on horseback in Ethiopia, and can bear witness there is no experience quite so gratifying to the pride.

7 It may seem that Francis' attitude to property was hypocritical. He could hardly claim to live 'without property' when he not only accepted but asked for a church and land for huts. The distinction between outright ownership and usufruct was academic in practice. This is a question that has always baffled the Franciscan Order and kept it in a state of perpetual tension. Father von Essen's view is that by the force of circumstances, as numbers expanded a

community of monastic-style life grew up with (a) fixed dwellings (b) punitive powers (c) studies. Certainly, at the present day, there is no distinction at all, as regards the possession of communal property, between the Franciscans and the Benedictines. The Order has completely abandoned not only the objections to outright ownership but the rule-of-thumb that Francis evolved – small, not large, churches; minimal furniture; dwelling-places in wood and clay, not in brick or stone; no estates or properties or houses bringing in rent. There has been a surrender to materialism all along the line; and, most shockingly of all, present-day Franciscans with their worldly common sense seem to have not the slightest uneasiness of conscience. The commercialization of the Portiuncula is particularly repellent.

8 Who, as Francis' original companion on the road, appears more than any other of the fraternity to have adopted, much more openly than Francis, the language and similes of chivalry. Cf. his *Sayings* (passim).

9 See the *Life of Fra Juniper* (chapter VII) for the story of Fra Giles and the three ways of dealing with 'the traitor carnal desire', which I have somewhat simplified. See *Fra Giles' Sayings* (the chapter on Holy Chastity) for his full views on 'the flesh, which is the devil's knight.' He obviously disapproved of Francis' rather exhibitionistic methods. 'If we would conquer carnal sins and obtain the virtues of chastity,' he told an enquiring brother, 'we may better obtain them by humility and by good and wise spiritual regimen than by our presumptuous austerity and violence of penance.' In fact Fra Giles, like a crusty Sancho Panza, came to disapprove more and more of his leader's quixotism.

10 First and foremost to the shades of G. K. Chesterton, in whose view there is no story about which even the most sympathetic critics have been more bewildered and misleading than 'the beautiful friendship of St. Francis and St. Clare.'
 'What is the matter with those critics is that they will not believe that a heavenly love can be as real as an earthly love? The moment it is treated as real, like an earthly love, their whole riddle is easily resolved.'

11 The sources for the life of St. Clare are basically two: (1) the *Legend of St. Clare*, probably written by Thomas of Celano, particularly the apparently purer version which Fra François Dupuis translated into French in the sixteenth century; (2) the *Acts* of the process of her canonization, and the Bull of canonization itself. The best short study in English is the pamphlet entitled *The First Lady Poverty*, written by Sister Felicity and published in 1973 by the Mater Dei Press, St. Augustine's Abbey, Ramsgate.

12 See chapter 13 of the *Second Rule*. It reads: 'If a brother is tempted and commits fornication, he must be deprived of his habit. By his wickedness he has lost the right to wear it and so he must lay it aside completely and be dismissed from the Order. Then he should do penance for his sins.' This seems shakingly emotional in tone and shockingly unlike Francis in its lack of compassion. Fornication is the one mortal sin which, he implies, cannot be forgiven, is indeed unforgivable. The only other case in which he directs expulsion is in the case of non-Catholic faith or practices – i.e. Catharism. But here he qualifies the order for expulsion with the saving phrase: 'Unless he repents.' Even heresy is less dangerous, therefore, Francis felt, than the sexual urge.

13 The interpretation I have given here is obviously romanticized; it is based, however, on the facts as we know them, and in my view is the only interpretation that can explain these facts.

Francis was (1) tormented by sexual urges (2) in later life suspiciously misogynistic (3) always self-conscious about his own middle-class origins.

Clare was (1) nubile (2) in later life always pathetically eager to see an elusive Francis (3) noble.

The two, each with a companion, met secretly for a year.

On Palm Sunday 1212 Clare abandoned her family home, came down by night to the Portiuncula, exchanged her finery for the habit of poverty, and cut her hair. She took refuge at the Benedictine convent of San Paolo, from which her family tried unsuccessfully to retrieve her; then at the Benedictine convent of Panzo, where she was joined by her sister and a violent episode occurred. Finally the girls were installed at San Damiano, the little church about half a mile outside Assisi that Francis had restored; and there, for the rest of their lives, they lived.

These are the bare bones of the story, and of the situation. Various attitudes, both at the time and in later years, need to be explained away; and this is what I have attempted to do.

I have, I believe, incorporated into my account every major incident – except the famous scene in the cathedral on the morning of Palm Sunday, where Bishop Guido at high Mass came forward to give Clare a palm. Does this gesture signify that he was in the secret? If so, the night move from the Portiuncula to San Paolo was not a panic measure but carefully planned, with the previous consent of the Abbess (Sibilla? A papal Bull tells us a Sibilla was Abbess in 1201) and of the bishop; and, of course, of Francis and Clare. This is possible but seems less in character. The gaps in the accounts are such that hypotheses can never be entirely proved or disproved, and there is of course only a margin between imaginative sympathy and imaginative fantasy.

❧ The Questing Urge ❧

9: The Questing Urge

John of Brienne

Among the knights of Champagne who had set out with Walter of Brienne to Apulia was his brother John. With Walter killed, his following had dispersed; and John of Brienne drifted back to the rich lands of France. There Count Thibaud of Champagne had, on his sad death, left a young widow, Blanche, a Spanish princess, the daughter of Sancho of Navarre. She ruled from Troyes as Regent for her young son, the little Thibaud IV, and John of Brienne, that lusty knight, helped the young widow Regent to pass her days and, it was said, her nights agreeably.

Over the seas the Fourth Crusade, which Count Thibaud had inspired and would have led, had come to an impious halt with the sack of Constantinople and the conquest of the Eastern Empire. Yet this display of power, though not as it happened directed against them, had made the Saracens wary. The great Saladin was dead; Saphadin, his more cautious brother, had granted a five-year truce to the Christians of Outremer who held out in the coastal strip of the Holy Land. But the five-year truce was due to expire very soon. In great alarm the barons of Outremer sent appeals to the Pope and to the King of France.

Their young queen, Marie of Jerusalem, who in fact ruled from Acre, was in any case of the blood of the house of Champagne. She was cousin-germain to the little Thibaud IV, for her mother Queen Isabelle had married Henry of Champagne, on whose death at Acre Blanche and her husband had succeeded to the county. Outremer and Champagne were almost twinned; as for Blanche the Regent, she too had been brought up in a little kingdom continually warring against or negotiating with the Saracens. She, though no blood relation, could sympathize with the difficulties of a perpetually crusading and perpetually threatened outpost of Christendom.

Marie of Jerusalem was seventeen. What the barons wanted the King of France to provide was a husband, for a husband from France would mean expeditions, men and money. Philippe Auguste, however, was always careful to avoid entanglements that would distract him from his task of driving out the English. Just as ten years before he had virtually chosen Walter of Brienne to marry Sibylla and try the fairly hopeless adventure of reconquering Sicily, so now he designated the rather hoary John of Brienne as consort of Marie. Besides, it was his duty as overlord of the little Thibaud IV to put a stop to a situation that was scandalous and looked like becoming dangerous. Philippe Auguste was no partisan of troubadours, courts of love and adulterous devotion. John of Brienne would be better overseas.

The Pope welcomed Philippe Auguste's decision; he himself, he wrote to Paris, would be lending John of Brienne fourteen hundred marks of silver. And Philippe Auguste, obligingly, dowered him with an even greater sum. John of Brienne may not have been the answer to the barons' dreams: he was not a great noble, nor well known, nor rich in his own right; but he had support, and a reputation as a military leader, and they accepted him.

He may not have been the answer to Marie's dreams either; but she accepted him too.[1] They were married on 10 September 1210 at Acre; and on 3 October John of Brienne was crowned King of Jerusalem at Tyre. The five-year truce had ended in July; the Saracens did not renew it. John took the field.

With money, but without fresh men, John was soon in difficulties. Innocent followed events in Outremer with keen anxiety; and by June next year was writing with urgent desperation to the Christians in Georgia to beg them to arm an expedition and help. John's appeals to the Pope and to Christendom in general became more and more anguished; and though Innocent knew from sad experience that a crusade will not be improvised, Christendom responded.

It was the most extraordinary and most impressive of all the many responses to the many appeals from the Holy Land. A shepherd boy aged twelve, Stephen of Cloyes near Orleans, began preaching a crusade: by the end of June of the year 1212, thirty thousand children, not one in their teens, with their oriflammes and leaders had gathered at Vendome. They marched out of France into the lands of the Empire, from Tours first to Lyons and then down the valley of the Rhone, welcomed by the inhabitants everywhere; and at Marseilles they embarked for the Holy Land – and no more was heard of them. Meanwhile another boy, Nicholas, had collected another band of children, almost as large, in Germany; they gathered, and came down to Rome to ask for the Pope's blessing.

All Europe rang with stories of this adventure of adventures. For once the platitudes that statesmen in every age pour out, about the future being in the hands of the younger generation, were being taken literally: while knights and nobles and ecclesiastics hesitated, the children of Christendom were marching to the aid of the Kingdom of Jerusalem.

Inevitably Francis was caught up in the ferment. Years earlier he had set out on horseback and in armour to join Walter of Brienne. Now, when even the children were taking the Cross and setting out for the Holy Land, how could he fail to answer the appeal of John of Brienne? Crusades needed prayers as well as weapons, religion as well as knights. His guise was different but his heart was the same. And in any case it was becoming almost traditional that when things went too wrong or scandals and dissension caused by his activities blew up in Assisi, Francis should set off, north or south, on crusade. It is amazing only that he stayed to see Clare properly settled at San Damiano; when she was settled, he must have been ready for any excuse to set out on the road for simple adventure; and leave all the strain and complication of family quarrels and intrigues and reproaches far, far behind him. With a great sigh of relief, he dusted his hands, hitched up his tunic – and was off. According to Thomas of Celano, he was 'burning intensely with the desire for holy martyrdom.' Certainly he had itchy feet.

As far as one can make out from the very sketchy accounts, Francis found a ship and set out alone. This was against all his own rules for the brothers, of going two by two throughout the world. We do not even know how or where he found the ship, or anything at all about it. However, in the *Life of Fra Giles* there is a chapter that tells us how 'by leave of St. Francis, Fra Giles went to visit the Holy Sepulchre of Christ, and came to the port of Brindisi, and there he abode many days, because no ship was ready.' Giles, it is clear, was alone too. I think therefore that it is possible, indeed probable, that Francis and Giles set off together on the great adventure, as they had set off earlier on the road to Le Marche when there were only four brothers in all. On that first journey Giles the peasant had more or less been Francis' squire. But since then much had changed, and in particular a woman had appeared. Giles had been excluded from any contact with Clare and her adventures, to which Bernard and Philip, of better birth and less boorish manners, had been admitted. Being human, he was probably hurt; having a mind of his own, he almost certainly spoke out. It is hardly fanciful to picture Francis and Giles setting out together for the Holy Land in high spirits that gradually disappeared as Giles took the opportunity to lecture Francis, rather like the traditional British nanny, on his behaviour in the Clare affair. But even old family retainers can go too far; and even saints can lose their tempers when they are accused of faults of character and imprudence in action, particularly if they know the accusations to be justified. Francis and Giles split up; and each attempted to make his own way to the Holy Land.

Ironically enough, it was Giles who succeeded, and Francis who once again failed. His ship was blown off course, and anchored in the region of Slavonia, on the Adriatic coast of what is now Yugoslavia. It must have been late autumn or winter, for it was apparently impossible to find any other ship sailing for Cyprus or Acre that year. After various difficulties Francis managed to stow away on a ship returning to Ancona. His attempt to join John of Brienne in Outremer had been as abortive as his attempt ten years earlier to join Walter in Apulia.[2]

With his usual charm he appears to have enrolled a companion in Dalmatia. The two of them did not head back for Assisi from the coast, but set out preaching, all round Le Marche, heading slowly north. There he had a consolation for his disappointment, of just the sort that would appeal to him. A man gave him a mountain in Tuscany.

The story is told in the *Fioretti*, and is dated very firmly in 1224. However, communal archives show that the mountain was in fact transferred legally and in due form on 8 May 1213.[3] So, with due allowance being made for possible inaccuracy, here is the story as the *Fioretti* tells it.

Francis and his companion were passing by the foot of the *castello* of the Counts of Montefeltro, at which there was a great festival and banquet being held to celebrate the knighting of one of the sons of the Count. Francis joined in the celebrations by climbing on a little wall and preaching, naturally enough, of the sufferings of holy martyrs and the tribulations and temptations of holy virgins, so beautifully that it was 'as if it were the angel of God that spoke.' Among those listening enthralled was a great and rich noble of Tuscany, Messer Orlando of Chiusi in Casentino – who buttonholed Francis, consulted him in private about the salvation of his soul, and finally, late that night, said this to him: 'I have in Tuscany a mountain most apt for devotion, the which is called the mountain of La Verna, exceeding solitary and passing well fitted for such as would do penance in a place remote from men, and desire a life of solitude. If it pleases thee, gladly would I give it to thee and thy companions for the salvation of my soul.'

Technically, Francis should have refused such an offer. A mountain after all is property. Instead, 'St. Francis hearing so liberal an offer of a thing which he much desired' – charming admission of inconsistency – 'was exceeding joyful thereat, and praising and thanking first God, and then Messer Orlando, he spoke unto him thus: "Messer Orlando, when you shall have returned to your home, I will send unto you some of my companions and you shall show them that mountain: and if it shall seem to them fitted for prayer and for the doing of penance, even from this moment do I accept your charitable offer." '

And so Francis hurried back to the Portiuncula. He had no tales to tell of the Holy Land but he could at least announce something resembling a quest and an adventure. Two of the brothers – we do not know which two – immediately set out for Messer Orlando's castle of Chiusi. They were welcomed with great joy and sent off to inspect the mountain, with an escort of fifty armed men to defend them from the wild beasts – clearly there was no danger of the mountain becoming an income-bearing asset. Finally 'they came unto a part of the mountain exceedingly well fitted for devotion and for contemplation, in the which part there was some level ground, and that place they chose for their habitation and for that of St. Francis; and with the aid of those armed men which were in their company they made a little cell with the boughs of trees, and in this wise in the name of God they accepted and took possession of the mountain of La Verna and of the place of the brothers in that mountain, and departed and returned to St. Francis.'

This would seem to show that the two friars who had been sent out from the Portiuncula were there in Tuscany on 8 May when the deed of transfer was registered,[3] and that therefore they had time, just, to be back at the Portiuncula, with their mission accomplished, for the Pentecost Chapter.

When, before going to Rome and the Pope, the first eight brothers had set out in pairs towards all the points of the compass, they had no notion or plan about when to return, and it had been more luck than good sense (see page 120) that had brought them all back to the woods below Assisi at about the same time. Since then, Francis had set up a tradition: just as King Arthur had decreed for the knights of the Round Table, so Francis decided that his fellowship should reassemble at their base, at the Portiuncula, for the 'hyghe feste of Pentecost.' Wherever they had been on their quests, as Pentecost drew near, Sir Launcelot and Sir Gawain and Sir Percival and all the rest had abandoned their adventures and ridden back from east and west and south and north towards Camelot. Just so, the roads and paths leading towards Assisi were to see, as the years went by, year after year the grey brotherhood hastening in from all sides to gather around Santa Maria degli Angeli and tell the tales of their travels to their fellows.

So, at Pentecost in the year 1213, the brothers assembled to welcome the gift of a mountain – and, very possibly, to hear the tale of Fra Giles back from the Holy Land, with exemplary stories of how he had had to work as a water-carrier in Brindisi and as a basket-weaver on his return to Ancona, in exchange for bread on which to live – but never, of course, for money.

Meanwhile, though none on the Children's Crusade had ever reached the Holy Land,[4] John of Brienne had, on his own, justified his choice by Philippe Auguste, and beaten back the Saracens so successfully that they accepted, in July 1212, a new five-year truce. The pressure was off in Outremer, but, at the other end of Latin Christendom in Spain, the Muslim power was attacking.

The Route to Spain

In the year 1118 Ibn Tumart, a Berber of the Atlas mountains, went by foot from city to city in Morocco preaching penance and a life of Koranic purity and poverty. His followers were called the Al-Mowahhidun, the People of Unity, whom the Christians came to know as the Almohades. Though Ibn

Tumart, their founder, died in 1130, by the middle of the century his successor had rooted out the ruling dynasty in North Africa and was casting greedy eyes across the straits, at the land the Moors knew as Al-Andalus.[5]

The great days of the Caliphate of Cordoba, and the burning and sacking of the holy city of Santiago de Compostela by the Amir Mohammed al-Mansur the Victorious, were long over. The little Christian pockets in the north had regrouped themselves under Sancho III the Great, of Navarre and Leon; only to divide again as the inheritance of his four sons. On the west the Count of Oporto had become the King of Portugal; to the east the Count of Barcelona had become the King of Aragon; and, most important of all, in the centre the Counts of Castile, splitting away from the Kingdom of Leon, had become kings too in their own right. It was Alfonso VI of Castile who, in 1085, had occupied the centre of Arab learning and culture, Toledo, and declared himself – till intolerance on both sides rendered the title meaningless – 'Emperor of the Two Religions.'

But, 150 years later, that was still the spirit that governed much of the relations between the five Christian kingdoms and the power of the Moors reconstituted by the Berber Almohades and their overlord, the Amir al Mu'minin, as he was hereditarily entitled. Even Sancho of Navarre, the father of the Countess Blanche of Champagne, was known to have paid a suspiciously friendly visit to the 'Miramolin' and was believed to be in secret alliance with him. For the King of Castile, Alfonso VIII, had been abandoned by Leon and Navarre and terribly defeated at Alarcos by Yakub-al-Mansur, he for whom the Giralda had been erected at Seville. And Yakub's son and successor, the new 'Miramolin', Mohammed ibn Yakub al Nasir, had rolled the Christian powers back to Madrid and Guadalajura, and in the year 1211 had brought over so huge an army from Morocco, over half a million foot-soldiers and nearly a hundred thousand cavalry, that all Christendom below the Pyrenees, and possibly above it too, was threatened. As the armies of the Almohades, whose strength had been tested in the autumn campaign, prepared to come out of winter quarters, the Christian kings, even the pleasure-loving Pedro II of Aragon, banded together – and appealed to the Pope.

Never was there a man so snowed down with appeals for aid on all sides as Innocent. He reacted with his usual vigour; on 23 May 1212 he declared a crusade in Spain and announced a three-day fast throughout Christendom on bread and water. The chivalry of Spain, reinforced by the barons of northern France from an apparently pacified Languedoc, gathered in immense confusion but great numbers at Toledo. On 3 July, however, as the armies marched forward, 26,000 French, disappointed by the lack of booty, abandoned the Christian host, leaving only the Archbishop of Narbonne with 130 knights. Four days later, happily, Sancho of Navarre arrived, and the three kings, under the orders of Alfonso of Castile and the guidance of the Archbishop of Toledo, led their own hosts and the military Orders of the Knights of Santiago, of San Juan, of Calatrava, and of Alcantara, towards an encounter that appeared to be hopeless. On Monday, 16 July the 'Miramolin' set up his golden throne by the field of Las Navas de Tolosa, near Jaen, as his enormous armies moved forward to crush the Christians. That night that golden throne was on its way to Innocent, an outward sign of the greatest triumph that Christian paladins had won over the Moors since Poitiers and Roncesvalles; and the greatest empire in the Muslim world began to break up.

'The Emperor Charles, Roland and Oliver,' Francis would, as the *Fioretti* reports, tell his friars, 'all paladins and valiant knights, who were mighty in battle, pressed the infidels even to death, sparing neither toil nor fatigue and gained a memorable victory for themselves, and by way of conclusion these holy martyrs died fighting for the faith of Christ.' The news of the fantastic triumph in Spain, the first real Christian success to counter the fall of Jerusalem to Saladin, set all Christendom abuzz. Alfonso, Pedro and Sancho, the kings, were the worthy heirs and successors of Charles, Roland and Oliver. Francis may have been at sea or in Slavonia at the time, but certainly by the winter of 1212 he would have heard the great news from Spain, and at the assembly of the brotherhood at Pentecost in the year 1213, it is natural that he should have decided on his next adventure. Like the paladins and valiant knights whom he praised, 'the prize of martyrdom still attracted him so strongly,' says the *Three Companions,* 'that the thought of dying for Christ meant more to him than any merit he might earn by the practice of virtue.' And so, Thomas of Celano adds, 'After a not very long time he started on a journey toward Morocco, to preach the gospel of Christ to Miramolin and his people.' Once again Francis was off on a crusade, and once again it was to end, though not so pathetically as before, in anticlimax.

At least he knew he could get there. There were Saracens within walking distance, no seas to cross, or winds to blow him off course. But it was a long, long walk. And it must not be forgotten that the walk inevitably took him along the shores of the Mediterranean, through Provence across into Languedoc, and almost certainly Aragon as well. For he followed the road to Santiago de Compostela.

It was the natural road to follow. After Rome itself and leaving aside the Holy Land, the pilgrimage to the shrine of St. James was the most famous in Christendom. And before seeking martyrdom among the Moors, any man would naturally go to celebrate the great triumph of Christian arms and Spanish chivalry at Santiago – and Francis in particular.

The feast of St. James falls on 25 July, and if Francis and his companions had set out after the Pentecost gathering of the year 1213, they could have been there in time for the great celebrations. I believe, however, that they did not set out until, at earliest, the winter and, at latest, the following year; and the reason was this: that their route lay through Toulouse.

The *Camino de Santiago* – the Road to Santiago – strictly speaking indicates only the very last stretch of the route, the road that ran right across the north of Spain, from Navarre into Leon, Castile and Galicia. All over Europe, however, other *caminos* wound, like a spider's web, to join together at different points, the greatest meeting-place being at St. Jean Pied-du-Port north of Roncesvalles, where the three great routes leading down through France, from the sanctuaries at Vezelay, Orleans and Le Poys, converged. It was not, however, till well inside Spain, at Puente la Reina, south of Pamplona, that the southern route linked up like some delayed tributary with the main stream of pilgrimage. This was the route that Francis took. There were, of course, other roads that he and his companions could have used to reach the north-west tip of Spain, but in a sense there was something sacrosanct about the *caminos*. They were laid out specially for pilgrims, with hospices for their (poor) comfort all along the way and, more significantly, passed through sanctuaries a visit to which formed an essential part of the pilgrimage. In other words it is almost inconceivable that Francis and his companions, who would have been in their element among the throng of barefoot, ragged, penitential but triumphantly joyous pilgrims, should have diverged from the proper route. And the proper route, the *Camino del Sud*, led them from Italy to Arles, the seat of an archbishopric, then straight west across the Massif Central to Toulouse, and from Toulouse down through the County of Comminges to cross the Pyrenees at the Col de Semport, and pass through the ancient capital of the Kingdom of Aragon, Jaca.

This, for all pilgrims from Italy and Provence, was the road to Santiago; and if there is one thing certain about an episode of Francis' life that remains extremely sketchy, it is that it was not in the summer of 1213 that he and his companions followed that route. Why? Because it would have taken them through lands where a most brutal civil war between Christians was being fought.

Pedro of Aragon

King Pedro of Aragon, energetic, amorous, bold, gay-hearted and warlike, was an attractive figure of chivalry, though by no means a perfect Christian. Yet whatever sins men might rightly accuse him of, none could accuse him of heresy or of feebleness in supporting the Catholic faith and the Catholic Church. He

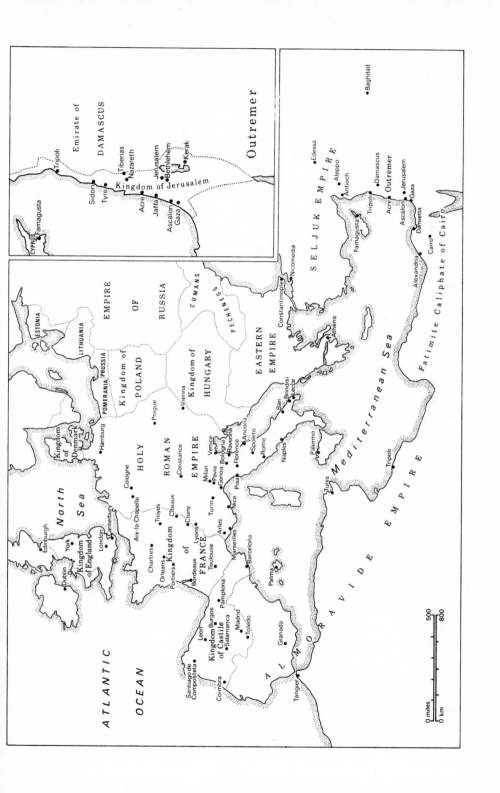

had become one of the several princes in Christendom to swear direct feudal allegiance for his kingdom to the Pope. 'I will be true and loyal to my Lord the Pope Innocent,' he had sworn in Rome, at the little church of San Pancrazio, where the Pope had crowned him king; and the ties between the two of them had continued very close.

There was never the slightest suspicion that Pedro was infected by the beliefs of the Cathars; yet the invasion of the County of Toulouse by the barons of northern France had left him distinctly uneasy. His sister was married to the irresolute and dissolute Count Raymond, a man 'mistrusted by all, mistrusting himself'; he himself had married the heiress Marie of Montpellier, and the Counts of Foix and Comminges owed feudal duty for their territories to himself as well as to his brother-in-law Count Raymond. Therefore the King of Aragon watched with an uneasy eye as the Frenchmen sacked Beziers and captured yet another of his own fiefs, Carcassonne; and his uneasiness grew, as, with the Cathar power apparently crushed in a brief two months, the northern barons and prelates proceeded none the less to harry Count Raymond's territories and to harry the count himself, using heresy as a pretext for what was becoming more and more clearly a campaign designed to acquire power and territory.

Pedro himself was present, a cynical onlooker, at the Synod of Alers in 1211 when the two papal legates imposed fourteen demands, many of them outrageous, upon Count Raymond as a price of lifting the excommunication that lay upon his person and the interdict that lay over his lands. Not only were all his castles to be dismantled and all his troops disbanded but all his subjects – he in whose vast territories there were, in a famous phrase, 'as many cities as there are days in a year' – were to pay extra taxes to the Church, have fasting imposed, and, worst insult of all in the homeland of the troubadours, wear only dark cloth, whatever their condition or status. Furthermore, Count Raymond was then to expiate his past faults by going on crusade until such time as the legates should give him permission to return. Such an ultimatum was an insult to the whole south. Count Raymond, with the approval of the King of Aragon, rejected the conditions and quitted the Synod. The legates declared him an enemy of the Church and his possessions open to whoever might take them. Innocent confirmed the decree. Land-greedy 'crusaders' appeared from France, Germany, Lombardy and even Slavonia to join Simon de Monfort's ranks. Dominic of Guzman was at his side, as were Count Raymond's two bitterest enemies, Fulques, Bishop of Toulouse, and the Abbot Arnold-Amanry of Cîteaux. They were joined by the Archbishop of Reims, the Archbishop of Rouen, the Bishop of Paris and many other prelates. There was civil war in Toulouse itself, and sieges and massacres all over Languedoc. On 5 May Lavaur fell. 'Our pilgrims', recorded a chronicler, 'with immense pleasure burnt a very great number of heretics.'

This is the sort of atmosphere that may have appealed to Dominic; it could never have attracted Francis. Quite apart from his personal chivalrous character, all the evidence indicates that his only concern with Catharism was to keep all his brothers as far away from it as he possibly could and to avoid the slightest contagion of a heresy that he knew only too well to be extremely attractive. What he never, ever, showed was the least desire to set out and convert the Cathars. Francis drew a clear line, even if Christendom did not, between a real crusade and a persecution dressed up in the finery of a crusade. Of the one he was all in favour; the other he shunned as he had once shunned the lepers' hospitals, holding his metaphorical nose and looking the other way.

The threat of the Saracens diverted, momentarily, Pedro of Aragon's attention from the threat to his northern flank. After the great victory at Las Navas, in the summer of 1212, Pedro was one of the heroes of Christendom: a defender of the faith, if ever a king merited that title. He looked back over his shoulder to find Simon of Montfort besieging Toulouse; and defending Toulouse not only his brother-in-law Count Raymond but his vassals the Counts of Foix and Comminges, who looked to him for protection. The counts appealed to Pedro of Aragon; and Pedro of Aragon appealed to the Pope. Innocent hesitated and seemed to relent. In January 1213 letters were sent out from Rome ordering, on Pedro's request, a local council, a halt to the persecution, and that Simon of Montfort should only be allowed to hold Carcassonne if he swore allegiance to the King of Aragon. But at the same time the papal legates had themselves called a Council at Lavaur; and their letters to Rome screaming abuse, heresy and treachery, crossed with the Pope's. 'Arm yourself, my Lord Pope', they wrote, 'with the zeal of Phinees, annihilate Toulouse, that Sodom, that Gomorrah, with all the wretches it contains; let not the tyrant, the heretic Raymond, nor even his young son, lift up his hand; already more than half crushed, crush him to the utmost.'

Was this the sort of atmosphere in which Francis could possibly have chosen to cross the lands of Toulouse, Comminges and Aragon?

While sieges and fighting continued, the Pope and Pedro exchanged messages. It is impossible not to sympathize with Innocent's predicament. He relied on messages and reports; but utterly conflicting reports were coming in from two sides – on the one from great prelates of France and his own legates, on the other from a most Christian king, his own vassal. He hesitated as long as he could; but on 1 June he made up his mind against the legate-murderer Count Raymond and wrote to King Pedro blaming him for the suppression of the truth and adjuring him to abandon the cause of the Count of Toulouse.

King Pedro, the victor of Las Navas de Tolosa, ignored the Pope and rode out to the wars. Even less likely is it that peace-loving Catholic pilgrims should have ventured along the *Camino del Sud* that summer. By the castle of Muret, south of Toulouse, de Montfort with only 400 squires and 1,000 men-at-arms fell on the Aragonese and the southern French. It is said that Dominic, who had assisted at the council of war before the battle, was praying during the battle at the Church of Saint James and that there the devotion of the rosary was revealed to him.

What we may be quite sure of is that Francis was nowhere near, on no side, praying for none. It was more a skirmish or an ambush than a full-scale battle; but in the fight King Pedro fell. And with his death the second phase of the armed resistance of Languedoc ended. His young son Jaime was captured – though very soon, on the Pope's express orders, released and restored to Aragon. The Counts of Foix and Comminges submitted, Count Raymond and his son, after a brief flight to England, returned and submitted too. A new papal legate, the Cardinal-Deacon of Santa Maria, Peter of Benevento, was sent out from Rome to supervise the pacification both in Toulouse and Aragon. Cardinal Robert de Courçon, the papal legate in France, descended and confirmed Simon de Montfort in his conquest; and the peace of exhaustion settled temporarily over the whole south.

It is only then, I believe, – that is to say, not before the winter of 1213–14 – that Francis could have set out happily, first for Santiago and then for martyrdom among the Moors.

In fact I would place his departure later, after the Pentecost meeting of 1214. For at the best of times it is a long trek from Assisi to Santiago and winter would have been the worst of times. Furthermore, like all pilgrims, he would surely have preferred to arrive in Santiago for the feast of the apostle.

I have myself covered, with my sister, on foot and on horseback part of the *camino*, from St. Jean Pied-du-Port to Santiago. We set out on 5 July, and arrived on the eve of the feast of the apostle, nineteen days later. I believe it took us twelve days from Puente la Reine, where Francis would have joined the main stream, to cross the breadth of northern Spain. It is difficult to calculate how much difference walking barefoot would have made for someone whose feet were as hardened as his; but surely the journey must have taken at least three weeks from Assisi to Arles, ten days from Arles to Toulouse, and another three weeks across the mountains from Toulouse to Puente la Reina. If the Pentecost Chapter of 1214 was short and sharp that would just about have had Francis and his companions, if they hurried, and if they had an uneventful journey, reaching Santiago by 25 July.

Old Companions – and New

According to the *Fioretti*, Francis took with him certain brothers including his first companion Bernard of Quintavalle; but poor Bernard was left behind in an unspecified town en route to look after a sick beggar. 'And Fra Bernard, humbly kneeling and bowing his head, received the obedience of the holy father and remained in that place.' Giles went to Santiago too – 'Once, in process of time, by leave of St. Francis,' as his *Life* puts it – but there is not the slightest hint that he set out with the other two, or the slightest extraneous reason to suppose that he did. Indeed it is hinted that he was becoming more and more of a lone wolf and a solitary, for there is no mention at all of the usual companion but simply of his starvation, sacrifice and humiliation – 'And so, as he went through the world, he was much derided and as ever he bore it with all tranquillity.'

The *Fioretti* knows nothing of Francis' intention to convert the Moors; but treats the episode merely as a simple pilgrimage to Santiago, with Francis finding Bernard again on the way back and giving him permission to go to Saint James the following year. However, Thomas of Celano writes that: 'The good God . . . withstood him to his face when he had travelled as far as Spain; and that he might not go any further, he recalled him from the journey he had begun by a prolonged illness.'

This is the first talk of any illness, the first outward sign of Francis' ever more feeble physical condition that was to bring him to an early death. If he had hurried to Santiago under the scalding summer sun of those endless Spanish plains, it is not surprising. It means that this Spanish expedition must have taken up most of the year – over two months to get there, a prolonged illness, and presumably a much slower journey back.

Once again it had been a failure. Despite heartening visions of the brotherhood's expansion that came to him in the cathedral of St. James itself Francis had still never set eyes on a Moor or a Saracen, though he had been so eager to get at them that, in Thomas of Celano's words, 'at times he left his companions on the trip behind and hurried to accomplish his purpose, drunk as it were in spirit.' The implication in the *Fioretti* is that he had, besides Bernard, at least two other companions on the trip, Masseo and Elias; for when they finally returned to the valley of Spoleto they went and dwelled together in a hermitage, where they spent much time in prayer and were visited by an angel disguised as a youth who zoomed Bernard over a river in the twinkling of an eye and whose name was Wonderful.[6]

Masseo was one of Francis' favourites, tall and handsome, but very much under Francis' thumb. He was the perfect foil for Francis' wild sense of humour and an old companion of local journeys, as the following famous story of the *Fioretti*, my own favourite, tells:

'One day, while St. Francis journeyed with the Fra Masseo, the said Fra Masseo went a little before: and arriving at a certain place where three roads met, which led to Florence, to Siena and to Arezzo, Fra Masseo said: "Father, by which way must we go?" St. Francis made answer: "By that which God shall will." Said Fra Masseo: "And how shall we be able to know the will of God?" St. Francis answered: "By the sign that I shall show thee. Wherefore I command thee by the duty of holy obedience, that in this place where three roads meet, on the spot where now thy feet are set, thou turn round and round as children do, and stop not from turning thyself unless I bid thee do so." ' And so Masseo twirled round and round and became dizzy and fell down and got up, and fell down again and got up again, until finally Francis told him to stop. He was facing Siena. 'St. Francis said: "That is the way whereby God wills that we go." Now, as they went by that way, Fra Masseo marvelled that St. Francis had made him do even as children do, before the worldly folk who were passing by: nevertheless, for reverence' sake, he ventured not to say anything to the holy father.'

Masseo was not the sort of character to persuade Francis, at Santiago de Compostela, to give up his idea of preaching to the Moors and return to Assisi again. But there must have been somebody capable of doing so: and, assuming that he was there, it could only have been Elias.

Elias is a key figure in the history of the Franciscan Order, and indeed from this time onwards in the story of Francis' life as well; but a key that baffles rather than reveals. For, unfortunately, he was to become so controversial that none of the writings about him can be taken *au pied de la lettre*; or at least none except perhaps for the references in the *First Life*, the only document written before his own disastrous period as Minister-General. He came, probably, from the hamlet of Beviglia outside Assisi; he may have earned his living as a young man in Assisi by making mattresses and teaching children to read, though Fortini judges this a later slander; he may have been, as Sabatier believed, Francis' companion as a treasure-seeker; he may have been Assisi's first consul (see page 56); he probably went to Bologna as a *scriptor* and, if not a lawyer, at least came to know something of the law for which the university was so famous. What attracted him to Francis' way of life is obscure, for he appears to have been, or to have become, ambitious. All we can say, with reasonable assurance, is that he was most energetic and capable, that the links between him and Francis became very close, that Francis came to rely on him more and more, and that he was devoted to Francis personally, though not to all of Francis' ideas. What we can also deduce from later events is that, like Francis, he was passionately interested in joining a crusade and preaching to the Saracens. Indeed it was probably only because his interest was as sincere and his determination as great that he succeeded in turning Francis homewards at Santiago and diverting him, one imagines with promises and assurances of a joint venture in the future, from the great longing, which even though ill, Francis must have had to go south and still further south, until he reached the Moors and martyrdom.

There was, however, more than mere personal assurances to back up Elias' persuasions. For as early as the spring of 1213, a new crusade was in the air. Though there was a five-year truce in the Holy Land, '*Li Rois Jehan, qui a Acre estoit, manda a l'apostole, por Diu, qu'il le secourust.*' Both John of Brienne and Pope Innocent knew that it needed a good four years or so to make the dispositions for a real crusade, to preach it, plan it, finance it, assemble it and finally to ship it. Together they looked ahead, as Saphadin and the Sultans on their side were doing, to 1217 and the end of the truce; and Pope Innocent, that man of immense energy, began to plan the second great crusade of his papacy. In the early months of the year 1213 'he sent word throughout Christendom to the best clerks whom he knew to preach the Cross.' Cardinal Robert de Courçon was sent as papal legate to France to preach the new crusade there, in the heartland that had always provided the core of crusaders; and so he did, till he was diverted by what seemed to be more pressing needs in Languedoc. Jacques de Vitry, a Canon of Oignies, and a great letter-writer and historian to-be, was appointed as future Bishop of Acre and meanwhile preached the Cross most fervently. But the preaching as such was merely a sideshow. On 19 April Innocent sent letters out from the Vatican to all the prelates and princes and great nobles of Christendom, announcing that, as a prelude to the reform of the Church and the reconquest of Jerusalem and the Holy Land, he was summoning a great Council to be held in Rome at the Lateran in two and a half years time: on 1 November 1215; and to it he, the Vicar of Christ on earth, summoned all to come, cardinals, archbishops, bishops, abbots, and representatives of all the kings, princes, dukes, great nobles and military Orders of Christendom. It was to be, as he intended it to be, the greatest ecclesiastical assembly of the Middle Ages. And a week later he sent a letter to Saphadin himself enjoining him to restore the holy places to the Christians; and this was the context in which a week later still he sent out that letter to Pedro of Aragon which urged him to abandon the quarrels of Toulouse and as a great Moor-slayer to turn all his energies to future preparations for what Innocent hoped would be the greatest and most carefully planned crusade of all time. To further men's concentration, the indulgences granted to those who went 'crusading' against the Moors in Spain or the heretics in Languedoc were revoked; only on this new crusade to save the Holy Land, could such indulgences in future be hoped for and gained.

The death of Pedro of Aragon, his own vassal, a king, a warrior and a potential leader of the crusade, was of course a stiff blow to Innocent. Yet it did at least mean that the civil war between Christian lords that might have spread from southern France and engulfed the energies and passions of Western Europe was suddenly and effectively snuffed out. Moreover, even before the fight at Muret, the Pope had been watching with pride and a joy that was almost paternal in its narrowest sense, the emergence of a young man that he believed and hoped and trusted would become the leader of his new crusade, the future Emperor Frederick II.

It is no part of this history to do more than sketch in the portrait of the greatest and most complex of the Hohenstaufens. Let it suffice to say that the hopes of half Christendom, and all the hopes of Pope Innocent, were centred on Frederick Roger. He was an extraordinarily talented and graceful young man, who seemed to combine the sense of loyalty and chivalry of his grand-father Barbarossa with the dash of the Hautevilles, all overlaid with the attrac-tive veneer of polyglot and polycultural civilization that a boyhood in Sicily perhaps alone could confer. Only son of an elderly mother, ward of an authori-tarian Pope, plaything of ambitious noblemen, married at the age of fifteen to the sister of Pedro of Aragon, herself already a king's widow, he might have turned out to be a very poor thing indeed, moody, weak and ineffectual. Instead, at the age of eighteen, he surprised all Europe with a sudden dash from Sicily to Swabia,[7] and a meteoric ascent thereafter. Chosen and crowned German King at Frankfurt and Mainz, he went on, with the support of Philippe Auguste, to defeat his rival Otto and capture the imperial Golden Eagle at Bouvines, and eventually to be crowned a second time, with the full ceremony of tradition, on the marble throne of Charlemagne at Aix-la-Chapelle. And not only was this young man graceful, he was also grateful. On 15 July 1215, less than four months before the great council at the Lateran was due to open, on the day of his coronation at Aix the new ruler, the young hero of twenty, solemnly took the Cross. Innocent's joy was unbounded. For here was an Emperor after any Pope's heart, devout, knightly and above all obedient, the secular ruler of Christendom, ready, willing and able to lead Christendom wherever its spiritual ruler might direct. Innocent, now in his middle fifties, had his heart's desire. The Fifth Crusade, led by a young Hohenstaufen and supported by all the chivalry of Europe could hardly fail to be the greatest crusade of all time, and to liberate Jerusalem. Old John of Brienne must have reflected with some amusement that it was the little baby whom his brother and he had set out to deprive of one kingdom nearly two decades earlier on whose help he was now counting to establish him firmly in another.

As for Francis, on that long and halting trudge back from the far corner of Spain, in the company of the ever-changing confraternity of the pilgrims' way, hardly a day could have passed without rumours and news and gossip of Barbarossa's grandson and his exploits in the north, and of the preparations for the great council that was to plan in Rome the reconquest of Jerusalem. In his boyhood he had hated the Germans as any high-spirited boy would hate a foreign occupier; in his manhood he had mistrusted the German Emperors and shown his mistrust, as any liege-man of the Lord Pope was bound to show his mistrust for the Pope's enemies in arms. But the new Emperor-to-be had been born in Le Marche, a baby in Umbria, brought up in Sicily. He was half-French by ancestry and the Lord Pope's ward, loyal and faithful to his guardian. He was the sort of Emperor Francis could hardly fail to approve.

Francis was certainly back in the woods below Assisi for the Pentecost assembly of the year 1215; and when a few weeks later Frederick was crowned in the city of Charlemagne and, with his paladins, vowed to go on crusade, and the news of this came to the valley of Spoleto, no-one's heart can have leapt with greater excitement than Francis'. Here was a crusade that he would not miss; and from this time forward his thoughts and all his intensity of feeling were directed towards the Fifth Crusade. He had set out so often, in so many guises, in so many directions, as one who had taken the Cross; and every time he had failed, for one reason or another, to arrive. This time, when the time came, he was determined not to fail.

Only a mile or two away from Santa Maria degli Angeli, almost looking down on Francis and his companions, Clare was waiting. All her life, she and her sisters, enclosed in the narrow confines of San Damiano, were to pass waiting with compassion and anxiety, for news; but she can never have been more anxious or found the waiting more agonizing than in those long months that passed while Francis was away seeking and perhaps winning martyrdom among the Moors. When she learnt that he was back, that he was back safe and un-martyred but ill and worn-out, her heart must have gone out to him: what else could she hope for but that he would come to her and allow her to nurse him back to health? Had she not at least a right to expect that? Surely he would come, and surely he would tell her the great tale of his journey to St. James, and talk over his future plans.

So the eager girl of twenty waited. But Francis, though he must often have gazed up at San Damiano, did not come. It was only a short walk to the place he had first shaped and loved and to the woman he had also shaped and also loved. But did he love her in Christ or in the flesh? Francis was prudent in this, in his relations with women, and perhaps in this alone was he circumspect –

hateful virtue – but, being Francis, he carried his prudence to extremes. Neither then nor for many years afterwards did he ever set foot in San Damiano or set eyes on Clare.

However, not being totally heartless, he did the next best thing: he sent Masseo to see her. And Masseo delighted her not only by his account of their journey to Spain and back but by telling her that Francis desired her advice. 'Dear brother,' he had said to Masseo, 'go to Sister Clare and tell her to pray devoutly to God, with one of her purer and more spiritual companions, that he may deign to show me what is best: either that I preach sometimes or that I devote myself only to prayer.' It was a most flattering request. It gave Clare something to think about. At the same time she must have realized instinctively that it was as much a test for her as a genuine request – indeed almost a trap; particularly when she learnt that, as if to ensure against wrong advice from her, Francis had also told Masseo to put the same question to Fra Silvester, the cathedral canon and the first priest to join the Order, who had retired from the city and was staying higher up still, near the Benedictines, up Monte Subasio.

Clare wisely waited till she had learnt what God had advised Silvester; and then even more wisely informed Masseo, on his second visit, that she and her companion had had the very same answer from God.

'Fra Masseo,' the *Fioretti* relates, 'therefore returned to St. Francis. And the Saint received him with great charity; he washed his feet and prepared a meal for him. And after he had eaten, St. Francis called Fra Masseo into the woods. And he knelt down before Fra Masseo, and baring his head and crossing his arms, St. Francis asked him: "What does my Lord Jesus Christ order me to do?"' Masseo repeated Silvester's reply: 'The Lord says that you are to tell brother Francis this: that God has not called him to this state only on his own account but that he may reap a harvest of souls and that many may be saved through him,' and added that Clare, too, wanted him to go about the world preaching.

This was the answer that Francis had been hoping for: in a way Clare's permission and Clare's approval and indeed Clare's command were necessary to him: heaven knows to what degree of morose depression he would have been reduced had she bidden him sit still. As it was, delighted at her loosening of what was a possible chain, 'he got to his feet all aflame with divine power, and said to Fra Masseo with great fervour: "So let's go – in the name of the Lord".'

The preaching tour that followed was the most successful ever. Francis 'set out like a bolt of lightning' with Masseo and Angelo, hushed the twittering swallows at Cannara who were interrupting his preaching, and a little further down the road, at Bevagna, left his companions, saying: 'Wait for me here on the road. I am going to preach to our sisters, the birds'.

This episode, perhaps the most famous of Francis' life, was really the beginning of his legend. The birds on the trees came down to him, and the birds in the fields stayed motionless, and Masseo loved to relate in later years how, after St. Francis had told them most beautifully to praise the Lord, and, making the sign of the Cross over them, had given them leave to depart, they rose into the air simultaneously; and how in the air, before flying away, they sang a wonderful song.[8]

Francis went on south to Alviano, Narni and the valley of Rieti that he so loved and where, in remote hermitages, he was to spend so many months of his last years, and in the end he went north towards Arezzo and 'his' mountain. But there his illness returned and he had to ride homewards on horseback. His greatest success, however, came in Le Marche, to the east, where he and Giles had tried to preach so unsuccessfully on their very first journey as penitents six years before.

This time all was different, and not merely the companions he took with him. 'When he entered any town,' the *First Life* relates, 'the clergy rejoiced, the bells were rung, the men were filled with happiness, the women rejoiced together, the children clapped their hands, and after taking branches from the trees they went to meet him singing.' And, Thomas of Celano adds rather significantly, 'while the faithful rejoiced, the heretics' – who in this region could only have been Cathars – 'slipped secretly away.' Francis by his sanctity was achieving in Italy what Dominic with all his intelligence and sincerity had failed to achieve in France; and that without ever a hint of bloodshed or burning. The first miracles of healing occurred; or at least were believed to occur. 'The people would offer Francis bread to bless, which they would then keep for a long time; and upon eating it they were cured of various illnesses. So also they very often cut off parts of his tunic in their very great faith, so much so that he was sometimes left almost naked.' At Ascoli Piceno thirty men, including significantly many priests, joined the fraternity. And then Thomas of Celano really launches out in his tales triumphant: 'How Francis healed a cripple at Toscanella and a paralytic at Narni;' 'How Francis gave sight to a blind woman; and how at Gubbio he straightened the hands of a crippled woman;' 'How Francis also cast out a devil at Città di Castello;' and so on and so forth, detailing numerous incidents.

But probably what Francis himself enjoyed most was a chance encounter at the monastery of San Severino near Ancona. There he met a *jongleur* who, in the shocked words of Thomas of Celano, 'was the most outstanding of those who sang impure songs'; or rather the *jongleur*, who was also a *troubador* and composed his own songs, met him. This fellow, or so at least he gave out, had been crowned King of the Verses by the Emperor; but none seemed to know which Emperor or when. He was probably one of those Italianized Frenchmen who lived impudently on their wits and their talents and who delighted an audience still largely influenced by the Cathars with satirical lampoons on the Catholic Church. The newly famed miracle-worker from Assisi must have seemed a good subject for the exercise of his talents. But on hearing Francis preach, 'there and then he said goodbye to popular renown and joined Francis by professing his Rule.' Francis re-christened him Pacificus 'in as much as he had been brought back to the peace of God.' 'The conversion of this man,' Thomas of Celano adds with portentous pomposity, 'was so much the more edifying to many in that the circle of his vain companions had been so large.' He may have been the first non-Italian to join the Order; he was certainly the first cosmopolite.

Francis loved Pacificus and loved to have him with him. Pacificus may have been half a goliard, but he was also a master of courtly song and a man who, knowing all the lays of chivalry, could sympathize with Francis' fantasies. Like Francis, too, he was a great man for visions: only his visions were usually blindingly colourful. Indeed when he had first heard Francis preach, he had seen fire flickering like two crossed swords from head to foot and from arm to arm in front of the preacher. And later he saw a cross on Francis' forehead 'which gave off from many coloured circles the beauty of a peacock.' But it was by Trevi, where he and Francis were travelling together, in the delight of new-found *camaraderie* (presumably having dispatched Masseo and Angelo elsewhere), that he had his greatest vision. Francis was keeping a vigil inside a little church; when he came out, Pacificus threw himself at Francis' feet, his arms in the form of a cross. 'He seemed to be completely transformed and spoke to Francis not as to a man living here on earth but as one of the elect already reigning in Heaven.' He had just come out of a trance in which he had been snatched up to the skies and seen a host of thrones, with one higher than all the others, empty, radiant, ablaze with all kinds of precious stones. Like the knights of Camelot, he had admired the splendour of this Siege Perilous and wondered what the throne was and for whom it was prepared. And a voice had told him that this was indeed the most perilous seat of all eternity, for it was the throne from which Lucifer had been hurled down because of his pride, and it was the seat that Francis, exalted higher than any Galahad, would occupy after his death because he believed himself to be the greatest of sinners. God's accolade had descended on Francis through the person of a troubadour. Nothing could have been more suitably devised by the Almighty to give both his servants pleasure.[9] It was the best of omens for what both anticipated would be the greatest of crusades.

NOTES

1 Marie of Jerusalem died in 1212, but not before giving birth to a daughter, Yolande of Brienne – thus making an extraordinary run of four hereditary queens, no male heirs intervening. Yolande was to die even younger than her unfortunate mother or grandmother, after the most illustrious marriage possible – to the Emperor Frederick II.

2 Francis' journeys to Slavonia and to Spain (see page 192) are only very cursorily referred to by the early biographers. Yet there is no reason to doubt that they did take place. For his first journey on crusade has all the air of being legendary if we were to go by those accounts alone – yet, fortunately, there is an independent confirmation. This indicates *first* that the fact that there are no outside accounts of the first two journeys does not mean to say that they were mere legends; *secondly*, that the biographers were more concerned with what Francis became than what he aspired to be. Hence their disinterest in his travels.

3 The *Intrumentum donationis Montis Alvernae* is in the communal archives of Borgo San Sepolcro.

4 The French boys after sailing from Marseilles simply disappeared; and for eighteen whole years there was no news of them – till a few survivors, living in Egypt, told how they had all been betrayed by the shipowners and sold to the infidel as slaves. The German boys had been gently discouraged and turned back by Pope Innocent at Rome; their leader, Nicholas, was on his return to Germany hanged by hysterically anxious parents.

5 Islam, like Christianity, was continually stirred by movements of reform; the impulse, as in the Christian world, came from the desire to get back to the principles of the Founder of the Book. The Almoravides, the 'Vowed to God', had themselves been reformers before they had been replaced by the Almohades. The principal difference was that in Islam, with its more fluid structures, these reforming movements often succeeded in taking political power whereas in Christendom, till the time of the Reformation, they were absorbed or repressed. But the impulse was the same. It is fascinating to note that St. Francis considered Roland and Oliver and the paladins 'martyrs'. This is in itself a concept borrowed from Islam: that those who die as warriors in a holy war for their faith go straight to paradies, their sins forgiven. It is not the orthodox Christian idea of martyrdom. And so Francis considered all crusaders potential martyrs; and when he talked of 'seeking martyrdom', we cannot rule out the possibility that he meant, initially at least, to seek it sword in hand.

6 This is one of the first angels with whom the brothers had dealings and certainly the most communicative.

7 He entered Constance with only sixty knights three hours before Otto of Brunswick and his forces arrived.

8 In Francis' love of animals, undeniable and much insisted on, psychologists might find certain interpretations that would offend the sentimentalists. Both, in my view, would be wrong. Francis loved having pets, particularly birds and lambs and rabbits, but realized it was a weakness (cf. chapter 15 of the *Second Rule*: 'The Brothers may not keep animals'). Like the Abbot Joachim, who led his congregation out to salute the rising sun with a *'Veni, Creator,'* he had a great feeling for nature, flowers and landscape. But he was not a sentimentalist. He disliked mice because they tormented him in the straw-bedding, sows and pigs for their habits, and ants for showing so much care for the future. He liked lambs for sym-

bolic reasons, worms for scriptural reasons (*Psalms*, 21,7), and larks best of all birds because he could draw parables from them. Larks wore a hood like the clerks, scavenged for food even in dung, went singing gaily, and wore dark-coloured dirty feathers: Hence 'If I could talk to the Emperor,' said Francis, 'I would beg him for the love of God to grant my prayer and to publish an edict forbidding anyone from trapping our sisters the larks or from inflicting any harm on them.' As for the two legendary occasions of the preaching to the birds, the first had a very practical moral: let congregations stop chattering and twittering till the preacher has finished. And in the second Francis was theoretically speaking to the birds but in fact addressing himself indirectly to men. 'Wherefore doth your Creator love you, seeing that he giveth you so many benefits. Guard yourselves, therefore, my sisters the birds, from the sin of ingratitude and be ye ever mindful to give praise to God.' This was allegory, not sentiment.

The well loved story of how St. Francis 'converted the very fierce Wolf of Gubbio', in the *Fioretti*, is, alas, probably embroidered from a little incident recounted in the contemporary *Chronicle of the Passion of San Verecondo*, where Francis, warned that wolves were about, continued on his journey with his donkey. 'I have done no evil to Brother Wolf,' he told the worried peasants by the priory of San Verecondo, 'he will not dare devour our Brother Donkey. Good night, my children, and fear God!' (See the 1926 collection by Fra Leonardo Lemmens of *Testimonia Minora* – published at Quaracchi, Italy.)

9 Masseo, Elias, Silvester and Pacificus – as always with Francis' companions it is impossible to be absolutely sure when they joined the Order. The *Legenda Antiqua*, however, states specifically that when Pacificus had his vision of Lucifer's throne, the church in which St. Francis kept his vigil 'had no resident priest, for at that time Trevi was in ruins and had only a few inhabitants.' From other sources we know that Dipold the German destroyed Trevi in September 1213, and that rebuilding began in 1215. This is the sort of 'outside' clue on which all the chronology of this period and indeed the very sequence of events must, *per forza*, be based.

❧ Lord Preserve Us ❧

10: Lord Preserve Us

The Great Council at the Lateran

In the autumn of the year 1215 it seemed as if the whole world was converging on Rome. Seventy-one archbishops, 412 bishops and no less than 800 abbots, with their servants, their retinues and their escorts rode in. From Outremer came the Patriarch of Jerusalem and the Patriarch of the Maronites. Count Raymond of Toulouse, flanked by the Counts of Foix and Comminges, appeared with letters from the King of England; not only the affairs of southern France but those of England and of Spain were settled, or at least discussed, before the council opened.

On 11 November, the feast of St. Martin, that most knightly and courteous of Christian saints, Innocent preached his famous opening sermon. He took as his text Luke, 22, 15: 'With desire I have desired to eat this passover with you.' Truly might the council be called a passover, he said, for the word passover means passage, and there would be a threefold passage of the nations – from vice to virtue, from temporal to eternal life, and from Christendom to the holy places.

This, the fourth Lateran and twelfth Ecumenical, was the greatest reforming council of the Middle Ages.[1] In its three sessions seventy canons were proclaimed. Many of them (like canon 21, which laid down the obligation for confession and communion once a year, and the secrecy of the confessional) shaped the Catholic religion and its practices as they now are. Many others (like canon 2, which condemned the Abbot Joachim's teachings on the Trinity, but those alone) dealt with more immediate issues. One, canon 68, which ordained that Jews and Saracens living in Christian lands should wear a distinctive form of dress, created a fearsome precedent. Perhaps most important of all the faith was defined, the doctrine of the eucharist discussed and trans-substantiation proclaimed, in the very first canon. As a corollary, all bishops were ordered to search out and punish heretics, and all rulers upon pain of excommunication to cleanse their realms of heresy by the sword, for which they should be granted the same indulgences as those who set forth to the help of the Holy Land. Canons against unchaste clerics, against clerics who drank and hunted, against clerics who sat up all night chattering and were late for Matins, were interspersed with two canons that particularly affected, or might have affected, the Friars Minor: canon 13, which forbade the establishment of any new Orders, and canon 10, by which the bishops were enjoined to appoint fixed preachers in cathedrals and converted churches. But all this, important though it was, was overshadowed by formal announcement of the great crusade.

'Jerusalem the city of sorrows,' cried the Pope, 'is calling to all who pass by the way to come and see if there be sorrow like unto hers: and shame and disgrace will be the lot of those who pass by unheeding.' Tournaments were forbidden for three years lest they might interfere with the crusade; there was to be peace in Christendom for four years. Indulgences would be granted to those who contributed money as well as those who more literally took the Cross. To set an example the clergy would contribute one-twentieth of their revenues for three years, and the Pope and cardinals one-tenth. And the crusaders were to assemble and be ready to set sail for the Holy Land on 1 June 1217 – eighteen months ahead.

Was Francis there to hear this proclamation? The evidence that he was is late and scanty, or indirect. 'Francis seems to have been present,' says Jorgensen. 'It is not improbable that Francis was present,' writes Father Cuthbert. Sabatier wisely stays silent.[2] In a sense it is unlikely that he was summoned to the council, where the authorities of the Church and the ambassadors of the kings were in attendance, but probable enough that he was hovering excitedly on its flanks; and he may even have met, as the later chronicles like to suppose, both Dominic and Cardinal Ugolino, the Lord Bishop of Ostia and a relative of Pope Innocent, at the time. It matters little. He would have known the news soon enough. Everyone heard the news. In Acre John of Brienne heard it, and rejoiced. At Damascus, Cairo and Jerusalem the Ayubite Sultans heard it, and trembled. An important Arab historian, Ibn Wasil, noted that the Franks were coming from *Roomiyya-al-Koubra*, Rome the Great, where reigned one of their most powerful sovereigns, who was known under the name of Pope.

With his usual immense energy Innocent threw himself and his letter-writers into the task of assembling a vast army and navy. Sicily, Frederick's personal domain, was closer to the rendezvous for those crusaders who wished to travel by sea; and the Pope announced that he himself would be there to organize the army and to bless it. Those who decided to go by land should set out, at the same time, and would be accompanied by a legate *a latere*. During their absence crusaders would be exempt from all taxes, secular or ecclesiastical, and from the paying of any interest to the Jews. False Christians who supplied the Saracens, enemies of Christ and of the Christian people, with arms or ships would be excommunicated. Prince Louis of France, who was threatening to invade England where both King John and his eldest son, the child Henry, had taken the Cross, was excommunicated, and his father King Philippe Auguste was threatened with excommunication. Worried about the fleet – which had caused so much difficulty in the previous crusade – the Pope moved north out of Rome, intending by his personal intervention to settle difficulties with the maritime cities of Genoa and Pisa. In the spring of 1216 he came to Perugia; and there, less than eleven months before his great crusade was due to set out, that crusade of which he was the inspirer, the organizer, indeed the dictator, by a cruel mischance that robbed history of great happenings, he died; and much of the enthusiasm for the crusade died with him.

Thomas of Eccleston (but he alone) relates that Francis was present at the Pope's death.[3] Certainly one who was present, or very nearly, was the newly appointed Bishop of Acre, Jacques de Vitry. He arrived on the afternoon of Saturday, 11 July, to learn that the Pope had died that morning; the open coffin containing the Pope's body was in the cathedral awaiting burial on the Sunday. 'It was on that day,' wrote the Frenchman, 'that I really understood the nothingness of grandeur here below. The night before the funeral thieves broke in and stripped the Pope of everything precious upon him. I saw with my own eyes his body, half naked, lying in the midst of the church, already stinking.'

So ended a great Pope; and one who influenced directly all the characters who have appeared in this history, and none more directly than Francis. There were nineteen cardinals in Perugia and within two days they had elected a new Pope: the unworldly Cencio Savelli of Rome. 'He is an excellent and pious old man,' Jacques de Vitry wrote, 'and he is besides, simple and kindly, having given almost all his fortune to the poor.'

On 24 July he was consecrated and took the name of Honorius III. On the following day he wrote to John of Brienne to reassure him and the Barons of Outremer that the great crusade would take place as planned. But though in Cardinal Ugolino dei Conti – who was in due course to be his successor – he had a stout supporter and an ambitious administrator, he had himself neither Innocent's prestige nor his immense driving-power. A crusade of sorts would no doubt set out; but all men knew that it would not be the great crusade that Innocent had planned – not unless Frederick showed himself as loyal to the new Pope as he had been to his guardian and set off back from Germany to assume its direction himself.

An Outsider Looks in

Jacques de Vitry was not impressed by the prelates and clergy that surrounded the new Pope. 'They are so absorbed by temporal affairs,' he wrote, 'and by those which concern kings and states that it is impossible to touch on religious questions. All this saddens me. In the midst of this corruption I none the less found consolation in seeing a great number of men and women who renounced all their possessions and left the world for the love of Christ: "Friars Minor" and "Sisters Minor" as they are called.

During the day the brothers go into the towns and villages, giving themselves over to the active life of the apostolate; at night they return to their hermitage or withdraw into solitude to live the contemplative life.

'The women live near the towns in various hospices and refuges; they live a community life from the work of their hands but accept no income. The veneration that the clergy and laity show towards them is a burden and it chagrins and annoys them.'[4]

This is the first eye-witness account of any length written about the Friars Minor by one who was not a member of their Order. Therefore it is of immense importance. It proves that in October of 1216 (when Jacques de Vitry wrote his letter) the Friars Minor had become a notable movement; yet it was necessary to come within range of Assisi to hear of them; that the Pope and cardinals approved; that they were expanding fast, without any check or control over membership; that they were seen as something very different from the monastic Orders, rather as a lay movement than a clerical one; that their aims and methods were understood and appreciated; and finally that there was no hint of scandal in the relationship between the Friars Minor and the women of the Order[5] – a fact that, I suppose, justified Francis' uncharacteristic circumspection towards women, and apparent coldness towards Clare.

'I am convinced,' de Vitry winds up that part of his letter on this theme, 'that if the Lord has decided to use these simple and poor men, he has done so to save a great number of souls before the end of the world and to put to shame our prelates who are dumb dogs who do not even have the strength to bark.'[6] What the letter-writer omits to mention is almost as significant as what he does say. In particular one searches in vain for any reference to the person or name of Francis.

Fra Juniper, an early companion, was always playing see-saw or wandering about in his breeches, for humility's sake; or cooking meals destined to last fifteen days in order that more time might be available for prayer; or cutting off pigs' trotters as a dainty dish for sick friars, impervious to the uncharitable wrath of the pigs' owners; or worst of all giving away not only his tunic but books, vestments, mantles, even the little silver altar bells at Santa Maria degli Angeli, indeed whatever he could lay his hands on, to the poor. 'And for this reason,' writes his unknown biographer, 'the friars left nothing exposed to the public, because Fra Juniper gave everything away for the love of God and for his Glory.' 'Would to God, my brethren,' commented Francis after one of the more outrageous of his escapades, 'I had a forest of such Junipers!'

But by the very fact of its success the nature of the fraternity was changing. Even before the Lateran council, many noble and learned men, Thomas of Celano informs us, joined the Order. Of the learned men (who perhaps included

Fra Leo, later Francis' most constant companion and secretary), the most distinguished was a canon of the cathedral, Peter of Catania. But it was the joining of Leonardo di Gislerio, one of the lords of Sassorosso, that finally conferred the seal of social respectability upon the Order. Leonardo's name is not mentioned in the communal archives of Assisi after February 1215, so he almost certainly joined in that year. Probably he followed in the footsteps of his daughter Filippa, who went to join Clare at San Damiano; it was a time of peace in Assisi – the only ructions were between Bishop Guido and the Abbot of the Benedictines – and Leonardo had lived long enough in the world to see his castle at Sassorosso restored for his three sons. It might fairly be said that his was the most renowned noble family in Assisi; little wonder, then, that the papal court in Perugia, where he had lived so long and where his name and history were so well known, looked with favour on the fraternity. He must have been known personally to Cardinal Rainerio, the new Rector (i.e. ruler) of the Duchy of Spoleto.

But these were all men of Assisi who knew Francis personally; and even that other nobleman who joined them about this time, Illuminato, was from the valley of Rieti, where Francis had preached. However, as Jacques de Vitry's letter makes clear, they joined not a man but a brotherhood. There was no such thing as a 'Franciscan'. There were simply the Lesser Brothers and Francis had no right of veto – there was no restriction on membership.

Indeed, in a way, nothing was simpler than to join the *Fratres Minores*. One group of friends, as de Vitry put it, simply brought another. Any Friar Minor was entitled to admit anyone else to the fraternity. The formalities were relatively few: if you wished to join, you threw away your shoes, your purse, your staff, your clothes and your food, you put on a shapeless bit of sacking, tied yourself together with a cord, and had your hair cut – hey presto, you were transformed. Naturally you had to take vows of poverty, chastity and obedience. But oath-taking was a common part of medieval life, not as solemn and unusual an affair as it would be nowadays. There was admittedly the *conditio sine qua non*, which was rather more of a hurdle: the giving of all goods to the poor. But, compared with the usual lengthy and complex processes of medieval life, the whole process was simplicity itself; no documents, no examinations, no trial-periods, no legalisms. A man could become a Friar Minor in an afternoon.

Inevitably this meant that there were Friar Minors who had never seen Francis, at least till the Pentecost meeting. And there were others who were not all that impressed even when they did see him; Giordano of Giano, who joined about this time, admits that he only really began to appreciate Francis' importance after his death; and Fra Salimbene, a later chronicler, hardly refers to him at all in his vast work. There were still those, like Brother John the Simple, who followed Francis around like a sheepish slave, genuflected when he genuflected, coughed when he coughed, and spat when he spat, on the grounds that 'I promised to do all that you would do; and therefore I want to do it.' But the trees were being lost in the wood. The personal ties and the loyalties that Francis had loved and that he had assumed would always bind the fraternity together were inevitably disappearing. The brotherhood was becoming an Order; because Francis had not had the foresight, nor indeed the wish, to restrict the number of seats at his Round Table.

Camps and Armies of the Knights of God

If there is any doubt about the regularity of the Pentecost Chapters, they are removed by Jacques de Vitry. He had reached Perugia in July, and wrote his letter in October; so he could not have been present at one himself. Yet, from hearsay, he knew all about them and realized their importance, as the following passage of his letter shows:

'Once a year, in a place on which they agree, the men of this Order assemble to rejoice in the Lord and eat together, and they profit greatly from these gatherings. They seek the counsel of virtuous and upright men; they draw up and promulgate holy laws and submit them for approval to the Holy Father; then they disband again for a year and go through Lombardy, Tuscany, Apulia and Sicily.'

This is a most informative passage. It implies that there was growing control over the fraternity; for not only did outsiders – 'virtuous and upright men' – attend their assemblies and give their advice but new rules and regulations – constitutions, as they were called – had to be submitted to the papal Curia for approval. And it implies that before 1216 the brothers, as they scattered for their year's wanderings, were inevitably accepting at least a *de facto* provincial organization.

What were these early Chapters like? One thing is certain: they were nothing like the later Chapters General (so often referred to in the first chapter of this book), which were limited to the administrators of the Order. Everyone who was a Friar Minor could and normally did attend. There were great open-air meetings; and though they were usually held in the woods by the Portiuncula, they could, as Jacques de Vitry states, be held in any place agreed upon.

One of these earlier Chapters was held near Gubbio, by the monastery of San Verecondo. It was there that 'the blessed Francis assembled his first three hundred Friars Minor in a Chapter; the abbot and his monks' – very probably 'virtuous and upright men' who were invited to join in – 'amiably procured food and lodging for them according to their means. Messer Andrew, now a very elderly man, who happened to be there at the time, has testified that the brothers received barley bread, fine wheaten bread, winter barley, millet, drinking water, quince wine mixed with water for the sick, and a quantity of two varieties of beans.'[7]

Could this have been the Chapter of 1216? I believe it was. Three hundred friars sounds about right. In 1210, when they went to Rome, there had been twelve of them. It is difficult to calculate the rate of expansion in the next five years; but all the indications are that it was limited to people from Assisi and nearby, and none too rapid from the period of Clare's escapade (Palm Sunday 1212) onwards, when Francis was mainly away on his vain attempts to reach the Holy Land or the Moors. The real break-through seems to have occurred at the time of his triumphant preaching tour after he had returned from Santiago de Compostela, that is to say, after Pentecost 1215. But even then the chronicler thinks that it is not merely worth noting but worth stressing that at Ascoli he enrolled thirty new members. (See page 199.) Le Marche was to become the great centre of the Franciscan spirit, even more so than Umbria; and it is reasonable to suppose that these thirty formed one of those groups who said to their friends: 'Come along!' All this is guesswork; but when one has immersed oneself in the biographies and chronicles of the period, one begins to get a feeling for something as nebulous even as numbers. Until Pentecost 1215 I would not imagine that there were more than a few dozen friars at most, all of whom knew Francis or Bernard personally. Then, in the year of the great council, came that sudden leap in numbers that means that a group (and its ideas) have become, instead of a mere bonhomie of friends and neighbours, an expanding and potentially powerful movement. This is an exulting experience for any group's founders. It is only a little later that they realize that they themselves – and, worse still, their ideas – are likely to be swamped.

In the five years that followed the number of brothers expanded geometrically; and according to St. Bonaventure and others often more than five thousand would assemble at the Pentecost Chapter; the Chapters of the Mats these were called, because all the groups – of sixty, or a hundred or two or three hundred – set up tents covered on top and round about with rushes and mats. They slept on straw or on the bare ground, with stones or pieces of wood for pillows; and when Cardinal Ugolino came to visit them and to preach to them from nearby Perugia 'marvelling at such a great crowd organized as an army camp, he would say' – the *Fioretti* tells us – ' with tears and great devotion: "Truly this is the camp and the army of the knights of God".'

Francis must have been delighted; no compliment could have given him greater pleasure. But even three hundred 'knights' were an army that needed a rôle and by next year's Chapter, the Chapter of 1217, these three hundred had probably swollen to two or three or even four times that number. So at this Chapter the 'army' was organized, with rather more formality than had been the case hitherto. Inevitably there is much confusion between the incidents that occurred and the decisions that were taken at each of these great 'Chapters of the Mats'; but, without entering into every detail, the outlines at least are clear.[8]

The 'army' was split into two: the garrison troops, so to speak, and the expeditionary forces. Perhaps Italy had already been divided into provinces informally; if so, the divisions were now made more formal, and Ministers-Provincial[9] were appointed to direct the activities of the Friars Minor in at least five regions – Tuscany, Le Marche, Lombardy, the Terra di Lavoro and Apulia. But what really caused excitement was the decision to move outside Italy; and to send groups of brothers over the Alps to France, Germany and Hungary – and over the seas to Outremer.

And now we come to a most extraordinary circumstance; and one which no historian has yet seriously attempted to explain. Francis was not the one to stay at home while others were going out and about: he chose to lead a group. And of course how could he choose otherwise than to lead a group which was setting out, at the same time as the crusaders, for the Holy Land? Impossible, yet he did. Elias was to lead the Friars Minor to Outremer; Francis, of all apparently useless places to go, chose to go to France.

This is so out of character as to be almost unbelievable. Had, then, the burning desire for martyrdom and his wish to preach to the infidel disappeared overnight? At the very moment a crusade was at long last setting out, he, who had so often taken the Cross, turned his back quite literally on his goal and went scurrying off towards the other end of Europe. Could it have been a sort of delayed repetition of his turning-back at Spoleto, a sudden return of cowardice when faced with reality? – hardly. He had after all proved his resolution in the intervening years by sailing to Dalmatia and walking to Spain. There must be some more convincing explanation of this apparently aberrant decision.

The chronicles give very little help. According to the *Speculum Perfectionis* Francis delayed his choice until the other friars had departed; then he begged those remaining to pray and help his choice, for 'as I have sent friars to distant lands to endure toil and abuse, hunger and thirst and other hardships, it is only right, and holy humility requires, that I should likewise go to some distant province.'

'And at once he said to them with joy "In the name of our Lord Jesus Christ, of the glorious Virgin his mother, and of all the Saints, I choose the Province of France, for it is a Catholic nation and they show an especial reverence to the body of Christ above other Catholics. This is a great joy to me and because of this I will most gladly live among them." '

This is the only full account we have; and coming from this late source it cannot be trusted in matters of detail or motive. Even if we were to admit that in a wave of emotion and longing for a land of which he had always dreamt Francis chose to go to France, the sequel then poses another almost insuperable difficulty. For, as the *Speculum Perfectionis* tells the story, Francis never reached France; he never even came within striking distance of France. He chose the brothers he wished to take with him, including his special companion Pacificus, and they set off in column of two. But when they reached Florence, they found there Cardinal Ugolino. 'Brother,' said the cardinal to Francis, 'I do not want you to cross the Alps, for there are many prelates who would willingly damage the prospects of your Order at the Roman Curia. But I and other cardinals who love your Order will protect and support it all the more willingly if you remain within the province.'[10] 'My Lord,' Francis answered indignantly, 'I should be very ashamed if I sent my brothers to distant provinces without sharing any of the hardships that they have to suffer for God's sake.'

'Well, why have you sent your friars to such distant places to die of hunger and undergo other hardships?'

'My Lord,' replied Francis with great fervour, 'do you imagine that God has raised up the friars solely for the benefit of these provinces? I solemnly assure you that God has chosen and sent the friars for the benefit and salvation of the souls of all men in this world. They will be welcomed not only in the countries of the faithful but in those of unbelievers as well, and they will win many souls.'

Now even if this conversation were accurately reported – and to my ears it has more the tang of a general statement of what was said on that particular occasion – the upshot is almost inexplicable. Despite his strong feelings, despite the brilliant way he had expressed them, despite the fact that he had, according to the account, convinced Cardinal Ugolino, Francis turned back, leaving Pacificus and the others to go on without him. So much for his fine words about setting an example to all the friars; so much for his proud choice of France. Can one imagine anything both more ignominious and therefore more unlikely than that Francis should turn back at Florence – at Florence! – abandoning his companions and his expedition because of some mythical threat of prelates being opposed to his Order? No, this cannot have been how it happened.

To understand the whys and wherefores of this episode we must fillet out the bare bones of the story; and the bare bones are these. The Chapter of 1217 decided to send groups of friars from Italy to four Christian countries, France, Germany, Hungary and Outremer. For some reason Francis chose to lead the group destined for France. When, however, this group reached Florence, Francis, as a result of an interview with Cardinal Ugolino, abandoned the project and returned to Assisi.

Why were those four countries chosen? Why did Francis not choose to go, as might have been expected, to Outremer? Why did he select France? And why, when he was en route to France, did he turn back towards Assisi?

The impending crusade dominated his life. And it is in the ups and downs of the preparations for this crusade that the answers to these four questions must be sought and can be found.

Whose Enemies, the French

Old and feeble he might be, but Pope Honorius was quite determined that the crusade proclaimed and planned by his great predecessor would take place. In this determination he never wavered. Before the end of the year 1216 a circular letter had been dispatched to all the prelates and princes of Christendom reminding those who had already taken the Cross of their vows, those who had not of the decisions of the great council, and all of the threat to Outremer when the truce should expire and of the rendezvous of the crusaders in the following June. The Pope's efforts were backed by his legates everywhere. In Tuscany and Lombardy Cardinal Ugolino was much employed in settling the various minor wars between the cities of northern Italy, for it was essential that the decree of the Lateran Council should be respected and that there should be peace for four years between Christian peoples, cities and kings. Simon, Archbishop of Tyre, new legate in France replacing the tactless Englishman Cardinal Robert de Courçon, was ceaselessly preaching. He was supported both by the doctors of the Sorbonne (who issued a decree stating that anyone who had taken the vow to go to the Holy Land but then failed to do so was guilty of mortal sin) and by numerous signs and miracles – clouds for instance that took on the miraculous formation of crosses.

All this hubbub was not without its results. As far away as Norway, King Inge took the Cross – only to die the following spring. Prince Sigurd Konungsfraendi led the Norse crusaders in his stead; and with Casimir, Duke of Pomerania, the northern contingent headed down to the south. There, on the southern borders of the Empire, they found a king and a host of 15,000 crusaders assembled under arms.

This king was Andrew II of Hungary, that wildly extravagant monarch who lived up to the motto he had once proclaimed: 'The generosity of a king should be limitless.' With him he had the relatives of his first murdered wife, led by Duke Otto of Meran in the Tyrol. Duke Otto's more powerful neighbour, Duke Leopold VI, 'the Glorious', of Austria, himself son of a famous crusading father, and great patron of the minnesinger, led another contingent from the imperial lands. It was not a negligible force that was moving in the spring of 1217 towards the shores of the Adriatic, to negotiate, like their predecessors of the Fourth Crusade, with a wily Doge, for shipping to the Holy Land, but it was not that mighty and overwhelming assembly that Innocent had been counting on. The lords of France and England, the backbone of all past crusades, were absent; Gervase Abbot of Prémontré reported sadly that the Dukes of Burgundy and Lorraine were ignoring their vows – and above all, the crusade's leader, the Emperor-elect, was not there and obviously would not be there by 1 June to lead the great expedition.

The aged Honorius trusted the young Frederick, who was always very courteous towards him. There were reasons for his holding back: in particular Otto of Brunswick was still in arms in northern Germany and still claiming the throne – and Frederick's absence on crusade might give Otto a hell-sent opportunity to recover all that he had lost. Honorius and Frederick were in constant correspondence with one another; and in the Pope's registries is a letter from Honorius dated 8 April 1217, thanking Frederick for congratulations on his election, and announcing that he would be sending him a legate to treat of the Holy Land. In other words, by April 1217 two things were clear: first, that a large body of crusaders led by a Christian King were assembling and that a crusade of sorts would set out; secondly, that the main crusading expedition, led by the Emperor, and comprising hopefully not only imperial forces but the chivalry of England and France, was unavoidably delayed.

It was five weeks, then, after this letter of Honorius's had been sent to Frederick that Francis and his 'army' met in the woods beneath Assisi. Perugia and the Pope's court, the whole buzzing hive of crusading propaganda, lay only a few miles away across the plain. And even if Francis was no political expert, he had at his side a man whose political capacities his later career was to prove – Elias. And what we have no right to doubt is that Elias was as sincere and passionate a crusader in heart as Francis himself. Francis trusted Elias – and rightly. He knew him to be, in this at least, such a kindred spirit that he agreed that Elias should lead the group of friars who were to set out with the crusaders of King Andrew; and this he could only have accepted if he felt, genuinely, that his *alter ego* was going, that he would be with the crusaders at least by proxy; and, most swaying argument of all, if he thought that he in person could help the crusade better elsewhere.

It now becomes clear why France, Germany, Hungary and Outremer were chosen as the destinations for the commando groups of Francis' 'army'. These were the lands that were providing, or would (so everyone believed) provide, the knights and leaders of the crusade; but they needed, as everyone from the Pope downwards recognized, to be stirred into action. The Friars Minor, then, must do their bit to help. The groups went out from Assisi not with the purpose of establishing their Order in other lands, as the chroniclers with hindsight believed, but for a far simpler reason: to add their voices to the chorus calling all Christian men to take the Cross.

Even in Outremer this was most necessary. It might be imagined that all the men of the reduced Kingdom[11] were awaiting with great eagerness the arrival of the crusaders and the chance to hurl themselves at the enemy. Not a bit of it. After twenty years of virtual peace the merchants and traders had never been so prosperous; the quays of Tyre and Acre and Beirut were piled high with merchandise, and Jacques de Vitry found to his digust that the Italian communities were far less interested in recovering the holy places than in making money. As for the descendants of the original Latin settlers, they were thoroughly degenerate – debauched, corrupt, sly and not above spying for the infidel. No sooner had he arrived to take up his new post as Bishop of Acre than he set about preaching, preaching and preaching again. It is not unreasonable to suppose that during his long stay the previous summer at Perugia he and Elias had become acquainted; and that he heard the news that Elias was leading a band of Friars Minor to help his efforts at raising the moral tone in Outremer – which, incidentally, he did succeed in doing – with enthusiasm. More preachers were needed, even in Outremer – and preachers whose way of life would be an example to merely nominal Christians.

This explains why friars were going to Outremer as well as to the crusading heartlands of Europe. It does not explain why Francis was not going with them. Why France?

The answer, when one hits upon it, is simplicity itself. Francis was heading towards France not because he was named after the land, nor because he had so long admired it, nor even because it was a Catholic nation that held the eucharist in reverence; he was hurrying there because the greatest threat to the eventual success of the crusade had blown up in France, and he wanted to do what he could to stop it. And he turned back at Florence, not because Cardinal Ugolino told him to or warned him of intrigues against the Order but because he learnt that the threat in France had blown over, and there was no longer any need for his presence there. The nature of the threat was very simple: it was the possibility of a war between France and England, a war that would have engulfed the efforts of all the chivalry of these two nations. And what Francis proposed to do about it was clearly to do as he had done in his first days as a penitent in Assisi: to go knocking on doors but on rather a wider and grander scale and preach to all who would listen to him on the theme: 'God give you peace.'

Very briefly the situation was this. King John's reign had ended in confusion, revolt and sporadic civil war. The rebellious barons had called in to lead them a prince with a rival claim to the throne – none other than Louis of France, son and heir of Philippe Auguste. Louis landed at Sandwich, marched on Canterbury, and with the help and protection of the rebels installed himself in London. King John died three months after Pope Innocent. He left as his heir a boy of nine, Henry III, who, on 28 October 1216 was crowned at Gloucester. All south-eastern England, Winchester included, was in the hands of the Frenchman and his followers. Yet the sympathy of the English now veered to the child king; Earl Ranulf of Chester, the greatest magnate of the realm and knight-errant of renown, came hastening to Gloucester to pay homage; as did the head of the Ferrers family Earl William of Derby. The papal legate Cardinal Gualo assumed the direction of the realm, or what was left of it, and on Pope Honorius' orders excommunicated Prince Louis and all his followers. For not only was the peace of Christendom being troubled, contrary to the decree of the council, but the realm of England had, like Aragon, been put under the special protection of Innocent and become a papal fief; furthermore on Ash Wednesday 1214, the child Henry had, with his father, taken the Cross. Therefore Pope Honorius declared that the child king as 'a ward and an orphan and *crucesignatus*' was 'under the special protection of the Holy See.'

In the winter of 1216 and the early months of 1217 letter after letter was sent by Honorius to Philippe Auguste enjoining him to call off his son. But with his usual guile the King of France had made it clear publicly that he washed his hands of the whole affair: in private he had charters prepared that would define the rights and duties of father and son when the one sat on the throne of France and the other on the throne of England. The whole slow, cautious, patient aim of Philippe Auguste during his long reign had been to drive the English out of Normandy, Brittany and Flanders. To culminate his policy with the seating of his eldest son on the throne of the Plantagenets would have been the master-stroke of French history. And he was too old a hand to feel the slightest enthusiasm for a new crusade. It needed but little for all the chivalry of France to be launched, officially or unofficially, into the English adventure.

This was the situation on 14 May, when the Chapter of the Friars Minor was held at Assisi. And this, no doubt, was why Francis decided to go and preach peace among Christian princes in France and, if necessary, in England. They should be on their way to the crusades, those warring nobles. God, and the Pope, wished it.

On 19 May, five days later, Saer de Quincy, Earl of Winchester and the leading magnate among the rebels, was routed at Lincoln. This was the decisive battle of the war. The nobles were sick of squabbling, the people were longing for peace, and Philippe Auguste immediately started looking for a settlement. By the time Francis and Pacificus reached Florence, news of Lincoln and its results would have reached Cardinal Ugolino. It was right that a group of friars should continue and, like the other groups, should go and preach the crusade in a land of potential but dilatory crusaders; however, there was now no need, as Francis must have realized, for he himself to go with them. The menace of a ruinous conflagration had disappeared. France and England would keep the peace. He waved Pacificus and the other brothers on – and returned to base, to Assisi.

Meanwhile, in the Holy Land

It would have been too much to expect the crusaders actually to set sail on the planned date of 1 June.[12] Very rarely, if ever, does a military expedition of any size involving land-sea co-operation set off on schedule. King Andrew had to conduct lengthy long-range negotiations with the Doge before it was agreed – at the price of the cession of the seaport of Zara – that Venetian galleys should be at Spalato, a seaport eighty miles further down the coast of Dalmatia, by 25 July.

There, we may assume, Elias and the group of brothers who had volunteered to go to the Holy Land were already waiting. They had probably sailed from Ancona with the group destined for Hungary.[13] The shortest passage across the Adriatic was the crossing from Ancona to Zara. And it would be logical that at Zara the two groups should split, Elias and his companions continuing down the coast to Spalato, and the Hungarian group heading inland, across territories that owed a vague allegiance to the King of Hungary, towards Budapest. If they reached Zara by the end of June – and it can hardly have been later than that – they would have heard that King Andrew was nowhere near the coast (indeed he did not reach Spalato till the third week in August) – and with renewed zeal they would have hurried off into the interior to urge on his tardy followers. Rude shocks awaited them.

As for the group heading towards Germany, consisting (again according to Fra Giordano) of no less than sixty friars led by Giovanni di Penna, their probable route would have taken them first to the Adriatic coast with the rest, and then up past Venice, heading north and inland via Verona up the Adige Valley towards Trent, with Meran, Duke Otto's capital, as their first obvious destination. Rude shocks awaited them too. In their naive simplicity and indeed parochialism the Friars Minor had overlooked one vital point: that in both Germany and Hungary men did not speak and could not understand Italian.

Francis himself must have been waiting restlessly and anxiously at Assisi for news of how his various groups were faring; though he knew he could hardly expect news to come till the next Pentecost gathering when the groups, or at least some of them, would return to Assisi to tell the tale of their year's adventures. What he was bound to hear, however, were the reports that, from the autumn onwards, flooded into Italy: and, first of all, the good news that the crusaders had set sail from Dalmatia and were expected to arrive in the Holy Land by the feast of the Nativity of Our Lady in September.

Duke Leopold of Austria had been the first to set sail; and had crossed the Mediterranean in a record time of only just over two weeks. A little later King Andrew, Duke Otto, Duke Casimir, Prince Sigurd and their hosts followed. They found Hugh I, the young King of Cyprus, already at Acre with his Turcopoles, where King John of Brienne and the barons had been joined by Bohemond VI, Count of Tripoli and Prince of Antioch. The tents of the crusaders filled the plains outside the walled city of Acre. The Masters of the three great Military Orders, Garin of Montaigu, Master of the Hospitallers, William of Chartres, Master of the Templars, and Hermann of Salza, Master of the Teutonic Knights, rode in from their great fortress-castles. And on 3 November, under the leadership of King Andrew, the knights rode out over the *Jisr Bennt Jacob*, the bridge of the Daughters of Jacob, across the Jordan, up into the Golan Heights, and down into the vast plain of the Hauran that leads to the gates of Damascus.

This was curious strategy.[12] For instead of heading south to free Jerusalem, the aim and object of the whole crusade, the host had apparently turned its back on Jerusalem and was heading north into the undisputed territories of Saphadin. It seems that there were two reasons for this: first of all, the crusaders, ablaze with the tales of romance, wished less to liberate the holy places than to perform exploits of glory and smite the infidel; secondly, a more practical reason, they had no siege engines of the sort that would be necessary if any serious assault upon the walled city of Jerusalem was even to be envisaged, let alone succeed. But whatever the reasons were, it must all have sounded very odd to the masses of enthusiasts back in Europe. And as autumn turned into winter and the year ended, and it became apparent that no great battle had been fought and that the holy places were no nearer being liberated than before, disappointment began to edge towards disillusion.

For, to the extreme annoyance of the Christians, the Saracens had very wisely refused to meet them in pitched battle. The *chevauchée* towards Damascus had turned back in disgust; and the two following enterprises, the siege of the great Saracen fortress of Mount Thabor, with its seventy-seven bastions, that lay across the plain of Esdraelon threatening Acre, and a long raid up from Tyre and the Château de Beaufort into Merdjayoun and the Bekaa, failed. For still the Saracens would not fight.

Famine, and the problems of a divided command, discouraged the crusaders.

After Christmas, despite the anathemas of Ralph de Merncourt, the Latin Patriach of Jerusalem, King Andrew decided to abandon the crusade. He left for Hungary by the land route, taking with him as a trophy the head of Hungary's patron St. Stephen, escorted by King Hugh of Cyprus and Prince Bohemond. At Tripoli, in Bohemond's territory, King Hugh fell sick; and on 10 January, died, leaving a nine-month-old son as heir to his kingdom. It was a bad beginning for the year 1218 in the Holy Land.

Yet John of Brienne at any rate heaved a great sigh of relief. His position had been very difficult. He was by birth only a minor noble of Champagne; while his wife lived he had indeed been King-Consort of the Kingdom of Jerusalem. But she was six years dead; and since her death their baby daughter Yolande was technically the queen and John of Brienne merely the queen's father. In practice the barons and the Masters of the Military Orders recognized him as their real ruler; but vis-à-vis crowned kings from Christian kingdoms overseas he was not, by all the conventions of the feudal world, entitled to claim or to exercise leadership. Yet he was the most experienced and *rusé* of the war-leaders; and whereas the crusading kings and nobles were, inevitably, mere passers-through, he was bound to stay. So the departure of King Andrew and King Hugh was not altogether a disaster: particularly as Duke Leopold of Austria stayed on and the second wave of crusaders was expected in the spring. John of Brienne turned his gaze towards the south; and in the first months of the year 1218 set to work, with the Hospitallers and Duke Leopold, rebuilding and refortifying the deserted city of Caesarea on the coast as a springboard for an eventual assault on Jerusalem. Meanwhile the Templars set to work on the construction of that enormous fortress at Athlith on Mount Carmel that was to become the headquarters of their Order.

In April 1218 the second wave of crusaders arrived. First came a fleet from the Low Countries, eighty Frisian ships. They had set off on the appointed date in June the previous year, wintered at Civitavecchia in papal territory, and brought with them many Italian crusaders. Shortly afterwards 180 ships arrived from north Germany. Oliver the Scholastic of Cologne, who had preached the crusade fervently in those parts, was acknowledged despite his clerical status as their virtual leader; they had set out with the Frisians but stopped off in Portugal to help Queen Urraca there in a successful attack against the Moors. No kings, no great nobles accompanied them; for which John of Brienne was profoundly grateful. The crusade was now equipped with a more powerful and efficient fleet, there to fight, not merely to transport for payment like the ships of the Italian maritime powers. John de Brienne called a great conference of war: and, on his suggestion, it was agreed that the crusaders, whose strength now lay in their sea-power, should postpone any direct assault on Jerusalem and attack the

Saracen power at the point Richard the Lion Heart had on his departure, as all Outremer remembered, advised that it should be attacked – in Egypt.

The Ferocity of the Germans

In the year of 1218 the feast of Pentecost fell late, on 3 June. Cardinal Ugolino again rode out every day from Perugia with a train of monks, knights and clerics to sing Mass and to preach. He had spent a busy but fascinating winter in Rome, occupying himself with the affairs of the Friars Minor and of St. Dominic's 'new' Order, the Friars Preacher.

'New' in inverted commas because, although Dominic's design was original, he had in accordance with canon 13 of the Lateran council chosen the already existing Rule of the Augustinians. After the council he had journeyed back to Languedoc, to Notre Dame de Proville, to have his discreet choice confirmed by other members of his group; and certainly by February 1218 he was back in Rome, for he had taken possession of the church of Santa Sabina and was being showered with favours and privileges by the papal court.

Dominic was a man after the authorities' own heart; original but not eccentric, devoted to the Church, respectful of established rules and procedures, a wise administrator. It was almost inevitable that Cardinal Ugolino should hit upon a scheme that appeared to have everything in its favour and nothing to be said against it: the amalgamation of the two new Orders of friars. For why duplicate effort when, combined, that effort may be twice as effective? The fraternities had many points in common and were, as time went on, to develop more. Their founders complemented each other admirably, for whereas Francis could inspire enthusiasm and attract followers in great numbers, Dominic, who lacked this gift – there were less than twenty Friars Preacher at Proville, despite his long years of work in Languedoc – could channel and direct such fervour with a clear head.

It is impossible to deny that Ugolino was probably right; and the subsequent history of the Franciscans might have been less disturbed, and that of the Dominicans more radiant, if their two founders had agreed to join forces. But the Cardinal had reckoned without that stubborn addiction to their own precise notions that characterizes the founders of groups of activists. Dominic and Francis met in Rome – Francis had been invited to preach before Honorius and his cardinals. which he did *extempore*, throwing away the sermon prepared for him, and•with great success – under Ugolino's auspices. Ugolino set the scene very carefully and Francis was much impressed with Dominic's humility, which resembled his own. As they left Dominic asked Francis to give him the cord he wore around his waist: this was a touching gesture coming from an older and wiser man, and a priest at that. And as he was tying the cord round his own waist, Dominic said to the other: 'Brother Francis, I wish that your order and mine might be made one and that we might live in the Church according to the same Rule.'[15]

Francis no doubt replied more courteously than he did to a group of friars who at the 1218 Chapter came to him with a similar proposal, but the gist of the reply was the same: 'My brothers! my brothers! God has called me by the way of simplicity and humility and has in truth revealed this way for me and for all who are willing to trust and follow me. So I do not want you to quote any other Rule to me, whether that of Saint Benedict, Saint Augustine or Saint Bernard, or to recommend any other way or form of life except this way which God in his mercy has revealed and given to me. The Lord told me that he wished me to be a new kind of simpleton in this world . . . God will confound you through your prudence and learning.' Nevertheless, Cardinal Ugolino was not a man to be easily deterred. He brought Dominic with him to the Chapter; and we may perhaps infer that he was hoping that if Francis would not accept any compromise, Dominic seeing the numbers and the fervour of the gathering by Assisi might join, with his handful of followers, the Friars Minor.

In fact, Dominic was rather shocked; for not only had Francis apparently made not the slightest attempt to organize food and drink for a multitude that, according to the *Fioretti*, numbered five thousand but in a sermon he even boasted of this improvidence, 'Give yourselves wholly to prayer and to praising God,' was his theme, 'and all the care of your bodies leave to him.' The miracle of the loaves was not repeated; but from Assisi, Spello, Foligno, Spoleto and even Perugia 'came men with pack animals, horses and carts laden with bread and wine and beans and cheese and other good things to eat, according to that which was necessary for the poor of Christ. Besides this, they brought table-cloths, pitchers, bowls, glasses and other vessels which were needful for so great a multitude, so that even knights, barons and other gentlemen, who came to see, waited upon them at table with great humility and obedience.'

Dominic was confounded; generously admitted his error; and decided there and then – or so the account has it – that holy poverty should be the rule in his Order too. But he went on his way unrepentant; spontaneous poverty perhaps was attractive but culpable inefficiency could hardly fail to put him off. He, like all who attended the Chapter, could see for himself the pitiful end of the ill-prepared expeditions that had set out a year earlier to Germany and Hungary.

They were back; and it looked as if nothing would induce them to set foot outside Italy again. Their tales of woe damped down everybody's enthusiasm; but perhaps none the less appealed, as the story of other people's disasters does appeal, to the sense of humour of those who had stayed behind – who included Fra Giordano. Here is his account in full – first of the brothers who went to Germany.

'Being ignorant of the language, when they were asked if they wished to be sheltered or to eat, or the like, they answered *ja*; they were accordingly treated kindly by some of the people. And seeing that because of the word *ja* they were treated kindly, they resolved to answer *ja* to whatever question they would be asked. Where it happened that they were asked if they were heretics and if they had come to corrupt Germany and they replied *ja*, some of them were cast into prison, others were stripped and led naked to a dance and made a ludicrous spectacle before their fellow-men. The brothers, therefore, seeing that they would not be able to gather a harvest in Germany, returned to Italy. As a result of these things, Germany had a reputation among the brothers of being so cruel that they would not dare to return there except they were filled with a desire for martyrdom.'

In Hungary the local inhabitants, though less interested in suspected Cathars, were even more uncouth.

'As they walked through the fields, they were derided, and the shepherds set their dogs upon them and kept striking them with their staves, the point, however, being turned away. And when the brothers debated among themselves why they were being treated like this, one said: "Perhaps they wish to have our tunics." But when they had given them these they did not leave off their blows. He added: "Perhaps they wish to have our vests too." But when they had given them these, they did not cease their blows. He then said: "Perhaps they want our breeches too." ' Eureka! For 'when they gave them these, they stopped their blows and let them go away naked.' It was just as well it was high summer. 'One of these brothers told me he had lost his breeches fifteen times in this way. And since, overcome by shame and modesty, he regretted losing his breeches more than his other clothing, he soiled the breeches with the dung of oxen and other filth, and thus the shepherds themselves were filled with nausea and allowed him to keep his breeches.' It was possibly fortunate that these naked if persevering Italians never came anywhere near King Andrew and his host: one can imagine the mighty gale of Hungarian guffaws that would have swept over the crusaders. And so 'these brothers, afflicted with other insults too, returned to Italy.'[16]

It is not surprising, then, that at the Chapter of 1218 there was no enthusiasm for sending new groups out. 'Lord preserve us,' prayed the massed friars, 'from the heresy of the Lombards[17] and the ferocity of the Germans.' Besides, the crusade appeared to be stagnating in the Holy Land. The Emperor was still in the north, among his ferocious compatriots, whom none now wished to beard, and they had no notion that John of Brienne was planning an assault on Egypt.

NOTES

1 For a full account of the Fourth Lateran Council, with the full texts of all the seventy canons, and the papal decree proclaiming the new crusade, see *Histoire des Conciles, Tome V Deuxième Partie* by C-J. Hefele, in the corrected French translation by Dom H. Leclercq (Le Touzey et Ané, Paris, 1913). See also for interesting accounts of the period and of Pope Innocent, the *Lives of the Popes in the Middle Ages*, Vol. XI, by the Rev. H. K. Mann (Kegan Paul, London, 1925, second edition) and the *History of Latin Christianity*, Vol. VI, by H. H. Milman (John Murray, 1887, fourth edition).

2 The only direct evidence that Francis was at the council lies in the assertions made by a Dominican friar, Gérard de Fachet, in his *Vita Fratrum* and, much later, by Angelo Clareno in his work. The indirect evidence, which is much more convincing, is bound up with Francis' strange devotion to the letter Tau: with which he always used to mark his own writings, and in particular the famous *Blessing to Brother Leo*, the actual sheet of which is preserved in Assisi, carefully folded, with a note by Leo, 'Blessed Francis wrote this blessing with his own hand for me, Brother Leo.'

What has all this to do with the council? Simply this, that in his dramatic opening speech the Pope quoted the vision of Ezekiel (IX, 1–4) in which the Lord tells the man clothed in linen, with the writer's ink-horn by his side, 'Go through the midst of Jerusalem and set a Tau upon the foreheads of men that sigh and cry for all the abominations that be done in the midst thereof.' The Tau was merely a form of the Cross; 'Only those will be marked with this sign and will obtain mercy,' added the Pope, 'who have mortified their flesh and conformed their life to that of the Crucified Saviour.' Certainly, if Francis was at the council, this would explain his often-mentioned devotion to this letter. But of course it is no proof; he may have heard Innocent's speech reported elsewhere – or read Ezekiel himself.

3 It has been suggested that Francis had gone to Perugia to discuss with Pope Innocent the difficulties raised by canon 13 of the council, which forbade the proliferation of new Orders and hence was present at his deathbed. (In fact it seems that Innocent's verbal acceptance of the *First Rule* before the council was considered valid enough to free Francis from the obligation that compelled Dominic to accept the Rule of St. Augustine for *his* Order.) It is also held that Francis was at Perugia shortly after Honorius' election to beg for a special plenary indulgence for the Portiuncula. This controversial but really rather unimportant question merits a chapter in most biographies and many articles in learned magazines.

4 The critical edition of the *Lettres de Jacques de Vitry* by R. B. C. Hoygens was published at Leiden in 1960.

5 Jacques de Vitry was wrong, technically, in calling them Sisters Minor (see page 207).

6 Echoes of the late Innocent here. It was he who first used that very phrase to condemn the Catholic hierarchy of Languedoc.

7 The description of the Chapter held near Gubbio is given by the anonymous writer of the *Passion of San Verecondo*. It does not seem that it may refer to a time later in Francis' life when,

after receiving the stigmata, he travelled about on a donkey. Yet, if so, how are we to explain the very explicit reference to Francis assembling 'his first three hundred Friars Minor'? Probably the elder Messer Andrew ran the two periods together in his reminiscences.

8 There is much confusion about the Chapter of the Mats; it is now, however, generally accepted that the medieval accounts lumped together a whole series of events that occurred at several similar Chapters; and it is also generally accepted that the first Chapter deserving the title was the Chapter of 1217.

9 It is also generally accepted that the title of Minister-Provincial was first instituted at the Chapter of 1217. It would seem to follow therefore that the title of Minister-General (which had absolutely no military connotations) was also instituted at the time. Yet though Francis has always been recognized as the first Minister-General, it is quite possible that as early as 1217 or before Peter of Catania had become in name as in fact his Vicar General, or stand-in. The third layer of authority was that of the '*Custodes*,' or guardians, in charge of a particular district or community. These are still the titles that the contemporary Franciscan Orders use.

10 When Cardinal Giovanni of San Paolo died in the year following Innocent's death, Cardinal Ugolino more and more assumed the role of Protector of the Order, which became formalized in 1220. There is a suggestion in Francis' request at that time to Pope Honorius to give his Order one special 'Pope' rather than many that between 1216 and 1220 there was some sort of commission of cardinals and prelates overseeing the Friars Minor. Hence Ugolino's warning at Florence of opposition at the Roman Curia: a remark for which there must be some explanation, even if the remark was not made at this precise time.

11 A coastal strip of only about 440 square miles was all that remained in the hands of John of Brienne and the barons. Admittedly it was bordered on the north by the County of Tripoli, the Principality of Antioch and the Christian Kingdom of Armenia; and backed by the independent Kingdom of Cyprus.

12 For the Fifth Crusade and its history, see especially *A History of the Crusades*, Vol. 11 by K. M. Setton and H. C. Lea (University of Pennsylvania, 1962) and the *Histoire du Royaume Latin de Jerusalem*, Vol. 11 by J. Prawer (C.N.R.S., Paris, 1970). The contemporary sources are the *Chronicles* of Matthew Paris, Ralph of Coggeshall and Roger of Wendover, already referred to, the *Chronicle* of Ernoul and of Bernard the Treasurer, *L'Estoire d'Eracles Empereur*, the *Historia Hierosolimitara* by the devoted Jacques de Vitry, and the *Historia Damiatina* by Oliver the Scholastic.

13 Who 'were conducted there by sea by a certain bishop from Hungary.' *Chronicle* of Giordano di Giano.

14 There is a most striking similarity that I had not noticed till writing this chapter between the strategy of the crusaders in the autumn of 1218 and the strategy of the British in the spring of 1941. Both launched three-pronged attacks from Palestine against the enemy: in 1218 the enemy being the Saracens, and in 1941 the Vichy French; and the three prongs were almost identical – the coast road, Merdjayoun and the Bekaa, the Golan Heights and Damascus. See, if interested, the present author's *Our Enemies the French* (Leo Cooper, 1976).

15 It is Sabatier who first insisted on Cardinal Ugolino's desire to unite the Orders founded by Dominic and Francis. See also Rosalind Brooke's *The Coming of the Friars* (Allen and Unwin, 1975) for a detailed and scholarly study of the relations between the two. It was in 1217 that

Dominic, too, dispersed his few followers; but his purpose was avowedly to set up new centres at the university cities of Bologna and Paris (*op. cit.*, p. 93 ff.) – as the same result followed from Francis' missions, at least in Paris, his motives were believed, incorrectly, to have been the same. Miss Brooke agrees that Dominic and Francis probably met in Rome in the early months of 1217.

16 The *Anonymous of Perugia* confirms Fra Giordano's account:

'*A quibusdam vero expellebantur quia timebant ne fratres non essent Christiani fideles, quia adhuc non habebant Fratres confirmatam a Papa regulam sed concessam . . . reversi sunt ad beatum Franciscum, angustiati plurimum et afflicti.*'

('They were expelled by some because they feared that the brothers were not faithful Christians, seeing that their Rule had still not been confirmed by the Pope, but was only conditional . . . they came back to the blessed Francis in the greatest affliction and distress.')

17 Pacificus' group had, unlike the others, at least reached its destination. But when they tried to begin preaching at Paris they were suspected of being Cathars – as Giordano reports – and so their mission was as ineffective as the rest. In Germany such suspicions might have been based on mere verbal misunderstanding; not so in France. In their way of life and in their tendancies, the Friars Minor were only too close to the Cathars. Presumably reports of this 'misunderstanding' came back from Pacificus to a horrified Francis: hence the chorus of prayer to the Lord to protect his followers not only from the suspicion but from the taint of the 'heresy of the Lombards'.

Crusader –
🌱 The Climax of a Life 🌱

11: Crusader – The Climax of a Life[1]

Arrival at Acre

A year had rolled by, and in May 1219 the Friars Minor once again gathered beneath Assisi. This was one of the more momentous Chapters of the Order; the inactivity and depression of the previous Pentecost gave way to new vigour and new decisions. Groups of friars were sent out not indeed to unintelligible Germany or Hungary but to the lands of the *langue d'oc*, Aquitaine and Provence. And this time they were to be provided, probably at the insistence of Cardinal Ugolino and the more level-headed friars, with a papal safe-conduct – a letter which Pope Honorius duly signed and sealed at Rieti, affirming that 'our dear son, Brother Francis, and his companions of the life and order of the Friars Minor' were good Catholics and should be treated as such. But the great news was that missions were to be sent to the infidels and their lands: to Tunis a group led by Fra Giles, to the Moors a group led by Fra Vitale, and to join the crusaders a group led by Francis.[2]

A month after the Chapter ended Francis and his group were at Ancona, making ready to embark.

Why this change? Why had Francis after so long a time finally and belatedly decided to join the crusade? Or, to put it another way, why had he not followed Elias in the autumn of 1217 or, failing that, after the Chapter of 1218? Why this sudden spurt of decision?

I think we may take it that it was all to do with the Emperor. In a sense this is a curious assertion because Francis and Frederick, so far as we know, never met. Yet people's lives can be greatly influenced – an assertion so commonplace and obvious that it probably needs restating – by leaders whom they never meet, particularly when those leaders are idealized. Frederick was the hope of Christendom, it was natural that he should be the hope of Francis.

There is more than mere speculation here. Francis reached Ancona to embark on the feast of St. John, 24 June. Now on 12 January, from the High Diet of Fulda, Frederick II, counselled by Hermann of Salza, the Master of the Teutonic Order, had written to the Pope not only pledging that he himself would be setting out on that date but advising Honorius to excommunicate all those German princes who should not appear in arms ready to embark for the Holy Land next St. John's day.

There was no reason to doubt Frederick's enthusiasm, or his word. As he wrote later to the Pope: 'Who could be more obedient to the Church than he who was nursed at her breast and had nested in her lap? Who more loyal?' Sentiments of loyalty apart, the material situation had changed for the better.

First, the crusade was active; and the crusaders had achieved great successes in the summer of 1218 in Egypt. Secondly, and more importantly, the cause for Frederick's original delay had disappeared: for his great rival, Otto of Brunswick was dead.

Otto had died on 19 May 1218, in his castle of Wurtzburg near Goslar, aged forty-three, reconciled on his death-bed with Holy Church and at the end only regretting that he himself had failed to fulfil *his* pledge to go on crusade, for 'the devil had still thwarted his holy vow.' He died, beaten in self-chosen penance, by the rods of his own scullions. With his death Frederick's position was at long last secure in Germany: his realm settled, nobles and churchmen ready to follow him, he could at long last turn his attention to his long-promised crusade. Hence the famous and enthusiastic letter from Fulda; and hence, no doubt, Francis' desire to be at Ancona on St. John's Day to meet this longed-for Emperor and all the nobility of the German lands.

But here there must be a note of caution. Difficulties arose between the Pope and the Emperor: Frederick before he left wished his seven-year-old son Henry, already crowned King of Sicily, to be elected King of the Germans 'that the two realms may be more firmly governed in my absence.' This was against traditional papal policy; yet Honorius, with misgivings, agreed: and replied to Frederick's letter of 10 May eight days later, authorizing the Emperor for this purpose to postpone his sailing till Michaelmas, that is to say till 29 September. Now in 1219 Pentecost fell late, on 26 May; and it is likely therefore that Francis and the Friars Minor did know of the Pope's letter of 18 May and of the postponement of Frederick's departure.[3] Yet all the same Francis and his group were in Ancona on the earlier appointed day. Perhaps their impatience was too great; perhaps knowing that Frederick would follow in the September passage they did not worry about anticipating him by two or three months; perhaps they hoped to join a great concourse of German nobles. At any rate they left; and for once Francis not only left: he arrived.

There is a late, and perhaps true, story told by Bartholomew of Pisa: it seems that a great number of brothers came with Francis to Ancona, eager to go with him; and that, unwilling to make the choice himself, he asked a little boy to pick out the lucky thirteen. If this is so, God, or Francis, must have guided the little boy's finger: for his companions included Peter of Catania, that trusted administrator, as well as the two noblemen who knew something of warfare, Fra Leonardo di Gislerio, late of Sassorosso, and Fra Illuminato of Rieti.

Very little is known of the journey;[4] according to some sources they stopped off at Cyprus, for Fra Barbaro was there made by Francis to eat asses' dung for having spoken angrily to another friar. (But Fortini places this incident not at *insula Cypri* but at Isola Cipii, a hamlet across the valley from Assisi.) There is one suggestion that they called in at Crete. Wadding very probably supposes that they disembarked in mid-July at Acre; and that they were met by Elias.

It is impossible to suppose that Elias had been inactive or led a placid, undistinguished life in the two years he had been in Outremer. It was not in his character to be anything but energetic and passionate. Fra Giordano, our sole direct informant, merely tells us that he enrolled in the Order a cleric, Caesar of Speyer, who had nearly been burnt for suspected heresy in Germany where he had founded his own little group of 'poor ladies' – much to the annoyance of their husbands. We may deduce, indirectly, that Elias studied crusader architecture: for the *Sacro Convento* built by him at Assisi, so rapidly after Francis' death, has many of the features of a crusader castle. But what can hardly be doubted is that Elias, an intensely political animal, greeted Francis and his companions on the quayside with all the news of the past two years, and of his own experiences: and in the days that followed told Francis not only of the details of the crusades, its armies, leaders and exploits but also of his own much increased knowledge of the Saracens. For it would have been out of character for Elias to have limited his mission to mere preaching to the local Christians: he, too, initially at least, must have been bitten by the desire to preach to the Saracens and perhaps, to seek martyrdom. Elias was an intelligent man; and religiously speaking, as his later diplomatic dealings showed, both an enthusiastic dispatcher of missionaries and an unbigoted correspondent with Mohammedan *eminenti* as distant as the Caliph of Baghdad. Much of what he had to recount must have come as a surprise, indeed a shock, to Francis, and a most disturbing shock. For any intelligent observer could only have had this to say: that, whatever newcomers might think, black was not as pitch-black nor white as unspotted as they were painted – not all Saracens were devils and not all Christians angels.

Meanwhile there was the dazzling city of Acre to be seen, with its gardens, long rows of marble houses, terraced roofs that stretched from one end of the city to the other, overlooking the wide and airy streets down below, with its quarters divided by nations, into a minuscule pattern of all Christendom, with the great Xenodochia of the knights of the Hospital, the glory of the city. From its walls the plains stretched to the blue outlines of the hills that hid Nazareth. Acre was the dream city of chivalry; and Francis, barefoot and poorly clad, must have wandered around it in a haze of delayed delight. He stayed, however, only a few days – for Acre, picturesque as it was, was merely Christendom *couchant*; and in Egypt his heart's desire was awaiting him – Christendom with its claws outstretched, Christendom *rampant*.

It is not clear how many of his companions Francis took with him; Illuminato certainly, Leonardo and Peter of Catania probably, Elias possibly. They sailed from Acre in mid-summer; and certainly before the ill-fated assault of 29 August had joined the crusaders that were besieging Damietta in the Nile Delta. It is only possible to guess at Francis' emotion when he finally saw the commander of the crusading forces, John de Brienne. It was nearly fifteen years since he had set out so gaily to join his brother Walter in Apulia. Now he was in a very different dress; but at long last the tales of Champagne were coming true.

The Nephew of Saladin

The Sultan Melek-al-Kamil of Egypt was a complex man in a complicated position. Nephew of Saladin, eldest son of Saphadin, he was almost exactly the same age as Francis. He was an extremely cultivated person, with a taste for Sufi religious poetry and in particular for the poems of the great mystic Omar-ibn-al-Farid. He was no fanatic; he had always been on excellent terms with the Venetians – there were about 3,000 European traders in Egypt – and was criticized by his Arab contemporaries for not being a fervent enough Muslim. Indeed, as a boy he had been knighted one Palm Sunday by his uncle's great but courteous antagonist, Richard the Lion Heart. It is a commonplace of medieval history that crusaders who had come out simply to kill or be killed, paused to admire and often stayed to be seduced. Saracen civilization – not, strictly speaking, Arab, for the Ayubites were a Kurdish dynasty – was more refined and in many ways more tolerant; yet behind the easy tolerance of the ruling classes there were religious fanatics, on the Saracen as on the Christian side, who saw in their antagonists merely dogs and infidels, who proclaimed them as such in violently intemperate language and who succeeded in destroying any attempt at establishing a dialogue.

Refinement did not imply decadence, nor a taste for poetry incompetence in war. Melek-al-Kamil had not been expecting an attack on Egypt; and most certainly had he been expecting one, he would have imagined that the invaders would choose to try and seize as their base Alexandria to the west rather than Damietta, a city of 80,000 that lay on the eastern banks of one of the many branches of the Nile two miles from the sea.[5] Damietta was well fortified; defended by a triple ring of walls with many towers and, on the Nile side, by an island on which stood a tower linked by chains to the bank: the Burj-as-Silsilah. But within a week of their arrival off Damietta the crusaders had, under the very eyes of the Sultan, attacked and taken the chain-tower and island. This was the first disaster. The next disaster was political: heartbroken, apparently, at this news, the aged Saphadin had died at Damascus. On his death the usual semi-fratricidal contest had smouldered. Saphadin's third son, Al-Muazzam, had succeeded him in Syria; in Cairo there had been a conspiracy to replace Melek-al-Kamir by the second son, his brother Al-Faiz. All these intrigues had caused great confusion in the Muslim camp; and it was only because the crusaders had been hit first by floods and then by an epidemic which killed among others Cardinal Robert de Courçon that little had been lost.

By the spring of 1219 these internal differences were over. Al-Faiz had been arrested, with the Amirs who supported him, and had died mysteriously. The Sultan's other brother, Al-Muazzam, had proved himself a fairly loyal ally; the Sultan's son, Al Masud, was ruling in the Yemen. The Ayubite dynasty had settled, with surprisingly little difficulty, into its mould for the next generation.

Militarily, however, the situation had deteriorated. The crusaders, reinforced by a large French and English contingent, had totally surrounded Damietta; and the Sultan was forced to set up his camp at Fariskur, six miles further down the Nile, six miles – and this was the point – closer to Cairo. By the late spring Melek-al-Kamil was appealing, vainly, to the Caliph of Baghdad for aid; and in the Holy Land his brother Al-Muazzam had decided, for fear that the crusaders might take them, to dismantle his fortresses in Cisjordan and even to pull down the walls of Jerusalem – the panicky policy of the *terre brulée*.

This was the situation when, at the Pentecost Chapter, Francis decided to set out for the crusade – a situation full of hope for the crusaders, militarily. They needed just that final boost that the coming of the Emperor would give – and then the fall of Damietta was assured, and the drive to Cairo might begin. It was not, however, quite the same situation when Francis arrived.

For one thing Duke Leopold of Austria had left the host. He had been crusading for nearly two years, and none could criticize him. For another there had been two failed assaults on the walls of Damietta, on 20 July and 6 August, and many were dead, including Hugh of Lusignan, Comte de la Marche, and William of Chartres, the Master of the Temple. There were once more all the problems of a divided command in the Christian camp. While John of Brienne, supported by Leopold of Austria, had been totally in charge, all had gone well. But with the arrival, in mid-September 1218, of the papal legate with papal money and the papal fleet so long waiting at Messina, trouble had stirred. This man was a Spaniard, and a cardinal, overbearing and tactless, Pelagius of Santa Lucia. This is not the place to go into all the intricacies of the dispute. Suffice it to say that as the Pope's representative he claimed the overall direction of the whole crusade, at any rate until the Emperor should arrive.

Even so, when Francis reached the host, in the hottest days of that blazing summer, there was much to gladden his eye. With the peace established in England, there were four great Earls and their followers in Outremer: Earl Ranulf of Chester, that veteran crusader, with the loyal William Ferrers, Earl of Derby; and also Saer de Quincy, Earl of Winchester, the leader of the ex-rebels with his supporter Hugh d'Aubigny, Earl of Arundel.[6] France, admittedly, was less well represented: with the death of the leader of the Lusignans, there was only Hervé, Count of Nevers, of the great nobility – but to make up for this gap there were militant churchmen galore, the Archbishop of Bordeaux, the bishops of Paris, Laon and Angers. And above all there was John of Brienne himself, almost universally admired for his skill in war, to symbolize the chivalry of Champagne.

I imagine that Francis, out of loyalty, attached himself at once to John of Brienne; but almost immediately he must have been faced with a very painful dilemma. For the one man who most certainly did not share the universal admiration for John of Brienne was Cardinal Pelagius. The two differed not only about military strategy and about the questions of command; they differed, fundamentally, in their war aims. Pelagius wanted outright victory, the capture of Cairo, and the destruction of Saracen power; John of Brienne, more modestly, would have been content with the restoration of the Kingdom of Jerusalem. These differences, which might have lain latent, had come flaring to the surface since February, because in February the Sultan had made his first, tentative offers of peace. Since then there had been a sporadic interchange of envoys between one camp and the other; and the divisions in the Christian camp had hardened. For Melek-al-Kamil had offered to surrender the Kingdom of Jerusalem, with Jerusalem itself, much to the joy of the barons and of John of Brienne. The Military Orders, however, supported Cardinal Pelagius in his intransigence, largely because the Sultan refused to include their fortresses of Kerak and Krak de Montreal in his offer – though, before the end of August, he had offered an annual tribute of 30,000 besants in compensation.

It can hardly be supposed that Francis remained ignorant of, or unaffected by, all the complications. He had probably expected to find a crusade of the *chansons de geste*, with paladins and churchmen in brave array, eager only to smite the Saracens or win martyrdom in the attempt. Instead he found a divided camp, with the paladins confusingly in favour of peace and the churchmen disconcertingly intent on war. Whatever his loyalty to the Church and to the Pope, he can hardly have failed to prefer John of Brienne, a French-speaker and from Champagne, to the haughty Spanish cardinal. Then there was the additional confusion of the Saracens and their attitudes. He must have learnt very quickly from camp gossip, even if he had not learnt it already from Elias, that the followers of Islam could be more generous and more peace-loving than the leaders of Christianity. If he had been a younger man, no doubt impulse and the sight of banners could have swayed his heart and quelled his doubts. But Francis was nearly forty; and this is an age for reflection.

On 29 August, while Pelagius and John of Brienne were still wrangling over strategy, the common soldiers of the crusade, sick of waiting, launched an almost spontaneous attack. It ended disastrously. Despite Pelagius' urging, the Italian crusaders fled. Only a last-minute rally by John of Brienne, with the support of the English Earls and the Masters of the Military Orders, prevented a catastrophe. As it was, over 4,300 crusaders were killed.

According to Thomas of Celano, Francis had had a holy presentiment that the battle would turn out badly, and tried, despite a natural fear of being considered an interfering fool, to warn the soldiers off; naturally enough they refused to pay the least attention to him; and, Thomas of Celano almost implies, they deserved therefore the hammering they received. But there are two significant details in his account: first that Francis mourned especially over the Spanish knights and secondly that Francis would not watch the battle himself but made 'his companion' go and watch it for him, and report back. Now the first detail can be seen as an implied reproach to Cardinal Pelagius the warmonger, who had been responsible for the deaths of his fellow-countrymen; but the second undeniably shows that Francis was no longer fascinated by the panoply of war. He had changed from the young man of twenty; he was horrified by the reality of war; he was ready, perhaps, to apply his favourite saying, 'God give you peace', not merely to the Christians but also to the infidels.

Indeed, despite the killing of so many crusaders at the end of August, the Sultan was more than ever inclined to peace. There was famine in Egypt, quarrels in Syria, and above all the threat that Frederick II and the hosts of Germany would cross the Mediterranean in the autumn passage. He sent two captive knights with his new terms to the Christian camp. They arrived at the end of September. The terms offered were noble: Jerusalem, central Palestine and Galilee would be restored, concessions were made on the military castles on the far side of the river Jordan, the Sultan would pay for the reconstruction of the walls and fortifications of Jerusalem which his brother Al-Muazzam had begun to demolish, a portion of the True Cross would be handed back to the Christians, and twenty noble hostages would be offered by the Saracens as a guarantee of their good faith. In return the Sultan requested a truce for the unprecedentedly long period of thirty years – a generation.[7]

It is easy to see now, with historical hindsight, that such a truce ought immediately to have been accepted: it would have meant not only the liberation of the holy places but the re-establishment and the prosperity of the Latin Kingdom of Jerusalem. Yet it is easy to understand too, Cardinal Pelagius' refusal. He took the offer, rightly, as a sign more of weakness than magnanimity; he was backed by letters both from Pope Honorius and from the Emperor Frederick, condemning negotiations and forbidding explicitly the accepting of any truce; he was supported for reasons of principle by the Patriarch of Jerusalem, the prelate most directly concerned and for motives of self-interest by the Italians in the crusaders' camp. And furthermore, despite the opposition of John of Brienne and Earl Ranulf of Chester he was proved right in immediate practice. Less than a week after Melek-al-Kamil's offer had been made and rejected on 5 November, Damietta fell.

The crusaders had been besieging the city for nearly a year and a half, it had been a hot and unpleasant summer; the sack of Damietta was not especially chivalric. There had been 80,000 inhabitants of the place; by the time the siege and the sack were over there were less than 3,000; and of these only 100 were both alive and well. The lower ranks were as avaricious over the division of the spoils as the higher ranks were quarrelsome over the division of the city. Vices waxed, virtues waned. In the midst of all this came the totally disheartening news that Frederick II had failed to sail at Michaelmas; once again he had asked Pope Honorius for a postponement, and he would not be arriving till the following spring passage.

And so, in the rather laconic words of the *Estoire d'Eracles* 'This man, who started the Order of the Friars Minor, brother Francis by name, came to the army at Damietta and there did much good, and remained there until the city was taken. He saw the sin and evil which began to increase among the soldiers, and was displeased by it. For this reason he left there, stayed for a while in Syria, and then returned to his own land.'

This bold summary omits the most famous and most significant of all the episodes of this part of Francis' life: his visit to the Sultan's camp.

To be Martyred or not to be Martyred

When he had originally set out to preach penance to the Moors in Spain, Francis had been 'burning with the desire for holy martyrdom.' On the surface there is something illogical and contradictory here; for if a missionary is martyred, he is no longer in a position to preach, and if he preaches successfully, then presumably he will not be martyred. Yet this was the ideal not only of Francis but of all clerics who wished to go among the Saracens; and in fact it was not as illogical as it sounds. For the aim, curiously enough, was to preach penance not successfully, but unsuccessfully; indeed to drive Saracens and infidels into such a state of exasperation that they really could not *not* martyr the missionaries, if only to have a little peace from their clacking tongues. Preaching of this sort was equivalent to the knight's defiance on the field of battle: and it was no more expected that the Saracens should be converted by the declamations of the preacher than frightened by the challenge of the knight. There was a ritual in missionary work just as there was on the battlefield: and all true missionaries realized that their basic and conventional task was to be martyred. To do otherwise was to outrage the conventions of the time.

The group of Friars Minor who set off for Morocco at the same time as Francis set off for Egypt were very much a case in point. Their leader Fra Vitale fell ill, but the other five went boldly forward. At Seville they entered the mosque and began to preach against the Koran: they were merely beaten. They shouted down from the top of a tower that Mohammed was an imposter: they were only imprisoned. Expelled from Seville, they made their way to Morocco and condemned the Muslim faith as a pack of lies before the Mira-molin, Abu Yakub Yusuf II. Still martyrdom eluded them, though at least they were tortured. The Infante Don Pedro of Portugal was living in exile at the Miramolin's court, a refugee from his miserable brother Alfonso II the Fat: he did all he could to save the five and at his insistence they were expelled from the country. Yet, slipping their guard, they hurried back to Marrakesh and once again invaded the mosques. In desperation Abu Yakub offered them vast gifts; they merely attempted to convert their torturers. At long last they won their reward. They were successfully beheaded – the first martyrs of the Franciscan Order, Fras Bernardo, Otho, Pietro, Accurso and Adjuto.[8]

Now the fascinating thing is that this was considered the correct way to behave, and highly meritorious. Any lesser insistence on the crown of martyr-dom would have been considered unsuitable. The very day after they were beheaded an eye-witness from the household of the Infante wrote a long account of their sufferings. Even Don Pedro himself, who, it might have been imagined, would have been only too glad that the incident was over, rescued their bodies from the dogs and had them taken secretly to Coimbra, to the church of the Augustinian Canons, where crowds flocked to pray before them – including a young canon regular, the future Anthony of Padua.

Now contrast this with Francis' behaviour. He went to the Sultan's camp, he had a series of amiable discussions, and he came back not only unmartyred but virtually unmarked. No wonder his contemporaries and biographers passed fairly cursorily over these and subsequent events, for Francis had not behaved as a person in his position was expected to behave. They were bewildered, and they were embarrassed. To cover their embarrassment they emphasized the courtesy of the Sultan: indeed they imply that he became a Christian in all but name. What they never dare consider, what indeed was inconceivable, was that Francis may have had, or shown, a sympathy for Islam.

Yet consider the *Second Rule* that Francis, with the help of Caesar of Speyer, composed after his return to Italy. Chapter 16 is headed 'Missionaries among the Saracens and other unbelievers'. It is rather long, it certainly envisages the pos-sibility of martyrdom, but the least that can be said is that it is not crusading in tone. The motto is taken from Matthew: 'Behold, I am sending you forth like sheep in the midst of wolves. Be therefore as wise as serpents and guileless as doves,' and the middle section that lays down the guidelines for the missionaries' behaviour reads as follows:

'The brothers who go can conduct themselves among them [i.e. the Saracens] spiritually in two ways. One way is to avoid quarrels or disputes and be subject to every human creature for God's sake, so bearing witness to the fact that they are Christians. Another way is to proclaim the word of God openly, when they see that it is God's will, calling on their hearers to believe in God almighty, Father, Son and Holy Spirit, the Creator of all, and in the Son, the Redeemer and Saviour, that they may be baptized and become Christians, because unless a man may be born again of water, and the Spirit, he cannot enter into the Kingdom of God.'

This is not, and could not be, a disavowal of the five martyrs of Morocco. But, had they been alive to read the *Second Rule*, they would have certainly been disconcerted at the implied preference for the quieter method of simply setting the Saracens a good example rather than proclaiming the credo from the minarets. And they would certainly have been peeved to find no reference to their own heroic sufferings, or condemnation of the diabolical nature of Islam. And indeed, according to Fra Giordano, Francis later forbade the reading out aloud of their *Legend*. The very least we can conclude is that his attitude to the Mohammedans had become very different.

When precisely did Francis visit the Sultan's camp? Fra Giordano says that it was while the Christian army was beseiging Damietta – i.e. before 5 November, when Damietta fell. Personally I would plump for a later date, during the winter truce that followed the fall of Damietta, on the strength of Jacques de Vitry's sixth letter.

'Sire Rainerio,' he wrote, 'the prior of St. Michael, has just entered the Order of Friars Minor. They are an Order that is making great strides throughout the world, and this is so because it expressly follows the way of life of the primitive Church and its Apostles. . . . The master of these brothers, who is also the founder of the Order, is called Francis; he is loved by God and venerated by all men. He came into our camp and, burning with zeal for the faith, he was not afraid to go into the very camp of our enemy. For several days he preached the word of God to the Saracens, but with little success. The Sultan sent for him in particular and begged him to pray to the Lord for him, the ruler of Egypt, so that God might show him which religion he wished to embrace.

'Colin, the Englishman, our clerk, has also entered this Order along with two other companions of ours: Master Michael and Dom Matthew to whom I had entrusted the parish of the Holy Cross. . . . And I am having a difficult time holding on to the chanter, Henry, and a few others.'

The letter was written in early 1220, and this means that it is at least possible if not probable that Francis was still at Damietta at that time – for there is no mention of his having left – and that the visit could have taken place at any time up to the time of writing of the letter. Furthermore the chronicler Ernoul reports that Cardinal Pelagius specifically forbade Francis to try and get into the Sultan's camp when he first begged to do so on the grounds that it was too dangerous: hence it is more likely that he went in time of truce. But the date of the visit matters very little: it is only important in that the later the visit was, the more likely it is that Francis would have had both the time and inclination to learn or hear about the beliefs and history of the Saracens – to the point where his desire was not to preach and be martyred, but to preach and discuss and even to learn, while of course accepting the risk of a sticky end.

At any rate, truce or no truce, before or after the fall of Damietta, Francis set out for Fariskur and the Sultan's camp with one companion, Illuminato. They were fairly roughly handled at the outposts but by dint of shouting 'Soldan! Soldan!' were finally dragged into his presence.

Melek-al-Kamil apparently at first took the two rather dishevelled figures for would-be deserters from the Christian army who had come over to serve him and embrace the true faith. There had been many such cases; indeed there was a continual flow of renegade Christians, who were extremely well treated by the Sultan. He was immediately disillusioned: he was treated to a short lecture by Francis,[9] who announced very firmly that neither he nor his companion would ever become Saracens, and secondly that they were not envoys from the Christian camp but messengers sent by God to save the Sultan's soul.

Melek-al-Kamil was apparently rather tickled by these strange but sincere visitors, and decided to devote a few days to them – another indication that it was a time of truce, not activity – for he enjoyed philosophical discussion. But he clearly had a rather impish sense of humour, and felt that a test or two of Francis' sincerity and wit would not be out of place.

One of the tests involved walking over a beautiful multicoloured carpet embroidered with crosses – a useful item to have at hand to try out the sincerity of self-declared converts to Islam. To the Sultan's surprise Francis agreed to walk towards him treading on the crosses, without demur, and explained: 'Thieves were also crucified along with our Lord. We have the true Cross of our Lord and Saviour Jesus Christ; we adore it and show it great devotion; if the holy Cross of the Lord has been given to us, the cross of the thieves has been left to you as your share. That is why I had no scruple in walking over the symbols of brigands.'

So much for Francis' quick wit, which 'aroused the admiration of all spectators.' St. Bonaventure heard this story from Fra Illuminato. There is another tale that only appears in the *Fioretti* and that all reputable historians and biographers ignore. I do not know why. It was obviously a fine and stiff test of Francis' virtue, such as any Sultan worth his salt might be expected to enjoy arranging.

One night, while staying with the Saracens, Francis went up to rest. 'And there he found a certain woman who was very beautiful in face and body but very foul in mind and soul. That cursed woman solicited St. Francis to commit a most shameful act with her.'

So far, so bad. But it is no disproof of this story that the same tale is told of many saints, any more than the fact that the Copts have legends of carpets with crosses proves or disproves the preceding anecdote. And I like to imagine Francis face to face with a hardened houri. It is rather the sequel that strains modern credulity; for instead of rejecting the scarlet seductress with words of fire, as the best saints tend to do, Francis reverted to his old, bad habits.

'St. Francis answered her: "If you wish me to do what you want, you must also do what I want."

' "I agree," she said, "so let's go and prepare a bed!" and she led him towards a room.

'St. Francis said to her: "Come with me and I will show you a very beautiful bed." And he led her to a room where a very large fire was burning in the house at that time. And in fervour of spirit he stripped himself naked.'

As at previous critical moments, Francis resorted to nudity; but this was perhaps a more dangerous occasion than most. However, Francis – and one cannot help regretting it a little – even at this very late stage saved his chastity once more.

'He threw himself down on the fire in the fireplace as on a bed. And he called to her saying: "Undress and come quickly and enjoy this splendid flowery and wonderful bed, because you must be here if you wish to obey me!" And he remained there for a long time with a joyful face, resting on the fireplace as though on flowers, but the fire did not burn or singe him.'[10]

Now this of course is quite obviously nonsense. Or is it? As Chesterton said, 'The world is in a welter of the possible and impossible,' and to reject all the miracles in Francis' life is 'to try to tell the story of a saint without God.' Certainly the story is dubious; certainly it is late; certainly it has elements of a fairy-tale, probably it is exaggerated – but for all that I believe it to be based on truth. First because it sounds just like Francis' weird sense of humour, secondly because of his well known tendency to take off his clothes in public, thirdly because he did treat Brother Fire rather like a flower later in his life, and fourthly because some such minor miracle would have given him the confidence to risk the test that he now, of his own volition, proposed to the Sultan.

Truth, Dare but no Consequences

Islam – what a problem it has always posed, and still poses, for the Western world. Before the coming of Mohammed the Mediterranean could be, and often was, the centre of a culture and civilization that lapped it on all sides: since Mohammed Mediterranean civilization has been split in two by a curtain of contempt more long-lasting and impervious to change than any other single vision of humanity. As I write these lines, Christians and Muslims are once again killing each other with rabid enthusiasm in the Lebanon, and in the period in which this book is being written the uneasy balance of power and wealth is swinging back once more, after long centuries of subjection, to Islam. There have been exchanges between the two cultures but very rarely any feeling of ease. 'If Islam had been converted, the world would have been immeasurably more united and happy,' Chesterton wrote, in the context of Francis' visit to Melek-al-Kamil. Of course the converse is also true: if Christianity had been converted, the result would have been the same.

Which is true, Islam or Christianity – and how can we possibly tell? But if only it were possible to prove the truth of one side or the other convincingly! There was Francis, an honoured guest at the Sultan's court, the advocate of the Christian faith, allowed to talk, encouraged to expound, but totally unable to convince. In a sense Melek-al-Kamil stood for all humanity: he was both the umpire and the audience, prepared to be convinced if only the two antagonists could agree on their terms of reference and their methods of proof. But they could not. The Sultan had summoned, in the words of the chronicler Ernoul, 'his archbishops and bishops and good clerks of the law, without whom he could not discuss in matters of religion.' But they demanded that the opposite party should not be heard. 'Sire, we ask you in the name of Allah and Moham-med that you give orders for their heads to be cut off, for we must not even listen to them, for our law forbids us to listen to those who preach another law than ours. If anyone dares to preach or even simply to speak against our law, the law orders that his head should be cut off. And we bid you cut off their heads for thus our law ordains.'

Like the Red Queen's in *Alice in Wonderland*, this *prise de position* was an insoluble barrier to any sort of rational debate. But in any case rational debate was, in Francis' opinion too, no way of arriving at the objective truth. 'Our faith is above reason,' he told the Sultan, 'and human reason can only aid the man who already believes. Besides, I cannot take my arguments from holy scripture, because your doctors do not believe in it.' In other words, Francis' position was in its way just as intransigent as that of the advocates of Islam. Discussion and debate were in these circumstances impossible (though Francis kept his head). Was there, then, any more infallible way of arriving at the truth, of proving for certain which was the true religion, and of ending therefore – vast ambition – all religious wars, and indeed reuniting in one religion all mankind? Francis thought there was; and he proposed to the Sultan a trial by fire.[11] The advantage of this method was that it was a system of proving truth of falsehood used all over the world and one that, as Francis may have known, Mohammed himself had proposed in the tenth year of the Hegira to settle a debate on the nature and person of Christ, a question that had left him in great perplexity, between the Christians of Najran and the rabbis of Medina. In Islam this method was known as the *mubâhalä*;[12] in the West as the *ordalia*.

It is important to realize that it is common to all primitive societies, societies where the ability to write and read has not much developed, where documents are rare, and where the proof of the truth or falsity of an assertion rests on oaths and witnesses – as indeed it still largely does in developed societies. But without documents to back up or confound contradictory oaths and statements modern law-suits would either grind to an indecisive halt or come up with some very unsatisfactory verdicts. In this particular case, as Francis had pointed out, 'there could be no agreement on documents; therefore more primitive methods of establishing the truth were called for.

Francis may in fact have been planning such a confrontation even before he left the Christian camp: this would explain the rather curious terms in which Cardinal Pelagius, according to Ernoul, finally gave him permission to approach the Saracens: 'My sons, I do not know what you have in your hearts, nor what your intentions are: but if you want to go keep your hearts and your souls always turned towards the Lord.' For the Church officially disapproved of the *ordalia*; and canon 18 of the Lateran council expressedly forbade any cleric to take part in any blessing or consecration of any of the implements used. Indeed as Pope Honorius wrote in a letter only two years later: 'Such a judgement is strictly forbidden because it seems to want to tempt God.'

Nevertheless this was a comparatively recent view; earlier the Church (though not the theologians, who had always stressed the tempting-God aspect) had not only accepted trials by fire, burning iron, water and the rest but had published special rituals with prayers and blessings, and laid down that the *ordalia* should only be undertaken after confession and fasting. The principle behind the *ordalia* was this: that it was a means of establishing the truth or falsity of a statement, or a series of statements, by the direct interposition of God. For God, being omniscient and just, would not allow an innocent person to be branded as a liar, or vice-versa. And this is an idea that has been accepted by not only Christians and Mohammedans but also by Hindus, Jews and indeed Babylonians. In other words it is an idea common to those that believe in Gods or a God who is both interested in his creatures and their affairs and controls the forces of nature.

In the West there were two forms of this trial by ordeal. The first was that in which both parties to a dispute submitted to an action; and it was this that Francis proposed to the Sultan: that a fire should be lit and that he and Illuminato should go through it at the same time as the doctors of Islam.

This was an extremely rash thing to do, physical dangers apart. For obviously there was the awful possibility – and Francis must have considered it – that he and Illuminato would be burnt but that the Islamic doctors would emerge unscathed. *In that case Islam would be proved to be the true religion.* It is not good enough to say that Francis was so true a Christian that he could never even have imagined such a result, or to suggest that he would have been consoled by being very dead. I suggest that Francis took this test very seriously indeed; and that therefore he, who had proposed it, was prepared to accept Islam as true and abandon Christianity as false should God decide on such an apparently unthinkable judgement. This is clearly a most important and indeed, to some, a most alarming assumption; yet another view must imply either that Francis was an unintelligent fanatic, which is not the case, or else that his proposal was mere trickery, which is worse. If his proposal was sincere – and I assume that it was – he was genuinely proposing to test, not only for the Sultan and humanity in general, but also for himself, the truth or falsity of Christianity and Islam.

In any case it never came to the test. The *Qadi* and the *Ulema* refused; and St. Bonaventure, who had it from Illuminato, reports that the Sultan had just caught a glimpse of one of his priests, 'an old and highly esteemed man, who slipped away the moment he had heard Francis' proposal.' This was probably the Sultan's respected adviser, the ninety-year-old mystic Fakr-al-Din who, the chronicler Al Zayyat reports, 'was consulted by the Sultan in the well known affair of the famous *rahib* [monk].' It was not, however, as Bonaventure implies, cowardice on the part of the Islamic doctors. In the episode of the Najrani Christians it had been Bishop Abu Harith and his five followers who, on the morning set for the *mubâhalâ*, 15 January 631, had refused the trial by fire; and after this Mohammed had received a revelation that Allah reserved the right to himself to explain fully 'the mystery of Christ to angels and man.' It was therefore against Koranic law to accept such a challenge on such an issue. Francis had in a way compensated six centuries too late for an act of Christian cowardice, or prudence. But there was literally no way in which he or any Christian could prove or even attempt to prove the truth of Christianity to the doctors of Islam.

As Chesterton put it, this was 'a great effort that it is hard to judge, because it broke off short like the beginnings of a great bridge that might have united East and West, and remains one of the great might-have-beens of history.'

It was not, however, in Francis' nature to give up. It might be impossible to challenge the doctors of Islam either by word or deed, and thus the great question of the truth of Christianity or Islam could neither be tested nor resolved. But Francis after all was there as the advocate of Christianity; and, being human, he can hardly have failed to be relieved by the doctors' refusal to test the truth and at the same time to be confirmed by this very refusal in his own belief of the truth of Christianity. He therefore offered what was in a way a much braver thing physically; he offered to undergo the trial by fire in its second form, that is to say by himself alone.

This was a more dangerous affair, and therefore a braver offer, in this sense: that in the first instance, God, so to speak, would have had his back up against the wall and would have been forced to allow either the two Christians or the Mohammedan doctors to come out unscathed. But if Francis chose to brave the flames alone, then indeed he might be tempting God, and God might very well let him burn. He could hardly have been ignorant of what had happened to Peter Bartholomew, the discoverer of the Holy Lance, at the time of the First Crusade. Exasperated by constant carping and suspicion, this wretched Provençal peasant had offered to prove his good faith and genuineness of the Holy Lance (which had already led the Christian army to a great victory outside Antioch) by undergoing the ordeal by fire. Dressed in a tunic, the Lance in his hand, he had run through the fire and came out horribly burnt, to die twelve days later. Yet the Lance was still treated with reverence by most.

Francis must have realized that, for presuming too far on God's mercy, he might die the same horrible death. Yet it would be worth the risk if he could convert not indeed the doctors but Melek-al-Kamil himself and his followers, the nobles and the common people. It was in a way a more generous offer than his first one; it is not quite true to say that he was choosing, like Christ, to sacrifice himself for the people, for the whole point of the exercise was to come out of the flames unscathed. But he was still risking, at a moment when his antagonists had refused to take the same risk, and he might gracefully have retired with, so to speak, the honours of the encounter, a self-imposed and rather horrible form of death.

The object of this second exercise being no longer pure truth but simply conversion, it was logical for Francis to explain to the Sultan that, as had happened to Peter Bartholomew, there was a strong risk of failure because of the weakness of the instrument.

'If you are prepared to promise me that you and your people will embrace the Christian religion if I come out of the fire unharmed,' he said, 'I will enter it alone. But if I am burned, you must attribute it to my sins.' This, however, did not particularly appeal to Melek-al-Kamil. The gambling element of a challenge on equal terms between two opposing teams was lost; and in any case he did not want to be responsible, even indirectly, for the burning to death of Francis, which must have appeared to him inevitable in any case and doubly inevitable since the Christian himself was half-prepared for it. He replied tactfully and no doubt truthfully that he would not dare to accept such a choice, for fear of a revolt among his people.

So there was really nothing for Francis and Illuminato to do but to return rather bathetically to the crusaders' camp. Melek-al-Kamil in the chivalric tradition of his dynasty attempted to load them with gifts: but they refused his gold, his silver and his silken garments, though they were forced to accept an escort. And when they came back, they presumably told the story of the Sultan's generosity to the whole camp, for in his *History* Jacques de Vitry gives a rather fuller report than in his *Letter*, which I quote to show how Francis' account must have rattled the prejudices of even a northern Frenchman.

'Even the Saracens and men plunged into the darkness of unbelief admire their [i.e. the Friars Minors'] humility and virtue when the brothers come among them to preach without fear: they receive them very gladly and give them all they need. We have seen the founder and the master of this Order, the one whom all the others obey as their superior general; he was a simple, unlettered man, loved by God and men: he was called brother Francis. Spiritual fervour and ecstasy moved him to such excesses that, having arrived at the army of the Christians before Damietta in Egypt, with no fear whatsoever, fortified solely with the shield of faith, he set out for the camp of the Sultan of Egypt. The Saracens arrested him on his way. "I am a Christian," he said, "bring me to your master!" And so they brought him to him. On seeing the man of God, the Sultan, that cruel beast, became sweetness himself, kept him with him for a few days and with a great deal of attention listened to him preach the faith of Christ to him and to his followers. But in the end he was afraid of seeing some of his soldiers whom the effective words of this man would have converted to the Lord go over to the army of the Christians. He, therefore, had Francis led back to our camp with many signs of honour and with security precautions, but not without saying to him: "Pray for me, that God may reveal to me the law and the faith that is more pleasing to him."'

So it all came down to that in the end: no argument or challenge could convert the 'cruel beasts', but simply prayer, and perhaps example. And this appears to have been the lesson that Francis incorporated in chapter 18 of the *Second Rule*. And a slow, weary, unsuccessful solution it was to prove. I wish myself that Francis and Fakr-al-Din had tried the ordeal by fire: Allah knows how else one can possibly convince Christians of the greater truth of Islam, or Mohammedans of the greater truth of Christianity, or oneself of the greater truth of either.

The Missing Six Months

The most extraordinary silence now falls over the rest of Francis' time in the East. There is not a single reliable anecdote – merely two late and minor incidents placed by Bartholomew of Pisa and Angelo Clareno at Antioch and in Outremer respectively. Sabatier (and Jorgensen even more) have pleased themselves and their readers by picturing Francis' pilgrimages to the holy places, but as Sabatier most honestly admits, *'les documents nous font singulièrement défaut.'*

One explanation for this lacuna may have been political embarrassment. Cardinal Pelagius spent that winter hoping for help from such distant and nebulous potentates as King George of Georgia and Prester John,[13] and in the meanwhile disputing with John of Brienne over the administration of captured Damietta. By letter Pope Honorius supported his legate: John was informed that he owed obedience both spiritual and temporal to the Spaniard. At length, in early 1220, on the pretext of settling questions of matrimonial inheritance, he left the crusade: and it seems quite probable that Francis left with him. The chronology fits; the motive is there, and the silence of all can be explained by their unwillingness to present a Francis siding openly and defiantly with a lay prince against the legate of the Pope.

Francis, then, probably sailed from Egypt to Acre with John of Brienne by the spring crossing; and he probably sailed back from Acre to Venice by the autumn crossing. What of the intervening six months in the Holy Land? We know nothing, absolutely nothing. It is unlikely that he made the pilgrimage to Jerusalem, for two reasons: the first is that Pope Honorius had, as early as 24 July 1217, issued a Bull forbidding all crusaders under pain of excommunication to visit 'the burial-place of the Lord' for largely economic reasons, to avoid paying 'the customary tribute' to the Saracens. The second was far sadder: by the spring of the year 1220 Jerusalem had virtually been destroyed by Al-Muazzam of Damascus. Not only were all the walls, fortifications and great buildings demolished, bar the Tower of David, the Holy Sepulchre and the two great mosques but Jerusalem, like Nazareth, was practically a ghost town. The wells had been blocked up, the fruit trees and vines cut down, and even the marble columns of private houses had been carted off to adorn Damascus. No, there cannot have been much pilgrimage in the Holy Land that year. Besides, all over the burnt out plains and hills of Galilee there was ferocious if sporadic warfare. In John of Brienne's absence, rebuilt Caesarea had been recaptured by the Saracens and destroyed; and in the autumn 4,000 knights of the Temple were besieged outside Acre in their vast new fortress on Mount Carmel.

The other possible explanation of the chroniclers' silence may have been religious. Francis was at least six months in Outremer, presumably in the company of Elias and the other brothers, he cannot have been entirely idle; and yet he showed no disposition to return to Italy. It was (as in a Greek tragedy) outside events, the arrival of a messenger with bad news, that eventually drove him to leave. But if that messenger had not arrived, all the indications are that he would have stayed on in Outremer. What were his projects at this time, what was he waiting for? In one sense there was an obvious answer: he, like everyone else, both in Outremer and Egypt, was waiting for the Emperor to arrive – and all through that year, as through the preceding year, Frederick kept postponing his departure with fresh excuses. This is one explanation, but it is not entirely satisfying; it is, by itself, a little thin.

There is another explanation; it is pure speculation and there is no positive evidence whatsoever, only the deafening silence of Francis' contemporaries and followers supports it. It is just possible that Francis during those last six months may have been immersed in the study of Islam and in contacts with Mohammedan doctors, intending with his brothers to stay on in the East and somehow strive to unite the two religions – probably, as the *Second Rule* suggests, by living an exemplary Christian life, without preaching, without martyrdom, in the midst of Saracen communities. Such a project would have been so repugnant to the whole spirit of the age that it is not surprising that if it existed it was totally taboo in later accounts. As Fra Giordano, quoting Ecclesiastes, wrote of the Moroccan martyrs, all their mission came to nothing, 'perhaps because its time had not yet come, seeing that "the time for everything is inscribed in heaven".'

Towards the end of the summer a lay friar, Stephen, arrived secretly from Italy and immediately sought out Francis. He came with very bad news: in Francis' absence the whole Order had been thrown into confusion. The two brothers left behind as vicars-general to administer the Order in Francis' absence had had the presumption at that year's Pentecost Chapter to introduce new rules, or constitutions. Francis, Fra Giordano relates, was sitting at table while Stephen read out the text of these new constitutions. The most shocking one appears on the surface a mere triviality and unworthy of so great a commotion – until it is realized that it amounted to taking the first steps down the slippery slope that Francis had always particularly feared and dreaded, the Catharization of the Order. The new constitution virtually forbade the eating of meat on any occasion, and of milk products at most. This was a Cathar practice: no meat, no milk, no eggs, no cheese were consumed by the Perfect; their diet was confined to vegetables, bread and fish. Why? It was not a mere matter of asceticism but a practice based upon a belief: that the eating of any produce direct or indirect of coupling, of the sexual act, was of the same order of degradation as copulation itself: fish, being cold blooded, were not, it was believed, contaminated in this way. To anyone, like Francis, acquainted with Cathar beliefs there could only be one, terrifying explanation.[14]

Francis had a plate of meat before him. 'Master Peter,' he said, turning to Peter of Catania, 'what are we to do?' 'Ah, Master Francis,' replied Peter with equal courtesy, 'whatever pleases you, for it is you who have the authority.' 'Well then,' said Francis, 'let us do as the gospel says, and eat the foods that are set before us.'

Stephen, who had been sent out as emissary by a number of worried brothers, was overjoyed. It was not just a question of new constitutions, Fra Filippo had obtained from Cardinal Ugolino and the Curia privileges for the Poor Clares, which was utterly against Clare's own wishes and Francis' strict line forbidding such things. A certain Fra Giovanni da Campello had banded together a great number of lepers, both men and women, and set up a splinter group. Moreover it was rumoured in Italy that Francis was dead. In fact, as so often happens in the absence of a leader, whether of a group or a country, particularly an absence abroad, there had been a virtual *coup d'état*, followed by confusion. Francis at once embarked with Elias, Peter of Catania, Caesar of Speyer, Illuminato, Leonardo and several others to revive and restore his threatened Order. The crusade, that should have been the crowning point of his life's work and had turned out so strangely and unexpectedly, was over.

The Final Years

Francis lived for six years after returning from his crusade, but the story of his active years ends here. What remained was disillusion and sadness – balanced by increasing holiness. In those six years, as he retired more and more into a hermit's way of life, he became a saint. And the mystery of sanctity is something that is very difficult for the ordinary unholy biographer to describe, and almost impertinent to attempt to analyse.

The outward events of those years are quickly told. On Francis' return to Italy 'a long shout of joy,' in Sabatier's words, 'sounded up and down the peninsula.' It was soon followed by tears. For though the upstarts were humbled, and the divergences dissolved, Francis himself gave up the leadership of his Order. 'From today,' he told the next Chapter, 'I am dead for you. But here is Fra Peter of Catania whom you and I will all obey.'

'Then all the brothers,' the account continues, 'began to weep out loud and to shed abundant tears, for they saw themselves becoming in some sort orphans. Next blessed Francis bowed down before brother Peter and promised to show him respect and obedience. From that time on he was subject to him until his death, just like any one of the brothers.'[15]

Why did Francis resign? No doubt because he was totally and utterly disillusioned. The high aim of his lifelong quest had been achieved only to fail. He had gone on crusade but he had not found his personal Graal. He had returned from Egypt and Outremer disillusioned with politics and with the Emperor, who had failed to keep his word, disillusioned with the Church hierarchy, which in the form of Cardinal Pelagius – and with the support of the Pope – had turned the crusade aside from the saving of the holy places; and, worse still, uncertain in his own mind of the need to convert and lost to the cause of martyrdom. He returned to an Order, his own creation, influenced by heresy, abandoning its ideals, and needing an administrator at its head and a more legalistic structure to define its aims. For the next three years he tried, ever more half-heartedly, to write a new constitution. With the help of Caesar of Speyer he produced the passionate *Second Rule*,[16] his last attempt to keep the Order to his own ideals by the exertion of his own force of leadership – only to have it virtually rejected by Cardinal Ugolino and to see the highly formal *Third Rule* – which is still valid, but though less rigorous, hardly applied by present-day Franciscans – solemnly approved by papal Bull on 29 November 1223.[17]

Peter of Catania had died; and Elias became, till Francis' death, vicar-general and the real ruler of the Order. Francis himself turned, like his first companions Giles and Bernard, more and more to the life of a recluse: he went no more a-roving in the old sense but moved only from hermitage to hermitage in the central hills and valleys of Italy, favouring perhaps above all others the hermitages at Greccio and Fonte Colombo in the beautiful valley of Rieti.

Furthermore his health had been ruined by his journey to the East. Always frail, he became a semi-permanent invalid; in particular he appears to have contracted an eye disease that became progressively worse; and fearsome are the accounts of how the doctors of the time attempted to cure him by cauterization. 'Deal gently with me, Brother Fire,' he said as the red-hot iron approached his temples, 'for I have always been very courteous towards you.'[18]

The last Pentecost Chapter that Francis attended, plucking at Elias' habit from time to time in order to attract his attention, seems to have been that of the year 1224. Towards the height of the summer he made his way to the mountain that Count Orlando had given him, Monte La Verna; with him went Angelo and Masseo and the cleric who had become his closest companion and to whom he dictated the letters which were now his only means of influencing the world – Fra Leo. Leaving Angelo and Masseo in the huts long prepared, he retired with Leo to the remotest part of the mountain and then separated himself even from his companion by a ravine, over which ran only a log bridge: Leo had strict instructions not to disturb him but to cross merely once a day and to leave a little gruel and a little water: for Francis was preparing by forty days of fasting and prayers for the feast of St. Michael . . .

There, in the fourth week of his fast, on the feast of the Holy Cross, which fell on the 14 September, he received the stigmata – the first man to do so since Jesus Christ received the wounds on the Cross. Fra Leo saw a seraph, a 'Burning One', the six-winged angel that guards, in Isaiah's vision, the throne of Yahweh, appear in the sky above Francis' primitive hut of reeds. The feast of St. Michael came and went; and Francis set out back for the Portiuncula and Assisi; his hands were bandaged up to the finger-tips and from then on he was careful never to show the wound in his side.[19] He, the great walker, had to ride a donkey, for his bandaged and painful feet, in which fleshy excrescences shaped like long points had appeared, make it too painful for him even to walk upon the ground. He did not have very long to live after this; but right to the end he kept up his good humour, even when his eyesight failed to the extent that he could no longer look upon that Brother Sun – '*Messer lo Frate Sole*' – whom he so loved. At this stage it is comforting to know that he was at long last with Clare, living in a little hut – much bothered by his brothers the ants – in the surroundings of San Damiano and looked after devotedly by Clare and her sisters. It was there in this darkness that he set about composing, in the Umbrian dialect, the first surviving and perhaps the best loved of poems in any modern European language, the *Canticle to the Sun*, that in a final flurry of pathetic enthusiasm he wished Pacificus and other brothers (like Abbot Joachim's monks, furnished only with lyres) to go round the world singing, and only after singing to preach a little.[20]

Next year, the last of his life, he added a new verse to the *Canticle* – the famous greeting to Sister Death:

'*Laudato Si, Mi Signore, per Sora Nostra Morte Corporale*
Da la quale nullu homo vivente po skampare
Guai a quilli ke morrano ne le peccata mortali
Beati quilli ke se trovarà ne le Tue sanctissime voluntati
Ka la Morte Secunda nol 'arra male'[21]

He was a long, slow time dying: they kept him at the bishop's palace in Assisi, but when he felt the end approaching he had them carry him down to the woods, to Santa Maria degli Angeli, and there, on Saturday, 3 October 1226, at nightfall he died.

Next morning they carried his body in procession up to his parish church of

San Giorgio; the procession made a long detour around by San Damiano. They held the body of Francis up by the open grille through which Clare and her sisters received communion; and then they carried it up to the centre of Assisi to bury.

NOTES

1 It is my belief, as the title of this chapter indicates, that the culminating event of St. Francis' life was the event that his biographers of the Middle Ages dismiss very briefly and even his modern biographers treat as a mere *incident de parcours* – namely his going on crusade.

It is necessary to state this very firmly because the facts are not only, as always, disputable but also very few in number – bar the central and most important fact of all, that Francis went on crusade and was many months in or near the Holy Land. 'This expedition,' writes Sabatier, 'which lasted more than a year, is mentioned by the biographers in few lines. Happily we have a number of other papers regarding it; but their silence suffices to prove the sincerity of the primitive Franciscan authors; if they had wanted to amplify the deeds of their subject, where could they have found an easier opportunity or a more marvellous theme?'

Here I must part company with Sabatier. Why the silence? Why, why and why again is the question a biographer must never cease to ask. I believe it was not a sign of their sincerity; I would hazard that it was a sign of their embarrassment.

2 It is by no means clear which 'missions' went out in 1217 and which in 1219. Fra Giordano, our main informant, confirms that he cannot quite remember. For the short and friendly text of Pope Honorius' safe-conduct, see the collection of papal Bulls of that year (Sbalarea's compendium) – *Cum Dilecti Filii*.

3 Because Frederick was later to carry his requests for delays in setting out on crusade to ridiculous lengths, many (and in the first rank Cardinal Ugolino who, as Honorius' successor, excommunicated him for this reason) have suggested that he was insincere right from the beginning. This seems unjustified. There were good and valid reasons at least for the initial postponements; and nobody at the time suggested that Frederick was anything but eager to succeed where both his father and his grandfather, cut down by sudden death, had failed.

4 Fra Girolamo Golubovitch has collected all the relevant contemporary documents concerning Francis' journey to the East in his *Biblioteca Bio-bibliografia della Terra Santa e dell'Oriente Francescano* (Quaracchi, 4 vols, 1906–27). This chapter owes a great debt to Fra Giulio Bassetti-Sani and his *Mohammed et Saint François* (Commissariat de Terre-Sainte, Ottawa, 1959), though I cannot accept all his sometimes wildly extravagant theses. There have been numerous articles and studies of this episode in specialized journals.

5 In 1169 Amalric of Jerusalem had attempted to seize Cairo by way of Damietta. His siege had been foiled by the chain-tower, the Burj-as-Silsilah. It was almost impossible to be original on a crusade.

6 For Cardinal Pelagius see the excellent study by J. P. Donovan, *Pelagius and the Fifth Crusade* (Philadelphia, 1955). Of the French and English leaders, Saer de Quincy, Earl of Winchester, was killed on 3 November, due to the culpable negligence of Hervé, Count of Nevers, who was forced to leave the host as a result.

7 As the attentive reader will already have noted, it was one of the curiosities of Near Eastern diplomacy at this period that such truces were almost invariably observed.

8 The eye-witness account of the martyrdom of the Friars Minor in Morocco came to light only last century – *Passio Sanctorum martyrum Barnardi, Petri, Adiuti, Accursii, Othonis in Marochio martyrizatorum*. As for Fra Giles' expedition to Tunis, it proved – fortunately for him, I would say, as he was far more likely to have behaved like the five would-be martyrs than like Francis – abortive. The Christian merchants in Tunis turned him back, for fear of ruining their good relations with the Bey.

9 In French, suggests Englebert, for Fra Giordano specifically states that Francis knew no Arabic. But it seems rather more likely that one of the long established Genoese merchants mentioned by the Arab chroniclers acted as interpreter.

10 There are three long accounts of Francis' visit to the Sultan's camp, that of the *Chronicle* of Ernoul, that of the *Fioretti*, and that of the *Legenda Major*. In this one it appears wiser to rely on Bonaventure, who recounts what he was told by Francis' companion Fra Illuminato. The story of the multi-coloured carpet with crosses appears only in the anonymous *Verba Fratris Illuminati*, and of the seductress only in the *Fioretti*.

11 Ernoul does not mention the test by fire, and the *Fioretti* refers to it only *en passant*. But Bonaventure's account, which is both definite and detailed, seems enough to establish its truth – particularly as, from the lay chronicler's viewpoint, it was distinctly a non-event. It is Ernoul who tells us that the Islamic doctors refused as a matter of principle to enter into a debate; and Bonaventure in his *Second Sermon on St. Francis* (Section IX) quotes Francis' parallel rejection of rationalism.

12 For the mubâhalä of Najran, see the *Sîrat* of Ibn Ishagj, Mohammed's first biographer. For Mohammed's later attitude see also the Koran, Sura 3 (54–61) and Sura 43 (81–83).

13 The Pope had written to Prester John forty years earlier – but had had no reply. Apparently the Curia were still waiting in hope.

14 It may be asked why, if the new constitutions represented growing Cathar influence, this is never clearly brought out and condemned in any of the accounts. One answer is – why, if they did not, was there so great a fuss? More seriously, and more generally, it was too dangerous for any member of the Order ever to breathe a suspicion that it might be contaminated by Catharism (as opposed to being influenced by a non-heresy like the Joachimite movement). It would be much as if a chronicler of the Templars had admitted openly that his Order was contaminated by witchcraft and unnatural practices – an invitation to suppression.

15 For Francis' resignation see especially the *Speculum Perfectionis*, 39–41.

16 The *Second Rule*, which Francis probably composed in the winter of 1220–1 is, in the words of Sabatier, not so much a Rule as a 'series of impassioned appeals', 'chaotic and even contradictory.' It is enormously long, filling thirty-nine folios as opposed to the four folios of the third and final Rule. Its rejection, and with it the rejection of *his* idea of how *his* Order should live, seems to have been almost the final blow to Francis. Again to quote Sabatier (whose views are disputed, particularly – and it is only natural – by Franciscan writers and scholars), 'Almost everything which was done in the Order after 1221 was done either without Francis' knowledge or against his will. . . . The last five years of his life were only one incessant effort at protest, both by example and words.'

17 The *Third Rule* has only twelve chapters where the *Second Rule* had twenty-three. It is pithy where the Second Rule was prolix; it is both more elegant in style and more legalistic in content. There can be very little doubt therefore that it owed more to those who helped draft the text (including the canon lawyer Fra Bonizzo of Bologna) than to its nominal composer, St. Francis – and that Sabatier was right in attributing this, the *Rule* that is still valid, to the influence of Cardinal Ugolino.

There are well over 40,000 Franciscans scattered throughout the world today (to say nothing of the innumerable Franciscan nuns, and the hundreds of thousands of lay people who belong to the Third Order), and it is obviously therefore a sweeping generalization to assert that the *Rule* is hardly applied by present-day Franciscans – particularly on the basis of very limited knowledge. Yet the mere fact that those 40,000 Franciscans are divided into three distinct and separate Orders, each with its own Minister-General, is in flagrant contradiction to chapter VIII of the *Rule* and would certainly be as great a shock to St. Francis as it is to the outside observer, who can see no reason now, whatever the historical reasons may have been, why this rather scandalous division should be perpetuated.

Furthermore the *Third Rule* lays down (chapter II) a limit on clothing and restricts the use of shoes; this seems to be totally ignored. It lays down rules for fasting (chapter III); they have, apparently, fallen into abeyance. It restricts contacts with women (chapter XI); no doubt that is intolerable. And, above all, it lays down (chapter IV) that the brethren shall not receive money or coin, either themselves or through an interposed person. This prohibition is glossed over – despite the *cri de coeur* of St. Francis in his *Testament*: 'In virtue of obedience I strictly forbid any of my friars, clerics or lay brothers, to interpret the *Rule* or those words, saying "This is what they mean". God inspired me to write the *Rule* and these words plainly and simply and live by them doing good to the Lord.' Admittedly the *Testament* is not valid in canon law – but how can any genuine Franciscan ignore this appeal and accept the glosses that make life so much easier and so much more comfortable? As the voice of St. Francis said, three times repeated, to Fra Matteo, founder of the Capuchin reform: 'Observe the *Rule* to the letter.' Surely this simple precept is a better guide than any number of papers on Franciscan formation, plans of life, etc. – for all three branches of the Order seem to be weighed down at the present with complex studies that are in rather shocking contrast to the basic simplicity of St. Francis' message. Perhaps it is time that a new and simple reforming movement arose within the Order, as has always happened in the past. If – when – it does, will it spring yet again from the province of Le Marche, so often the real centre of Franciscan spiritual life and ideals?

Or might it come, paradoxically, from the flourishing but worldly provinces of North America? There must be many Franciscans who, consciously or unconsciously, are yearning for such a renewal – including perhaps the thousands who have left the Order over the past few years.

18 For Brother Fire, see especially the *Legend of Perugia*, 24, and 46–8. The red-hot iron seared St. Francis from ear to eyebrow: 'All of us who were with him had to leave because we were overcome by emotion and pity – only the doctor remained with him.'

19 The story of the stigmata is best told in the *Five Considerations on the Holy Stigmata* woven together by the author of the *Fioretti* from many different earlier accounts. This has been described as 'the most beautiful piece of Franciscan literature that we possess.'

Fra Leo alone was allowed to see and to touch and to bandage St. Francis' wounds. But Fra Rufino also managed one day while 'scratching St. Francis' back deliberately to put his large finger into the wound in the side. "God forgive you, Fra Rufino," ' St. Francis shouted in great pain, 'why did you do that?' Also Lady Jacopa de Settesoli saw and kissed the wounds many times – as did St. Clare and her nuns when Francis was dead.

20 'I want to compose a new Praise of the Lord and his Creatures' said St. Francis as he lay sick in the garden at San Damiano, 'for we daily make use of them and cannot live without them.' (*Speculum Perfectionis*, 100.) That was the origin of the hymn to '*Altissimu Onnipotente Bon Signore*' in honour not only of '*Messer lo Frate Sole*', but also of '*Sora Luna e la Stelle,*' '*Frate Vento*', '*Sor Acqua*' and '*Sora Nostra Matre Terra.*'

'He then composed a melody for it and frequently urged the brothers to sing it when out preaching' – which they do no longer, alas.

In the last year of his life as he lay at the bishop's palace, St. Francis added verses about pardon and peace that settled a dispute between the ever-quarrelsome Bishop Guido and the *Podestà*.

When he felt death approaching, he summoned Fra Leo and Fra Angelo to his bedside to sing the *Canticle*; and there composed that final greeting.

21 'All Praise be Yours, my Lord, for our Sister Bodily Death
From whose embrace no mortal can escape
Woe to those who die in mortal sin
Happy those she finds doing Your will
The second death can do no harm to them.'

Index

15